THE Song OF Shabbos

MOSAICA PRESS

THE Song OF Shabbos

A COMPREHENSIVE AND IN-DEPTH
STUDY, REVEALING THE SECRETS AND
SANCTITY OF SHABBOS

Culled from Sifrei Olas Yitzchok

RAV YITZCHOK ALSTER

TRANSLATED BY RABBI YEHOSHUA GRANT

Published by Mosaica Press, Inc.
www.mosaicapress.com
info@mosaicapress.com

In tribute to
a person of intellect, character, and charm,
my dear cousin and true friend

Dr. (Chaim) Donald Lewin

A man of letters and accomplishment, with a keen interest
in the dissemination of Torah literature to bring Jews closer
to their faith.
He is also the benefactor of *Sifrei Olas Yitzchok.*
May Hashem grant him many happy and healthy years,
and may he have continued success in these worthy endeavors.

RABBI MOISHE STERNBUCH	משה שטרנבוך
CHIEF RABBI	ראב"ד
and Vice President of	לכל מקהלות האשכנזים
of the Orthodox Rabbinical Courts	מחזיק מושיעים ומבוע וישרת חשבות והנהגות
JERUSALEM	רב בית הכנסת הגר"א, ר"מ במרכזו התורה הר-נוף
	מגן נשיא הער"ה התוררית
Rechov Mishkalov 13 Har-Nof Jerusalem Tel:02-651-9610	בעה"ק ירושלים ת"ו

בעזהי"ת _____

קבלתי בשמחה עלים מספרו "עולת יצחק" ח"ב שקבע על פרשיות התורה, וכן דברי הלכה ביאורים ופירושים להאיר לב המעיין, ואשריו ואשרי חלקו שהוא חושב שכתתינו הר נוף ועמל ויגע בתורה, ומוציא כאן לאור פרי הארץ לגאון ותפארת.

ובחלק ראשון צולל במים אדירים בסוגיות הש"ס, וכמעשהו בראשון כן מעשהו בשני, ובמקומות הרבה ניכר עקבות מורי ורבו ה"ה הגאון האדיר רבי יצחק הוטנער זצ"ל, ומביא גם מדבריו.

והנני לברך אותו שיזכה עוד להגדיל תורה ולהאדירה, תזכה לראות הרמת קרן התורה וביאת משיח צדקנו בקרוב.

הנני מצפה בכליון עינים לישועת ה'
ורחמי שמים מרובים

בס"ד יום ג' כסלו תשע"ה

הנ"ם כבוד ידי"נ יביב וחביב הרב ר' אברהם
אורי'ן, חי'ש'ו ועודו שלימה יאמר לגוליון לאור, בואתי לבני
דהלוך אחת את נעכי רית הכ'לט על חוקי הכולא שקם
יוי'ש שמעה השפולו קהית אד'ו'חן, ב'ה'אה על וחן
שם הכ'שלת פ'ש'נ, ומנען דא האו' ען שא ושולה לקוט
ולאלו מסבי"ז לן אולמין. והי' ו'כב בהם החס'ו תולו
ס'ו שום ואם ומא שאן דא להחק"ע ער' ומאד' א מות
הסיו'ל שלשף בהם והכ'נם ענען'הם לאור עיין האינין,
ודכל לחרן לסכר שי'חן צ'לאהי תורה
מפ'ס'ו' ו'ה'ש'ך לשלח בנא הא ל'אור' ימ'ם ב'ר'א
ום'ם ו'דו' ולהבשל

הכולם והוגא
נ'שוב כ'עוב ולא'ה'ו'
יונתן

MIRRER YESHIVA CENTRAL INSTITUTE

Beth Medrash • Post Graduate School • Kolel • High School
Sephardic Division • Teachers Institute

1791-5 Ocean Parkway • Brooklyn, N.Y. 11223 • (718) 645-0536-7 • Fax (718) 645-925

וח של מרן הגאון ר' אברהם קלמנוביץ זצ"ל

Founded
Rabbi Abraham Kalmanowitz ל

בס"ד

Rabbi Shrage Moshe Kalmanowitz
Rabbi Shmuel Berenbaum
Roshei Yeshiva

יום 3 לסדר קדושים תהיו

הנה כב"ג הרב הגאון מו"ה ר' נ.ג.ה. שליט"א אשר הסתיר הרבה לפני
קהלות מחותו באהלו לאור לנתיבו לשון הרב בהם בהלכה אב
דיינו הקהלון לנגו למשות ההם שיעלית לעצות מתלבא ודרך
וענג להם ולהן נ רב להתורית גם מקום ילא הדבון
א' שהורה מר שאורית לוקה ס' פסקו ובוא"ל להלכה רב אמנם
לעיין כל ומגע לבינו ברבו יגל להלכה שמינק חלה
לפעל ומקהל הם וגנק בהלכה
הכתבה ליומר לכבוד התורה ולכבוד ובה התוהר ס',ו'ו'
חשואל בן דגלוש

Rabbi Aaron M. Schechter   אהרן משה שכטר

ב"ה

כבוד ידידי הרב הג"מ

[...handwritten Hebrew letter...]

ידידו עוז אוהבו

Mesivta Yeshiva Rabbi Chaim Berlin / 1605 Coney Island Avenue / Brooklyn, N.Y. 11230

בית אולפנא רוממה

שע"י עמותת "שב שמעתתא" ע"ר 580098846

ראש הכולל הרב ר' משה שפירא שליט"א

טל': 02-5374337 פקס: 02-5374339

רח' תורת חסד 1, ירושלים 94464

בס"ד   ירושלים, י"ד מנ"א תש..

את ידידי בית הגאון הנעלה ר' יצחק אלכסנדר אליס... הנני וכו' ...
...
...

ולבנו ... אבו ... ובישועתו ... יהיו

ובזכות ... יזכו אקירו ... ונכתבו

[חתימה]

שלמה סירקין

הקבלן 13
עיה"ק ירושלם תובב

ב"ה _____

מן הקול הגיע רבני בלשון השכורום וכו' שלא לבית אלקים

בהקהלות גדולה לפורים שבהיה דבא? לבטא רבה ניקוה מה חשואות

שלא עול ע"כ הנה הבטון התעלה וכ' יצא? אולסוור אלקים. של

בבריות מלאכית מין שעולה. שבוע ביפי עניני את הנה הגעון

כל שלא העלעו ובמו בקבל לאיות אלת בבתא ה. שלא נשאר

שלא לבתב, ל' וג יום ל' וגב יולה? ואל ל' אל עלבאנט והיות לעד

לגבאי עוד לארברית בעזך הקול תלעהא בעוגא ה' כ נשות

וכל רבות לטובה

שלויה המשבר נאמן

חותם פ"ק _____

ל' שלות עלה דעך יולעף

RABBI YAAKOV PERLOW
1569 - 47TH STREET
BROOKLYN, N.Y. 11219

יעקב פרלוב
ביהמ"ד עדת יעקב נאוואמינסק
ברוקלין, נ.י.

בס"ד יום ב' ג' לסדר ה' מספר

חביבי ידי"נ האלוף והנעלה הרב הגאון ר' יצחק שליט"א ... ...
ומעולם לא יחסר לאור עיני... וזכינו... מקרוב... ...
... כבוד ... לאמיתו בדברי חכמים ... ... על ...
... ... נדבר בדברי ... ...
... נודע ... אורות ... בענין מה ... ...
... ... יתרה ... מאמר ... ... דבר ... ...
... ... על החולה אשר ... ...
... לאורך ... ... באהבה של ... ...
... ...

יוסף (?)פערלאוו

Table of Contents

Preface

A n observant Jew was always known as *"an ehrliche Yid"* (a loyal Jew). In the years of upheaval of the first half of the twentieth century, he was called a *"shomer Shabbos."*

At a time when strict adherence to Torah and mitzvos was ebbing, Shabbos was the anchor and pillar of *emunah.*

The goal of the most Orthodox Jewish girls was to marry a *shomer Shabbos*—a person who observed the Shabbos. Such a milieu was not conducive for understanding the deeper meaning and beauty of Shabbos.

How things have changed in the twenty-first century! A massive revolution has taken place in Jewish communities throughout the world. *Shemiras Shabbos* has turned into a minimum not a maximum. Not only is the deeper meaning and beauty of Shabbos studied but all of the mitzvos are. *Limud* and *kavod haTorah* have become the hallmark of the observant Jew. *Yeshivos* and *kollelim* are growing and prospering as never before in Jewish history.

This *sefer* will explain why Shabbos is and always was the cornerstone of Yiddishkeit.

When Rav Yehoshua Grant volunteered to translate some of my treatises on the beauty and depth of Shabbos featured in *Sifrei Olas Yitzchok*, and simultaneously my dear cousin and friend, Dr. Donald Lewin, volunteered to be the patron, a certain scene from the past came to mind.

Several years before his *petirah* (passing) in 5741 (1980), I had proposed to Rav Hutner, *zt"l*, to publish a series of excerpts from his *Sifrei Pachad Yitzchok* (eleven volumes).

The purpose would be to make available some of the basic principles and fundamentals of *emunah* to the broader Jewish public. In his *maamarim*, the Rosh Yeshiva repeatedly stressed the crucial significance of certain concepts that "must be known."

My claim put forth to him was to question how these *yesodei ha'das* (basics of our faith) could become known if his *maamarim* were always delivered to the limited groups of his *talmidim*. Part of the problem was solved with the publication of the *Sifrei Pachad Yitzchok*. But this still left many out in the cold, primarily two groups: those with limited knowledge of the Hebrew language, but also those with a keen understanding of Torah texts in halachah and *derush*, but not in sync with his uncanny depth of intellect and integration of the basic texts. His style of articulation and poetic language took years for even his most astute *talmidim* to absorb.

Upon finishing my proposal, he reacted immediately: "Do it, but you should know that it would be even better in English."

He was *niftar* less than two years later, and, somehow, this idea never reached fruition. But I felt I was given a mission.

With this publication, I hope in some way to fulfill this legacy. Most of the *maamarim* herein are based on the fundamentals of *emunah* and Yiddishkeit that he so skillfully espoused to the *talmidim* of Mesivta Rabbeinu Chaim Berlin for over forty years.[1]

My prayer to Hashem Yisbarach is that this *sefer* will attain its goal and reach people that are searching for a deeper meaning of the human existence and of their Jewish identity.

I am very grateful to two dear friends who carefully reviewed the manuscript and offered their comments. They are Hagaon Harav Aharon Feldman, Rosh Hayeshiva Ner Israel, Baltimore; and Hagaon

---

[1]   If my interpretations and expositions are correct, then they should be considered implied by his words. If they are not, I assume responsibility.

Harav Yisroel Meir Kirzner, Mara D'asra, Congregation Bnei Yehuda, Brooklyn, New York.

I am especially indebted to my children and grandchildren who provide me with immeasurable *nachas* and helped with many of the details in the publishing process. A special thank you to a very special and great *talmid chacham*, my son-in-law, Rav Chaim Yitzchak Kaplan, *shlita,* who reviewed the original *sefer* and added pertinent elucidations and sources.

Yehoshua Grant has done a superb job of translation. As a *chaver* of good standing of Kollel Nachalas Tzvi, Yerushalayim, which I am privileged to lead, and having been exposed to many of these ideas, he was able to capture the style and the profundities. Translation of Torah texts is never an easy task. In many cases, translating is more difficult that authoring.

My daughter, Gitel Rivka Kaplan; my son, Rav Amram Moshe Alster and his wife, Pnina, were supportive as always, in their inimitable and unassuming manner.

A special tribute to my granddaughter, Sarah Bluma Weinstock, for her genial expertise in the typesetting and jacket design.

Nevas bayis techalek shalal (Tehillim 68:13*).* My *nevas bayis,* Rochel Alster, contributed immensely to this *sefer.* She reviewed most of the material with an uncanny understanding, editing and adding to the unique *nusach* of the *maamarim.*

Translator's Preface

Said Rav Avahu in the name of Rabbi Yochanan: When Hashem gave the Torah, no baby bird tweeted, no bird flew, no ox uttered a cry; the Ofanim did not fly, the Serafim did not declare "Kadosh, Kadosh," the sea did not move, people did not speak. Instead, the world was silent and hushed, and the words "I am Hashem your G-d" rang out.[1]

This Midrash depicts the utter silence that reigned during the revelation at Sinai. According to Rav Shimshon Pincus, *zt"l*,[2] this statement of Chazal reveals a seminal message, namely, that **when silence reigns in the world, the message "I am Hashem your G-d" is revealed of its own accord**. It is only the clamor of human activity that hides this message from sight, only the hubbub of *kochi v'otzem yadi* that buries it in a mountain of falsehood and nonsense.

The same occurs on Shabbos. As the Jewish people put down their tools for the week and refrain from *melachah*, their world undergoes

---

1   *Shemos Rabbah* 29:9.
2   *Shabbos Malkesa*, Introduction, §4.

shevisah, a moment of pause and silence. This allows the voice of Matan Torah—"I am Hashem your G-d"—to ring out once more.[3]

Shabbos is uniquely connected to Moshe Rabbeinu. According to Chazal,[4] Moshe realized the importance of Shabbos already in Mitzrayim, which is why the *Amidah* of *Shacharis* describes Shabbos as Moshe's portion: "*Yismach Moshe b'matnas chelko.*" How appropriate it is that the man who utterly nullified himself to the will of G-d,[5] the man who made a veritable *shevisah* of his earthly body,[6] was the one to recognize the power of the *shevisah* of Shabbos even before it had been commanded.

In the past few months, I have been privileged to write this *sefer* together with my Rosh Kollel, Rav Yitzchok Alster, *shlita*. Doing so has been a pleasure, for it has exposed me to the breathtaking Torah of the great *gaon*, Rav Yitzchok Hutner, *zt"l*, as transmitted by his faithful *talmid*, the Rosh Kollel, *shlita*. Moshe Rabbeinu wanted nothing more than to faithfully convey the words of Hashem to the Jewish people, and the Rosh Kollel wishes to faithfully convey the Torah of Rav Hutner, *zt"l*, to the wider public. Moshe recognized the power of the *shevisah* of Shabbos, and the Rosh Kollel has taken it upon himself to spread the "song of Shabbos" to one and all, delighting us with his fascinating discourses and vignettes, spanning all aspects of the Shabbos experience.

As translator, I wanted to be sure to not interrupt the faithful flow from *rav* to *talmid*, not present a blockage to the *shevisah* that would prevent the unadulterated wisdom of Rav Hutner, *zt"l*, to emerge. I am mindful of the Italian saying, "*Traduttorre, Traditore,*" which means "the translator is the traitor," and *daven* that I too have been faithful to the cause.

---

3   And, as the Rosh Kollel discusses extensively in this *sefer*, Shabbos allows this seminal voice to permeate and uplift the *sheishes yemei ha'maaseh*, the weekdays.

4   *Shemos Rabbah* 1:28, cited by the *Tur, Orach Chaim* 281.

5   Moshe was the quintessential *eved Hashem*, servant of G-d (*Devarim* 34:5), for he utterly removed himself from the narrative. This is why his name is not mentioned in the Haggadah, despite his prominent role in the Exodus.

6   In fact, according to Chazal, Moshe's soul did not wish to part from his body upon his death.

May the Rosh Kollel, *shlita*, see *orech yamim v'shanim*, continued *nachas* from his children and children-in-law, including the *geonim* Rav Amram and Rav Chaim Yitzchak, *shlita*, and from the members of his Kollel Nachalas Tzvi (of which I count myself a member), *ad bias go'el tzeddek*, until the coming of Mashiach, speedily in our days.

Yehoshua Grant
Cheshvan 5781

Divrei Aggadah

The Gemara[1] relates that the community of Alexandria discussed twelve matters with Rabbi Yehoshua ben Chananyah. Three were matters of *chochmah*, three of Aggadah, three were nonsensical matters, and three were matters of *derech eretz*. *Rashi*[2] explains that the matters of *chochmah* pertained to the world of halachah. The *Maharsha*[3] contends that the matters of Aggadah referred to "hidden matters concerning the ways of Hashem and His traits."

In his *sefer Pachad Yitzchok*,[4] Rav Hutner elaborates upon and contrasts the study of halachah and Aggadah. The Torah[5] records that Moshe Rabbeinu urged the Jewish people to "love Hashem your G-d, to walk in all His ways, and to cleave to Him…," and the *Sifri* comments, "Is it your desire to know the One who created the world? Learn Aggadah, for you will thereby know Hashem and cleave to His ways."

The *Sifri* clearly states that G-d's ways and His approach to operating the world are revealed in the study of Aggadah. This stands in contrast to the study of halachah, which seeks to clarify the mitzvos and their complexities. Additionally, the *Sifri* reveals that the study of Aggadah

---

1   *Niddah* 69b.
2   Ad loc., s.v. *"Divrei chochmah."*
3   Ad loc., s.v. *"V'she'shaalu."*
4   *Sefer Ha'igros* (54).
5   *Devarim* 11:22.

is a more direct way to cleave to G-d. For while certainly the study and fulfillment of the mitzvos may lead a person to grasping the ways of G-d, the study of Aggadah leads a person directly to that attainment.

Rav Hutner also noted that "additional comprehension and deeper understanding into the events of history in general, and Jewish history in particular, through the lens of the Torah is nothing less than familiarizing oneself with the ways of G-d."

On Shavuos of 5715, Rav Hutner revealed another advantage of the study of Aggadah over that of halachah. The Gemara[6] cites the ominous words of Yeshayahu HaNavi[7] regarding the destruction of Yerushalayim, "For behold, the L-rd, Hashem, Master of Legions, is removing from Jerusalem...every support of bread and every support of water." The "support of bread," it asserts, refers to *"baalei Talmud,"* those who study the Gemara, as the verse[8] states, "For the one who lacks an understanding of heart...Come and partake of my bread." The "support of water" refers to *"baalei Aggadah,"* who draw people's hearts like water. The prophet Yeshayahu thus revealed that at the time of the destruction, Jerusalem was to be bereft of its eminent Torah scholars and *darshanim.*

Bread is only procured after employing a series of activities of sowing, plowing, harvesting, and so forth. The original wheat seeds only fulfill their purpose after many months, after undergoing several transformations. The same is true of the study of halachah by the *"baalei Talmud."* Only when they invest time and effort into understanding the profundity of the words of the Gemara do they produce conclusions that are confluent with halachah.

The same cannot be said of procuring water. In order to do so, a person merely lowers a bucket into a well and draws the water directly from its source. The water undergoes no transformations and necessitates no activities to ready it for use—it remains precisely as it was at the

---

6   *Chagigah* 14a.

7   *Yeshayahu* 3:1.

8   *Mishlei* 9:4, 5.

source. This is reflected perfectly in the study of Aggadah, which draws directly from the well of the wisdom of the Almighty.

This isn't to say that time and effort needn't be expended in the study of Aggadah. The waters of celestial wisdom do not rise of their own accord; they must be raised by the intrepid and earnest studier of G-d's ways and wisdom. However, unlike the valiant studiers of halachah, who must sow, reap, grind, and knead the kernels of wisdom they encounter, the students of Aggadah devote their energy to drawing wisdom from the most profound depths of the Torah.[9]

Perhaps we may add one further comment.

The mitzvah to cleave to Hashem is also referenced in a different verse in the Torah: "Hashem your G-d you shall fear, you shall serve Him, you shall cleave to Him, and you shall swear in His name."[10] Famously, the *Sifri* asks, "Is it possible to cleave to the Divine Presence? Surely it is a burning fire! Rather, the intent of the verse is that one should cleave to Torah scholars and to their students, and if one does so, it is considered as if one has cleaved to the Almighty."

We see that cleaving to Hashem can be achieved in one of two ways: through the study of Aggadah, as referenced by the *Sifri* above, or by attaching oneself to Torah scholars, as referenced by the *Sifri* here.[11] And the two are intimately connected. The study of Aggadah, as stated, is designed to imbue a person with a clearer perception of G-d and of His lofty ways. The same is true of forming an attachment with great Torah scholars. For in studying their ways and availing oneself of their wisdom, a person may similarly attain an understanding of Hashem and His wisdom.

And in truth, the two must work in tandem. The study in depth of the words of Aggadah **as understood** by the *Chachmei Ha'Aggadah* (the Torah scholars of the Aggadah) combine to present the unique opportunity for a *talmid* to cleave to Hashem.

---

9   This topic is discussed at great length in the general introduction to the *sifrei Pachad Yitzchok*.

10   *Devarim* 10:20.

11   Strangely, *Rashi* to 11:22 cites the *Sifri* to 10:20.

Erev Shabbos

1

Kah Ribon, composed by Rabbi Yisrael Najara, the prominent Kabbalist of the sixteenth century,[1] is one of the most famous and celebrated *zemiros* of Shabbos. However, it curiously fails to make mention of Shabbos in any of its five hallowed stanzas. This, as we will see, reveals a most profound idea about the nature of Shabbos.[2]

Creation on Shabbos

Rav Hutner in his *sefer Pachad Yitzhak*[3] elaborates upon a fundamental concept stated by the Vilna Gaon[4] regarding Shabbos. The Gaon discusses a seeming contradiction as to whether the Creation of the world also took place on Shabbos. On the one hand, the Torah states[5] explicitly that on the seventh day G-d was *"shavas va'yinafash—He rested and was refreshed,"* but on the other hand, G-d is described as renewing Creation each and every day, *"Mechadesh b'tuvo b'chol yom tamid*

---

1   And of whom the great Sages of Israel said, *"Lo kam b'Yisrael k'Yisrael*—And there never arose among Yisrael a person like Yisrael."
2   See *Maamar "Kah Ribon"* for an alternate explanation.
3   *Shabbos* 1:3.
4   *Aderes Eliyahu, Bereishis* 2:3.
5   *Shemos* 31:17.

maaseh Bereishis—In His goodness he renews daily and perpetually, the works of Creation."[6]

The *Gaon's* answer to this contradiction is cryptic in the extreme: He states simply that the Creation that occurs on Shabbos is *huchan mi'yom shishi* (prepared on Friday). Rav Hutner, in his inimitable way, explained the intent of the Gaon as follows.

On *yom ha'shishi*, G-d created Adam, a thoroughly unique creation. Unlike all other creations, inanimate or animate, man was endowed with intellect, making him capable of discerning between good and bad, holy and profane. Prior to this, all elements of creation could have been perceived to be equal for there was nobody to determine the good from the bad, or the *ikar* (those things that are of primary importance) from the *tafel* (those things that are secondary or subservient). This all changed with the creation of man.

Man's arrival set the stage for Shabbos. Shabbos seeks to place the natural world (*teva*) in its proper context, which is that it is *tafel*, subservient, to the spiritual world, which is the *ikar*. With the creation of man, G-d could roll out a hierarchical creation; a creation in which the notion of *ikar* and *tafel* could be appreciated by those who had the aptitude to place everything in its proper context.

G-d did not desist from physical Creation on the seventh day, for the world can only exist by dint of His continuous will. He is *"mechadesh b'tuvo b'chol yom tamid,"* recreating the world at every moment. However, He did indeed desist from the **philosophy** of the physical Creation, which advocates the supremacy of *teva*. Hashem sanctified the seventh day, *"Va'yekadesh oso,"*[7] and thereby revealed that the very purpose of Creation is *kedushah*, and that all other elements of Creation are secondary. For unlike science, which studies and gives precedence to nature and the physical world, *kedushah* reveals purpose.

This concept and modus operandi of Creation was *huchan mi'yom shishi* (prepared on the sixth day of Creation), for then, with the birth of mankind, the ability to discern between holy and profane emerged.

---

6   This is stated in the *Birkas K'rias Shema*, on weekdays and on Shabbos.

7   *Bereishis* 3:2.

Following that, Shabbos could arrive and infuse the week with meaning; for although it was the final element of Creation, it was the original goal of Creation and considered before everything else, *"b'machshavah techilah."*[8]

Now we can understand the cryptic words of the Gaon. This new perspective on Creation was **prepared on Erev Shabbos** with the creation of man and his intellect. And while G-d did not desist from Creation on Shabbos, He enjoined man to desist from the *ikriyus* of physical creation—the notion that *teva* is *ikar*.

2

The context of *ikar* and *tafel* that is the gift of Shabbos to the rest of the week is one of the **unconcealed** elements of Shabbos. Indeed, a *"Shabbos-dik Yid"* can tap into the feelings of *menuchah* that abound on Shabbos and allow them to transform the rest of his week and fill it with context and perspective.

Let us now consider the *zemer* of *Kah Ribon*.

Aside from giving purpose to the rest of the week, Shabbos also has a deeper and hidden factor. Shabbos informs us that the natural world and the six days of the working week **not only gain clarity and context from Shabbos but are holy in and of themselves. In other words, Shabbos has the capacity not just to reveal that the physical world is secondary but to reveal that there is holiness hidden amidst it as well.**

This might be the veiled message of *Kah Ribon*. Unlike the majority of the *zemiros* that focus on the **overt, unconcealed elements** of the holiness of Shabbos, *Kah Ribon* focuses on the **hidden** message of Shabbos, which is that holiness can be unearthed from beneath the profane. This may be the reason that it does not mention Shabbos explicitly.

---

8   Eternalized by Rabbi Shlomo Alkabetz (the *rebbi* of Rabbi Moshe Kordovero) in his poem, *Lechah Dodi*, by the words *"Sof maaseh b'machashavah techilah,"* the goal reveals the original intention.

This notion is apparent in the first two stanzas of the *zemer* which extol G-d's powerful and wondrous deeds in Creating the physical world, for example "*B'nei enasha, cheivas bera, v'ofei shemaya*—Sons of man, beasts of the field and birds of the sky." If the physical world is merely *tafel* and bereft of holiness, it would surely have been more pertinent to extol G-d for the Creation of Shabbos, which is the *ikar*, rather than praise His Creation of the *tafel*. We must say that the *zemer* alludes to the hidden message of Shabbos, namely, that there is holiness amidst the physical world, and that this in fact allows it to lose its status as *tafel* and becomes part of the *ikar*.

This is also alluded to in the penultimate stanza of *Kah Ribon*, which beseeches G-d to redeem us from the mires of exile, "*Prok yas anach mi'pum aryevasa, v'apek yas amech mi'go galusa*." When the Jewish people and the Shechinah (the Divine Presence) are in exile, **all elements of holiness in the world are thereby concealed**. Just as *kedushah* is hidden behind nature and the physical world of Creation, so are the Jewish people and the Shechinah hidden by the series of events of the world, namely history. In short, *teva* is to *kedushah* what *galus* is to *geulah* (redemption). Just as *kedushah* can be found in *teva*, so are the signs of *geulah* within the *galus*.[9]

But, as the final stanza declares, upon their actual *geulah* and their return to Jerusalem the "*Karta d'shufraya*" and their rebuilding of the Beis Hamikdash, "*L'Mikdashech tuv u'l'Kodesh Kudshin*," the holiness in the physical world will truly be revealed. Ultimately, in the rebuilt Jerusalem, the spiritual and the mundane will rejoice together for it is an "*asar di veih yechedun ruchin v'nafshin*—a place where the spiritual and physical rejoice."

The opening words of *Kah Ribon* depict how very concealed these miracles are. The word for "world" in Hebrew is "*olam*" which is related to the word "*he'elem*" meaning "hidden" or "concealed." The words "*Kah Ribon alam v'almaya*" therefore paint a picture of utter *he'elem*, a world of mystery and veiled secrets.

---

9   See *Makkos* 24a: "*Heim bachu v'Rabbi Akiva tzachak—They wept and Rabbi Akiva laughed.*"

But behind the veil is G-d Himself, the orchestrator of it all. The word "*alam,*" which depicts the "*he'elem,*" is spelled without a letter *vav,* which is the "*Os ha'chibbur* (the letter that acts as a conjunction). This alludes to the fact that G-d has no *chibbur* (conjunction) with the physical or spiritual worlds, for His holiness supersedes all.[10] But on Shabbos, the *machshavah techilah* (the original masterplan of the world) becomes revealed in the *sof maaseh.* On Shabbos one may find Hashem and get to know Him and his master-plot, for Shabbos is *me'ein Olam Haba,* in miniature.

It follows that the *zemer* of *Kah Ribon* is truly pertinent to every day of the week, for it tells of the Godliness hidden in our world. But it is nevertheless set aside for Shabbos because it is then that we may sense G-d's presence in our world and almost point to Him with our fingers, "*Ant Hu Malka Melech malchaya*—You are the King who reigns over kings."

The Midrash relates:[11] "*Kevod Elokim haster davar, u'chevod melachim chakor davar*—It is the honor of G-d to conceal, but it is the honor of kings to reveal."[12] Rabbi Levi commented: "Until this point [the onset of Shabbos], the honor of G-d was "*haster davar*—a concealed matter." **Thereafter, the honor of the King can be revealed.** During the week, the world is beset by *he'elem.* On Shabbos, it may perceive the "*Malka Melech malchaya*" amidst the "*alam v'almaya.*"

---

10   *Responsa Rashba* 5:52: "G-d is **revealed** in terms of His existence but **hidden** in terms of His essence."

11   *Bereishis Rabbah* 9:1.

12   *Mishlei* 25:2.

The Song of Shabbos

Lechah Dodi

The first two stanzas of *Lechah Dodi*, the celebrated song of *Kabbalas Shabbos*, appear at first glance to have been written out of order. The first stanza, which begins with the words "*Shamor v'zachor b'dibbur echad*," describes the Shabbos of Matan Torah (the revelation at Sinai) when G-d commanded the Jewish People to observe and commemorate Shabbos.[1] The second stanza, which contains the words "*Me'rosh mi'kedem nesuchah*—From the beginning, before anything, she was honored," references the seminal Shabbos of Creation. Why is the Shabbos of Creation only mentioned after that of Matan Torah?

The Gemara[2] states, "Said Rabbi Hamnuna: Any person who prays on Friday night and recites *Vayechulu*—the Torah considers it as though he becomes a partner with G-d in the acts of Creation." Simply understood, the Gemara's intent is that by observing Shabbos a person demonstrates that he believes that G-d created the world in six days and rested on the seventh, and that in so doing he ascribes to the Biblical account of creation. But how does this belief render him a "**partner** in creation"?

---

1   "*Shamor*" connotes the "don't do" aspects of the laws of Shabbos such as working, writing, or planting. "*Zachor*" heads the list of the "dos," such as Kiddush or *oneg Shabbos*. Ostensibly, dos and don'ts address opposite functions of the human psyche. Extroverts like the do's and introverts prefer the don'ts. Nevertheless, on Shabbos both fuse into one.

2   *Shabbos* 119b.

Further, if Shabbos is said to demonstrate the belief that G-d created the world, why was it only gifted to the Jewish People? Surely this matter is pertinent to any nation which ascribes to the story of creation.

Unity of Hashem

"*Shema Yisrael Hashem Elokeinu Hashem Echad*"—Hear O Israel, Hashem is our G-d, Hashem is One."[3] *Rashi*[4] explains that the reason that the name "Hashem" is repeated in this verse is to hint at a time in the future when all of the world's inhabitants will recognize Hashem as G-d. He writes: "Hashem, who is now our G-d and not the G-d of the idol worshippers, will, in the times to come, be the solitary G-d when the words—'Then I will transform all of the nations to speak a common language that they all call out in the name of G-d' come true."

When a person recites *Shema Yisrael* (the two most famous words in the Jewish lexicon), he accepts the yoke of Heaven upon himself. Why is it important that he mention the fact that Hashem is not currently the G-d of the idol worshippers?

Perhaps the verse wishes to stress that presently it is only through Torah that one can grasp the notion of G-d's all-encompassing unity, and the idolatrous nations will only realize this in the times to come. This may be the reason why our twice-daily declaration of faith and acceptance of the yoke of Heaven comprise this verse, for the belief in Hashem's unity in this world is exclusively felt by us. In fact, this may also be why the verse stresses that it is Israel who hears the message that G-d is One—"*Shema **Yisrael**.*"[5]

G-d's unity—namely, that He is unique and that there is no other being that is His equal (captured in the words of the second *Ani Maamin*, the thirteen tenets of our faith)—is grasped principally by the people who accept the Torah. They recognize that all of the world's forces, including those that are in conflict with one another, such as fire and water, are truly one. They know that all of the results of Providence,

---

3   *Devarim* 6:4.

4   Ad loc.

5   "*Shema Yisrael*" were the last two words uttered by those who sacrificed their lives for the Jewish faith throughout the millennia of Jewish history.

including the unfathomable suffering of the righteous, are one. And in fact, only they believe that at their root, these phenomena do not contradict one another at all.

The idolatrous nations may relate to the first *Ani Maamin*—namely, that G-d created the world—but the appreciation of G-d's unity, immortalized by the second *Ani Maamin*, is truly beyond them. (Though they might ascribe to it, their grasp is superficial.) Indeed, we witness how these nations defy elements of the created world, in stark contrast to the Jews who espouse the belief that "it is only fitting to pray to Hashem, and futile to pray to any other."

According to Rav Hutner, Shabbos is a day that reveals the unity of G-d. The Torah relates that when G-d saw that all that He had created was "very good,"[6] He created Shabbos. It is thus clearly a day when everything is unified and perfect. Shabbos demonstrates how the apparently mundane elements of the world are no contradiction to holiness and sanctity just as the six mundane days of Creation are mere stepping stones to Shabbos. It also expresses the belief that holiness is paramount—helping the world to see how nature, the mundane, and the sacrosanct all work together in perfect harmony. Through Shabbos, the world begins to appreciate that every component of Creation, even the tiniest of its elements (like the blades of grass over which each has a presiding angel), together form a testimony to G-d's unity.

This notion is beyond the grasp of the boor or the fool. The verse states,[7] "A boor cannot know nor can a fool understand this: when the wicked bloom like grass and all the doers of iniquity blossom, it is to destroy them until eternity." The *Metzudas David*[8] explains that the boor and fool do not realize that the reason that the wicked are sometimes successful in this world is that G-d wishes to reward them for their few good deeds so that they will be eternally punished in the World to Come. The chapter of *Tehillim* in which this verse is found (*Mizmor shir l'yom haShabbos*) is an apt choice to be the "Song of the Day" of Shabbos

---

6   *Bereishis* 1:31.

7   *Tehillim* 92:7.

8   Ad loc.

for its message is that there are no contradictions in G-d's running of the world.[9] This resonates with Shabbos, which, as stated, is a day that reveals G-d's unity—a day on which there are no questions, when everything is at rest, and when our minds are at ease from the storm of unanswered questions that overwhelm us during the week.

The phrase from the *Shema*, "Hashem Elokeinu," is ostensibly a contradiction in terms. The name "Hashem" connotes G-d's trait of mercy but "*Elokim*" (from which "*Elokeinu*" is derived) reflects His attribute of strict judgment. However, we know that the two are really no contradiction at all. Unlike the boor and fool, who remain blissfully unaware of G-d's utter unity, the Jewish people proclaim the words "*Hashem Elokeinu*" in the knowledge that those words are perfectly complementary. And in the times to come, as "the world is filled with the knowledge of G-d," the boor and the fool will know it too.

Shabbos is the exclusive domain of the believers in the Torah, and a person who observes Shabbos is considered a partner in Creation—not just a believer in G-d. Those who observe Shabbos grasp the notion of G-d's unity and truly believe in it. On Shabbos, G-d's unity and His perfect handiwork are in evidence, and those who observe Shabbos are strengthened in their beliefs. Thus, they become true partners in creation. Creation didn't end after seven days; G-d needed a partner to spread the word of his unity—the message of Shabbos.

The Midrash famously relates[10] that when the people of the world see the *Menorah* (candelabra) alit in the Temple they declare, "See how they [the Jewish People] kindle a light for Him who is a light unto the entire world." According to the *Zayis Raanan*,[11] the correct text of the Midrash states that the Jewish People also achieve this by kindling the Chanukah and Shabbos candles. Clearly, the Shabbos candles (which are symbolic of Shabbos observance) represent the Jewish People's unique ability to teach the world about G-d's unity. In fact, the nation's miraculous survival of two thousand years of persecution and expulsion prove that

---

9   *Pachad Yitzchok: Pesach, Maamar* 54, §5.
10   *Bamidbar Rabbah* 15:5.
11   Ad loc.

there is a G-d Almighty and that persecution and redemption are not contradictory, but two components of one unified world master plan.[12]

Shabbos of Creation and Shabbos of Matan Torah

The exalted song *Lechah Dodi*, which was to be accepted by the Jewish People as an introduction to Shabbos, had to begin with a description of Shabbos as a vehicle for insight into the uniqueness of G-d. Thus, the first stanza, "*Shamor v'zachor b'dibbur echad*," declares that the One who uttered the command to observe and commemorate Shabbos was the *Keil haMeyuchad*, "the Unique G-d." But this notion was only grasped in all of its profundity at Matan Torah, not at the original Shabbos of creation.

In fact, Matan Torah served to reveal G-d's intentions in Creation in a broader sense. The Ten Commandments that were uttered at Sinai are said to be a practical expression of G-d's intentions when He created the world with *Asarah Maamaros* (Ten Utterances).[13] Thus, in the presenting of the Tablets of Stone and the transmitting of the Ten Commandments, G-d revealed His objectives of Creation.[14] This was a powerful demonstration of His unity, namely that Creation was all geared to this moment of Sinaitic revelation. As the first stanza of *Lechah Dodi* goes on to declare: "*Hashem Echad u'Shemo Echad*—G-d is One and His name is One."

The reason that the first stanza of *Lechah Dodi* describes the Shabbos of Matan Torah and not the Shabbos of Creation **is that one cannot fathom the Shabbos of Creation without contemplating the revelations of Matan Torah.** In this, the commandment of Shabbos is reflective of all of the Ten Commandments, each of which reveals the essence of one of the Ten Utterances of Creation. It follows that the Jewish People, who experienced the revelations at Mount Sinai, **are not only the sole possessors of the Shabbos of Matan Torah but also of the Shabbos of Creation.** This is why the gift of Shabbos was given only to them.

---

12   *Maharal, Netzach Yisrael*, first chapters and throughout.
13   *Avos* 5:1.
14   *Pachad Yitzchok: Pesach, Maamar* 47, §5 and 7.

There is another layer to this too. At Matan Torah, G-d uttered the command to **observe** Shabbos (*shamor*, the negative precepts) and the command to **commemorate** Shabbos (*zachor*, the positive precepts) simultaneously—"*Shamor v'zachor b'dibbur echad.*" This miraculous feat announced to the entire world that the mitzvah of Shabbos was only relevant to those who ascribed to G-d's unity, to those who recognized that the two different commands of *shamor* and *zachor*, relating to contradicting forces, were both uttered by one G-d. The peoples' experience at Matan Torah, as they heard G-d utter *shamor* and *zachor* simultaneously, made the notion that "G-d is One and His name is One" a concrete belief rather than an intangible concept. This is true, on some level, of every Shabbos, which grants us an almost tangible feel of G-d's unity, quite unlike that which we experience during the week.

"*Shamor v'zachor b'dibbur echad*—Observe and commemorate Shabbos the unified G-d had us hear," for "*Hashem Echad u'Shemo Echad*—G-d is One and His name is One." He granted us the ability to hear something that is ordinarily impossible to hear, and that experience and the faith that it engendered made us partners with Him in Creation. This faith allows us to march directly to the second stanza of "*Likras Shabbos l'chu v'nelcha,*" and the Shabbos of Creation that it describes, "*Me'rosh mi'kedem nesuchah*—From **the beginning**, before anything, she was consecrated."

On Shabbos, we return to the deep understanding of the source of it all, which is the creation of the world. In fact, already prior to Creation G-d had decided to establish Shabbos in the world—"From the beginning, before anything, she was consecrated"—and although it was ultimately introduced last in Creation, it was first in G-d's master plan. Ultimately, Shabbos was introduced to the world to reveal the purpose of Creation, which is to create *kedushah* (holiness), as the verse states regarding Shabbos "*Va'yekadesh oso*—and He sanctified it."

Perhaps this sheds some more light on the famous comment of the *Gra* (the Gaon of Vilna) regarding the three prayers of Shabbos.[15] The *Gra*

---

15   *Aderes Eliyahu, Balak* 5:23; *Likuei HaGra, tefillas Minchah shel Shabbos.*

avers that the three prayers correspond to three notable Shabbosos in history. The *Maariv* prayer, which contains the paragraph of *Vayechulu* (a description of the completion of Creation), corresponds to the Shabbos of Creation, *Shabbos Bereishis*. *Shacharis*, which contains the paragraph of "*Yismach Moshe b'matnas chelko*" (which describes Matan Torah), corresponds to the Shabbos on which the Torah was given. *Minchah*, which describes the idyllic life of the World to Come ("*Atah Echad v'Shimcha Echad*"), corresponds to the Shabbos-like state that will exist after the final redemption.

These three Shabbosos do not only appear in chronological order but also in conceptual order. Nighttime is a time of *yediah* (knowledge), as the verse states regarding the *mann*, "In the **evening** and you will **know**."[16] Therefore, *Maariv*—the nighttime prayer, references the Shabbos of Creation which began at night as the verse states, "And it was evening and it was morning."[17] Nighttime is a time of *yediah*—the knowledge that Shabbos is holy. Knowledge is an inferior perception to that of *re'iyah* (seeing).

Daytime is a time of *re'iyah*, as the verse states regarding the mann, "In the **morning** you will **see**."[18] Therefore, the *Shacharis* prayer references Matan Torah when the Jewish People heard *shamor* and *zachor* uttered as one. The Sages say that at that time they understood that although Shabbos has a dual nature[19] (all aspects of Shabbos are *kefulim*, layered), all of its myriad dualities stem from one unified source of *kedushah*.

The Shabbos of the times to come, referenced in the *Minchah* prayer, refers to the era when the unity of G-d will be felt tangibly by all of the nations of the world, not just the Jews—"All of the inhabitants of the world will recognize and know that Hashem is G-d," meaning that the G-d of mercy is the very same as the G-d of justice.

The *Gra* also notes that each of the Shabbos prayers commands its own *nusach ha'neginah* that the *chazzan* sings. But on Yom Tov, all

---

16   *Shemos* 16:6.
17   *Bereishis* 1:5.
18   Ibid., 7.
19   See fn 1 above.

three of the prayers have the same text—"*Atah bechartanu*"—which delineates the singular chosenness of the Jewish people who are united in their pilgrimage to Jerusalem to "see and be seen" (*yireh v'yeira'eh*)[20] in the Beis Hamikdash. Moreover, there is only one *nusach ha'neginah* for all three of the prayers.

This is why Rabbi Shlomo Alkabetz, the great author of *Lechah Dodi*, began with "*Shamor v'zachor b'dibbur echad*"—the immortal words that describe the display of G-d's unity at Matan Torah. By appreciating G-d's unity a person can imbibe Shabbos to the full degree, attaching himself to *Shabbos Bereishis*, the Shabbos of Matan Torah, and ultimately the Shabbos of the end of days. The subsequent stanzas of *Lechah Dodi*, namely "*Mikdash Melech*" until the penultimate stanza, allude to the end of days when the unity that permeates creation, and which was envisaged by G-d before creation, will be gloriously evident; everything will come full circle, and the world will return to utopian times as it was before Adam committed his sin.

This idea helps answer a question on the aforementioned comment of the *Gra*. The Sages say[21] that Shabbos is *me'ein Olam Haba* (akin to the World to Come). Assumedly this is true of all of Shabbos—night, morning, and afternoon—how then can the *Gra* claim that only Shabbos *Minchah* corresponds to the Shabbos at the end of the days?

In light of the above, we may suggest that both *Shabbos Bereishis* and the Shabbos of Matan Torah which are invoked by the *Gra* also reflect a state of *me'ein Olam Haba*. *Shabbos Bereishis* represents the utopian times that existed before Adam's sin, the world residing in a state akin to the World to Come.[22] The Shabbos of Matan Torah was also akin to the World to Come as the stain of the original sin of Adam left the Jewish People ("*paskah zuhamasan*"),[23] and they entered a G-dly state as the verse states, "*Ani amarti Elokim atem, u'vnei Elyon kulchem.*"[24]

---

20 Mishnah *Arachin* 2:2.
21 *Berachos* 57b.
22 Although Adam's sin took place before the first Shabbos of Creation, the Torah describes it only afterwards. See below, chapter 17, *Nishmas Kol Chai*.
23 *Shabbos* 146:1.
24 *Tehillim* 82:6.

It follows that the three segments of Shabbos—evening, morning, and afternoon—each present a different aspect of the World to Come. At night there resides the knowledge of G-d's unity (the *yediah*); in the morning it is palpable (there is *re'iyah*); in the afternoon there is the overriding sense that the Jewish People are similarly unique and uniquely matched with G-d, "You are one, Your name is one, and who is like your nation Israel—a singular nation in the land?"

As we received from Chazal, "*Yisrael, v'Oraysa v'Kudsha Brich Hu chad hu*—Israel, the Torah, and G-d are One."

To Declare That
Hashem Is Just

The Song of the Day of Shabbos, chapter 92 of *Tehillim*, concludes with the words *"L'hagid ki yashar Hashem*—to declare that Hashem is just." What does the notion of G-d's justness have to do with Shabbos?

David HaMelech states, "Hashem, guide me in your righteous way…make Your way straight before me."[1] How could David ask for G-d to "make His ways straight"—are G-d's ways not inherently straight? The *Metzudas David* explains that in fact David was asking that G-d grant him an appreciation of how His ways are just—"Endow my heart that I shall understand the justice of your ways."

Rav Hutner would explain[2] that on Shabbos Hashem endows a person with this understanding that His ways are just. During the week man may struggle to comprehend why the righteous suffer and the wicked succeed, as *Tehillim* 92 indeed notes, "A boor cannot know, nor can a fool understand this: when the wicked bloom like grass and all the doers of iniquity blossom." But on Shabbos he has no questions, and his mind is at ease for he recognizes that "it is to destroy them until

---

1   *Tehillim* 5:9.
2   *Pachad Yitzchok: Pesach, Maamar* 54, §5.

eternity," as G-d wishes to reward them for their few good deeds so that they will be eternally punished in the World to Come.[3]

On Shabbos man may truly grasp that everything that G-d does is just and good. The song of Shabbos, "*Mizmor shir l'yom haShabbos*," begins with the word "*tov*" (good) for the very *mizmor* of Shabbos preaches the notion that everything in G-d's world is good. He will ensure that the wicked will ultimately receive their comeuppance and the righteous "will flourish like a date-palm, like a cedar in the Lebanon he will grow tall." On Shabbos, the prayer of *Tehillim* (5:9) "Make Your way straight before me" is answered emphatically—"*L'hagid ki yashar Hashem.*"

---

3   *Metzudas David* ad Loc. See above, "The Song of Shabbos" where we discuss this concept at length.

Good Shabbos

Greetings

The Mishnah in *Berachos*[1] records a fascinating *takanah* (enactment) of the Sages by which people would be permitted to greet one another using one of the names of Hashem. Proof for this *takanah* is adduced from the conduct of Boaz who, upon returning from Beis Lechem, greeted the harvesters with the words, "Hashem be with you."[2]

Rashi explains,[3] "A person may greet his fellowman using the name of Hashem; and we do not claim that [in so doing] he degrades the honor of the Almighty in the name of honoring people..."

Is there an **obligation** to greet others with G-d's name or is it merely **permissible**? This would seem to depend upon two different explanations offered by *Rashi* in *Makkos*[4]:

> *It is permissible for a person to greet his fellowman using the name of G-d, such as "G-d shall grant you peace." Doing so does not constitute uttering G-d's name in vain.[5]*

---

1. 54a.
2. *Rus* 2:4.
3. S.v. *"She'yehei."*
4. 23b.
5. This idea may help explain the curious expression *"sho'el es sh'lom chavero."* Why do Chazal use the term *"sho'el,"* meaning "to ask," to denote a greeting? The answer may be that using G-d's name as a form of greeting is actually fraught with danger, for people may come to

20

Alternatively, a person is obligated to greet his fellowman using the name of G-d. We similarly greet one another using G-d's name, for the word Shalom is one of the names of G-d, as the verse states, "And he called it 'G-d of peace' in the name of G-d."[6]

According to *Rashi's* second explanation, there is an **obligation** to use Hashem's name in a greeting. Why then are we accustomed today to using greetings such as "Good morning" or "*A gut yohr*" etc. rather than "*shalom aleichem*" or the like?

The Gemara rules[7] that it is forbidden to go to a person's home in order to greet him before *Shacharis*. In fact, if a person does so it is as though he built an altar for an idol! *Rashi* explains, "When it is incumbent upon you to occupy yourself with the honor of G-d, do not occupy yourself with the honor of man." This law is also codified by the *Shulchan Aruch.*[8]

The *Beis Yosef* cites Rabbeinu Yonah,[9] who contends that it is only forbidden to greet a person before *Shacharis* if one uses the word "*Shalom*" which is one of the names of Hashem. Merely wishing him a good morning is permissible.

---

utter His name in vain. Though Chazal ultimately permitted it, they dubbed it as "**sho'el es sh'lom chavero**" as if to hint at the care and concern that a person must show in doing so. In other words, it is as if on each occasion we "*ask permission from G-d*" to make use of His name in that fashion. (See *Shabbos* 89a and *Maharsha* ad loc. who discusses the difference between *nesinas shalom* and *she'eilas shalom*.)

This answer is reminiscent of a comment of Rav Hutner who noted that while the trait of loving G-d is dubbed "*ahavas Hashem*," the trait of fearing Him is dubbed "*yiras Shamayim*"—fear of Heaven (even though the term "*yiras Hashem*" is found in verses in *Tanach*). The reason for this is that refraining from uttering G-d's name in vain is an expression of fear. Therefore, in the very name of this trait we refrain from uttering His name, and instead call it "*yiras Shamayim*."

6 *Sefer Shoftim* 6:24.
7 *Berachos* 14a.
8 *Orach Chaim* 89:2.
9 Ibid.

The Mishnah in *Mo'ed Katan* rules[10] that *she'eilas shalom* (extending greetings) is prohibited to a mourner. The Gemara clarifies[11] that while a mourner may greet others for they are "in a state of *shalom*," others may not greet him for he is not. The *Tur* and *Shulchan Aruch*[12] therefore rule that if a person is mourning a parent then one may not greet him for the entire twelve months of *aveilus*.

The *Rama* cites opinions which permit greeting a mourner after the *shloshim* (the first thirty days of mourning). He posits that this is because they do not consider the traditional greetings to constitute *she'eilas shalom*. However, the *Shach* insists that this argument is flawed. For if our greetings do not constitute *she'eilas shalom* they should be permissible even within the *shloshim*!

The *Be'er Hetev* defends the reasoning of the *Rama*. He compares this halachah with that of greeting a person before *Shacharis* where greetings like "Good morning" are not considered to be *she'eilas shalom* as outlined above. Since our greetings are mostly of this sort, one may be lenient and greet a mourner in this fashion after the *shloshim*.

According to the *Be'er Hetev*, the sort of greeting which may not be extended to a person before *Shacharis* may similarly not be extended to a mourner. This may help answer the question we posed earlier. The reason that we are not accustomed to greeting others with the name of Hashem is to ensure that we don't accidentally use this form of greeting at a time when doing so is prohibited, such as before *Shacharis* or when in the company of a mourner. Our custom to refrain from using Hashem's name as a form of greeting reflects a natural sensitivity to preserve the sanctity of Hashem's name. This is somewhat reminiscent of our custom to use the term "*yiras Shamayim*" (fear of Heaven) rather than "*yiras Hashem*" (fear of G-d) which (as discussed in footnote 5) similarly reflects a desire to avoid the desecration of Hashem's name. Earlier generations, who were accustomed to using these greetings,

---

10   15a.

11   Ibid., 21a.

12   *Yoreh Deah* 385.

were on a higher level of *kedushah* and thus were able to be mindful and not err.

Good Shabbos

This may also shed some light on the advice offered by the Brisker Rav to wish a mourner *"Gut Shabbos"* rather than *"Shabbat shalom."*[13] The Rav may have held that *"Gut Shabbos"* is similar to "Good morning" which, according to the *Be'er Hetev*, may be addressed to a mourner.

However, according to the *Shach*, we cannot compare the laws of greeting somebody before *Shacharis* and greeting a mourner. Therefore, though a person may wish someone "Good morning" before *Shacharis*, he may nevertheless not greet a mourner in this fashion.

Why does the *Shach* hold that there is a difference between these two areas of halachah? Perhaps he understood the two prohibitions to be fundamentally different. The issue of greeting a person before *Shacharis* is that it is disrespectful of Hashem to use His name before having accepted His yoke upon oneself. For this reason, the *Orchos Chaim* rules[14] that if a person has already said some of the *Berachos* of *Shacharis*, thus accepting G-d's yoke upon himself, then he may be lenient and extend a greeting to somebody.

However, the issue of greeting a mourner is not one of disrespecting Hashem's name but due to the fact that a mourner "is not in a state of *shalom*." According to the *Shach*, it is logical to say that just as the state of mourning precludes *shalom* (thus one cannot greet him with the words *"shalom aleichem"*), it also precludes other positive concepts such as *tov* (goodness). Therefore, one also cannot wish him a "Good morning" or *"A gut yohr."*[15]

---

13   I heard this in 5733 from Rav Romm, a *rav* in Haifa and a *talmid* of the Brisker Rav.
It appears that the Brisker Rav held that *she'eilas shalom* is even forbidden on Shabbos. Though on Shabbos he may not publicly observe the laws of mourning, nevertheless since he still conducts himself like a mourner in private, he is still not considered to be "in a state of *shalom*."

14   Cited by the *Beis Yosef, Orach Chaim* 89.

15   This requires further study as a mourner who, for example, receives an inheritance, is still obligated in the *berachos* of *Hatov V'hameitiv* and *Shehecheyanu*.

According to the *Shach* it would presumably be forbidden to wish a mourner "Good Shabbos" too. Why then did the Brisker Rav advise people to wish a mourner "Good Shabbos"?

One possible answer is that the Rav would only *advise* people that they may conduct themselves in this manner but did not issue it as a halachic ruling. Since it at least fulfills the opinion of the *Be'er Hetev* (as explained above), he felt that a person could be lenient given that we are generally permitted to follow a more lenient opinion in the halachos of mourning. However, ideally a person would fulfill the opinion of the *Shach* and not wish a mourner "Good Shabbos."

Perhaps we may suggest a deeper answer.

Rabbi Akiva Eiger[16] famously contends that a person fulfills the Biblical obligation of Kiddush merely by declaring *Shabsa Tava* (Good Shabbos). Since the essential mitzvah of Kiddush is to make a special mention of Shabbos—"*Zachor es yom haShabbos l'kadsho,*" one may fulfill this mitzvah through praying *Maariv* or even by extending the greeting of "Good Shabbos."[17]

At first sight, this is a difficult ruling to understand. The *Rambam* explains[18] that the mitzvah of Kiddush is to declare a *zechiras shevach v'kiddush*, "a mention of praise and sanctity," and while the *tefillos* of Shabbos—which are replete with praises of the *yom ha'shevi'i*—clearly fulfill that condition, a casual "Good Shabbos" seemingly does not. How then can Rabbi Akiva Eiger contend that it fulfills the mitzvah of Kiddush?

Perhaps there is more to the simple greeting of "Good Shabbos" than meets the eye. Conceivably, "Good Shabbos" is not just a greeting equivalent to that of "Good morning" or "*A gut yohr,*" considered by

---

Perhaps we can distinguish between cases where he receives the "*tov*" automatically and those where it depends upon the active choice of the person bestowing the *tov*.

16   *Hagahos* on *Shulchan Aruch, Orach Chaim* 271.

17   According to Rabbi Akiva Eiger, if a person wishes another "Good Shabbos" on his way to shul on Friday, that would amount to an act of *kabbalas Shabbos* (accepting Shabbos upon himself). This would render him unable to perform *melachos* such as driving to shul! Perhaps it would be better for a person to decide in his mind that he has no intention of accepting Shabbos upon himself when he extends this greeting.

18   *Hilchos Shabbos* 29:1.

the *Shach* to be a *she'eilas shalom*, but is rather a statement extolling Shabbos—a declaration of *shevach* asserting that Shabbos is good! It therefore is a most appropriate phrase with which to fulfill the mitzvah of Kiddush.

If "Good Shabbos" is a declaration of *shevach*, why do we use it as a manner of greeting others? The answer may be that we wish to use the *shevach* of Shabbos to bless our fellowmen, "This good and blessed Shabbos shall be a source of blessing for you!" This is reminiscent of the custom of using the name of G-d to greet, and thereby bless, others whom we meet.

Perhaps this is why the Brisker Rav permitted wishing "Good Shabbos" to a mourner. For although it is generally used as a greeting, it is essentially a declaration of *shevach* rather than a form of *she'eilas shalom*.

If it is permissible to address a mourner with a statement of praise of Shabbos, why may we not similarly wish him "*Shabbat shalom*" which is also a declaration of *shevach*, namely that Shabbos is the source of peace?

The answer lies in a concept discussed extensively in this *sefer*.

Rav Hutner would explain that the source of the *kedushah* of Shabbos was the contentment (so to speak) felt by G-d when he observed that all that He had created was "very good." "*Va'yar Elokim es kol asher asah v'hinei tov me'od...Vayechulu haShamayim...Va'yevarech Elokim es yom ha'shevi'i va'yekadesh oso*—And G-d saw all that He had created and it was very good...And the Heavens were complete...And G-d blessed the seventh day and He sanctified it." In other words, the very definition of Shabbos is that it is the day on which all of creation is determined to be "very good."

This is also alluded to in the *Shir shel Yom* (the Song of the Day) of Shabbos which begins with the words "*Mizmor shir l'yom haShabbos, tov*—A song for the day of Shabbos, it is good." These words which serve as the prologue to the *mizmor* of Shabbos portray how the praise and song of Shabbos can truly be captured in one word—*tov*.

This may be why Rabbi Akiva Eiger held that the words "*Shabsa Tava*" fulfill the mitzvah of Kiddush. For in mentioning that Shabbos is *tov* a person has encapsulated the entire meaning of Shabbos and referenced the very source of its *kedushah*, namely, the "*tov me'od*" of creation.

In fact, Rabbi Akiva Eiger might have conceded that a statement, such as "*Shabbat shalom*" which does not mention *tov* would not have the same effect.

This is also why the Brisker Rav held that wishing a mourner "Good Shabbos" would not amount to *she'eilas shalom*, for the declaration that Shabbos is *tov* is the quintessential statement of *shevach* of Shabbos and not inherently a statement of greeting.

This is not the case with "*Shabbat shalom*" or the like. For although Shabbos is indeed the source of blessing and the source of positive ideals such as *shalom*, the statement that Shabbos brings peace does not capture the entire essence of Shabbos.[19] In fact, *shalom* as a blessing is pertinent on any day of the week. Therefore, it is viewed principally as a statement of greeting and constitutes *she'eilas shalom*.

If "Good Shabbos" captures the entire essence of Shabbos, why are some people (including some Ashkenazim) particular to use the phrase "*Shabbat shalom*"? Perhaps it is due to the fact that *shalom* is, as stated, one of the names of Hashem and it is preferable to bless one's fellow in that manner.

---

19   Moreover, *shalom* is said by Chazal (*Uktzin* 3:12) to be a *kli* (a vessel) of blessing rather than a blessing in and of itself. "*Lo matza kli tov hamachzik berachah ela hashalom.*" See also *Megillah* 18a: "The main *berachah* of G-d is *shalom.*"

Like Bride and Groom

1

Yasis Alayich

"The rejoicing of a bridegroom over his bride, your G-d will rejoice over you."[1]

These are the immortal words of the *navi* Yeshayahu describing the blissful relationship between Hashem and His people at the end of days. The *Targum Yonasan*, *Metzudas David*, and *Radak* all explain that the verse means to convey a parable, namely that the love of Hashem for his people at the end of days will **resemble** that of a *chassan* and *kallah* on their wedding day.

This also appears to have been the understanding of Rabbi Shlomo Alkabetz. In the eighth stanza of *Lechah Dodi* which recounts the joy and salvation that will abound in the times to come, he declares, *"Yasis alayich Elokayich, ki'msos chassan al kallah*—Your G-d will rejoice over you, **like** a *chassan* rejoices over his bride." By employing the *kaf ha'dimyon*, the letter *kaf* as a prefix that serves to compare one thing to another, Rav Alkabetz appeared to have understood the verse above to be a parable, just like the other commentators.

However, there may be a deeper concept at play.

---

1   *Yeshayahu* 62:5.

Simchah Bi'me'ono

Though the commentators clearly explain the verse to be speaking metaphorically, the verse itself noticeably refrains from employing a *kaf ha'dimyon*. Instead, it declares, "The rejoicing of a bridegroom over his bride, your G-d will rejoice over you." This implies that Hashem's love for His people is *precisely* that of a groom over his bride!

In the following paragraphs we will explore this remarkable idea, beginning with some extraordinary words of the *Aruch Hashulchan*:[2]

> *The reason for invoking the word "me'ono" (G-d's abode) [at a wedding or sheva berachos where we say she'hasimchah bi'me'ono in the zimun] is because it is from that place that G-d blesses the Jewish people, as the verse states, "Cast Your eyes down from Your holy abode, from the Heavens, and bless Your people Israel..."*
>
> *And it is only instituted to be mentioned at a wedding, and not at any other events [even those] that celebrate a mitzvah. [In fact] one great rabbi held that it should be mentioned at every siyum Maseches [celebration of completing a tractate of Talmud] arguing that there is no greater joy than that of the joy of Torah.*
>
> *It appears to me that on the contrary, the Sages instituted [that we invoke the word "me'ono"] specifically at a wedding. For if we give the matter some thought, we will realize that at a wedding our joy is incomplete...In fact, in this world our joy is [always] incomplete—only in Heaven [in G-d's abode] is there absolute joy, as the verse states, "[There is] might and delight in His place." [The addition of me'ono is consequently an admission to the limitation of the simchah (gladness) of chassan and kallah.]*
>
> *However, with regard to Torah study, it is possible to attain absolute joy in this world, as the Mishnah states,[3] "One hour*

---

2   *Even HaEzer, Hilchos Kiddushin 62:40.*
3   *Avos 4:17.*

*of repentance and good deeds in this world is greater than all
of life in the World to Come." This would be all the more true
of Torah study.[4] Therefore one should not say she'hasimchah
bi'me'ono, [at a siyum] for we too can experience joy that is
absolute...*

According to the *Aruch Hashulchan,* the joy of a wedding, or indeed
that of any of the mitzvos, is incomplete, for absolute joy can only be
attained *bi'me'ono* (in G-d's abode). This is the reason that we recite the
words "*she'hasimchah bi'me'ono*" at a wedding—to stress that our *simchah* does not approach that of the Heavenly abode. Mitzvos, of which
marriage is an example, only serve as a *means* to attain the absolute joy
of the World to Come; they do not afford us with that experience already
in this world. "*Ha'yom la'asosom u'l'machar l'kabbel secharam*—Today to
perform them, and tomorrow to receive the reward."[5]

Not so is the great joy of Torah study which already affords us a taste
of the *simchah bi'me'ono* (absolute joy of G-d's abode). Chazal describe[6]
how in the World to Come, "The righteous will sit, with their crowns on
their heads, and enjoy the radiance of the Shechinah (Divine Presence)";
but what enjoyment is there in contemplating the radiance of the
Shechinah? One can only assume that it is the enormous pleasure of
Torah study, for at that time the righteous will attain a far greater and
deeper perception of the Torah and of G-d[7] than they ever had before.
It follows, that the joy we feel when studying Torah in this world, is an

---

4   The *Aruch Hashulchan's* proof from the Mishnah that it is possible to experience absolute
joy in this world appears to contradict his theory that we may draw a distinction between
the joy of Torah and that of a wedding. Since a wedding is also a Mitzvah, why should it not
also be included in the Mishnah's statement that "one hour of repentance **and good deeds** is
greater..."

5   *Eruvin* 22a, cited by *Rashi* to *Devarim* 7:11.

6   Cited by the *Mesilas Yesharim* 1. See also *Taanis* 31a.

7   In the *berachah* of "*V'haarev na*" which we recite each morning, we ask that Hashem sweeten
the Torah for us. This sweetness is that experienced by the righteous in the World to Come as
they contemplate the Shechinah. Toward the end of the *berachah* we state that by means of
Torah study we will be considered *Yod'ei Shemecha*, those who know Your name. "Knowledge
of G-d's name" means attaining an understanding of G-d and is a taste of that which is
attained by the righteous in the World to Come.

experience in miniature of the delight[8] of the World to Come when the worthy will bask in the radiance of the Shechinah.

For this reason, the *Aruch Hashulchan* concluded that the words "*she'hasimchah bi'me'ono*" should not be invoked at a *siyum*. The sweet joy of a person who completes a tractate in Talmud is absolute for he is transported to G-d's abode in which *oz v'chedvah* abound. It is therefore not appropriate that he state at that time that absolute joy is only found *bi'me'ono*, and not in this world.

2

Hashem and Yisrael, a Marriage

L et us return to the words of Yeshayahu HaNavi.

Hashem's love for His people at the end of days will emanate from His Heavenly abode, a love that is absolute and complete. The *Navi*, in depicting that love, could not possibly compare it, even metaphorically, to the love of a regular *chassan* and *kallah*, for their joy is incomplete and unlike the *simchah bi'me'ono* (as the *Aruch Hashulchan* explained). A *kaf ha'dimyon* would therefore have been utterly inappropriate.

Instead, the *Navi* conveyed a far more profound idea—that the love of a *chassan* for his *kallah* emulates the love of Hashem for His people. The intensity of the love cannot be compared, but every marriage constitutes a Divine union that itself is a great cause for celebration—"The rejoicing of a bridegroom over his bride, your G-d will rejoice over you," without the *kaf ha'dimyon*.

This notion is alluded to in the concluding words of the *birkas ha'eirusin*, the *berachah* recited upon the betrothal of a *chassan* and *kallah*, which states, "*Mekadesh amo Yisrael al yedei chuppah v'kiddushin*—He sanctifies His people Israel, through *chuppah* and betrothal."

---

8   See the *Eglei Tal's* introduction to his *sefer* regarding *Torah lishmah*. See also the *sefer Igros Chazon Ish* (4) who describes the "*chiddushim* (of those who toil in Torah) which gladden the soul, and stimulate a supernal love, more elevated than all else."

The *Tashbetz HaKatan*[9] cites the *gedolei ha'poskim*, who explain that the *berachah* refers to the sanctity bestowed by G-d upon the Jewish people at Mount Sinai and that **this in fact comprised a *chuppah* and *kiddushin*.**[10]

If at Sinai G-d's love for the Jewish people was manifested in the form of a *chuppah* and *kiddushin*, it will certainly return in the same manner and in equal measure at the end of time. Yeshayahu HaNavi could therefore state that the love that G-d will feel for His people in the future **is** that of a *chassan* for His *kallah*.

When the *chassan* is Hashem and the *kallah* is His nation, the *simchah* engendered is the real *simchah bi'me'ono*. *Chuppah* is generally explained to be an act of *hachnasah l'beiso*—bringing the *kallah* into the home of the *chassan*. At the blessed moment of *chuppah* of Hashem and His people, *Am Yisrael* are, so to speak, taken into the sacred *me'ono* of Hashem—a *hachnasah l'beiso*."

The *simchah* of a regular *chassan* and *kallah,* however, cannot possibly reach these heights as the *Aruch Hashulchan* explained. Nonetheless, in light of the above, we may say that although their *simchah* is not quite like that of *me'ono*, it is nonetheless undiminished, for in marrying one another *they emulate the holy union between Hashem and Am Yisrael.* By invoking *she'hasimchah bi'me'ono* at a wedding, we do not mean to qualify their *simchah* or tactlessly note that the happiest day of their lives does not represent the ultimate joy of *me'ono*. On the contrary, we convey to them the glorious message that the *simchah* of their marriage is a Heavenly one and that they are emulating the Divine *simchah* of Hashem who was also a *chassan* to His *kallah*, the Jewish people.

However, we are still left with an obvious question. If the *navi* intended to describe Hashem and the Jewish people as an actual *chassan*

---

9 Cited in the *sefer Pachad Yitzchok: Sefer HaIgros* 76.

10 See also *Taanis* 26b: "Go forth you daughters of Zion and gaze upon the King of peace crowned with the crown His nation made for Him on the day of His wedding and on the day of the gladness of His heart" (*Shir HaShirim* 3:11). "On the day of His wedding" refers to Matan Torah, and "the day of the gladness of His heart" refers to the building of the holy Temple, may it be built speedily in our days."

and *kallah*, why do the commentators add a *kaf ha'dimyon* and interpret this verse in metaphorical terms?

Perhaps the answer is that the notion of the absolute joy of G-d's holy abode is not something that can be appreciated by the majority of people. Those who engage in serious Torah study and have experienced the ecstasy of doing so may perhaps grasp the idea; others will simply not. The *Mefarshim* therefore interpreted the verse metaphorically so that everybody could relate to it, even though a deeper idea is at play.

The same approach could be used to explain the citation of Rav Shlomo Alkabetz in *Lechah Dodi*. Perhaps he too employed the *kaf ha'dimyon* as a way of presenting this lofty concept to the masses.

However, there may be a deeper approach.

The *Iyun Tefillah* notes that although it is customary to recite *Lechah Dodi* at the commencement of Shabbos, only two of its nine stanzas refer to Shabbos at all! The final seven stanzas are devoted to discussing the holiness of the city of Yerushalayim and the future redemption. Why then is this poem so pertinent to Shabbos?

He answers that the custom may be based upon the famous adage of Chazal,[11] "If the Jewish people were to faithfully observe two Shabbosos they would immediately be redeemed." Since at the start of Shabbos the Jewish people accept upon themselves to faithfully observe Shabbos and adhere to its halachos, there is hope for the holy city of Yerushalayim and an anticipation of redemption. This hope is immortalized in the stanzas of "*Mikdash Melech*" and onwards.[12]

This lends us new perspective on the eighth stanza of *Lechah Dodi* which contains the reference to *chassan* and *kallah*. Since, according to the *Iyun Tefillah*, these stanzas which tell of the redemption are a result of the Jewish people's adherence to Shabbos, the reference to G-d's love for them has to be placed in that context. Shabbos, though certainly a taste of the World to Come, does not grant us the pleasure of the *simchah bi'me'ono* like Torah does, for ultimately it is only *me'ein Olam*

---

11   *Shabbos* 118b.

12   In fact, the first two stanzas that reference Shabbos overtly may allude to the observation of the two Shabbosos that will bring the redemption.

Haba—in miniature—whereas toiling in Torah grants us an actual experience of the World to Come. Therefore, in this stanza, we can only refer to Hashem's love for us with the *kaf ha'dimyon*.

Sasson and Simchah

The *Vilna Gaon* in his commentary to *Megillas Esther*[13] explains that there is a fundamental difference between *sasson* and *simchah*, though they both denote joy. *Simchah*, he notes, can be experienced when one is in the midst of a process or on the path to a destination, "*S'meichim b'tzeisam*—Joyous when they embark."[14] *Sasson* is only felt when the destination is reached or the goal achieved, "*Sassim b'vo'am*—Glad upon their arrival."[15]

The verse cited above describes Hashem's joy over His people Israel using the expression of *sasson*—"***Yasis alayich Elokayich*.**" In light of the above, this choice of wording is very apt, for it is meant to reflect the idea that the joy of the union of Hashem and the Jewish people in the times to come will be the absolute joy of *me'ono*, the ultimate destination and objective. At that time, the joy will transcend the *simchah* evoked on the path to perfection, and will reach a peak of completion and genuine *sasson*—"*Yasis alayich Elokayich ki'msos chassan al kallah*."

---

13   8:16.

14   *Tefillas Keil Adon.*

15   David HaMelech also declared, "***Sas anochi al Imrasecha k'motzei shalal rav*—**I rejoice over Your words like somebody who finds a great treasure." Discovering a treasure is a gift from Heaven, it doesn't occur by dint of a process or pathway. David therefore used the word "*sas*" (derived from *sasson*) to depict his joy rather than the word *simchah*. Specifically, *sasson* expresses the notion of reaching the ultimate perfection in relation to Torah study—"**I rejoice over Your words.**"

Panim Chadashos

1

Sheva Berachos

The final *berachah* of the *sheva berachos* praises Hashem for having created "*sasson v'simchah, chassan v'kallah, gilah, rinah, etc.*—joy and gladness, groom and bride, rejoicing, glad song, etc."[1] Given that a *chassan* and *kallah* were already created upon their respective births, why does the *berachah* describe them as being created upon their marriage? Further, why does the *berachah* place *chassan* and *kallah* between *simchah* and *gilah*?

Rav Hutner would say that the marriage of a *chassan* and *kallah* serves to create a new *neshamah* (soul).[2] If so, we may suggest that the "creation of *chassan* and *kallah*" invoked by the *berachah* is a reference to their newly created soul.

This also helps answer our second question, namely, why are *chassan* and *kallah* inserted between *simchah* and *gilah*? The *Vilna Gaon*[3] explains that *simchah* is a product of *chiddush* (novelty) whereas *gilah*

---

1   *Kesubos* 8a.
2   For this reason, he would recommend that his students walk down to the *chuppah* to the tune of the words "*neshamah shenassata bi*—the soul that you have placed in me."
3   In his commentary to *Mishlei* (23:24).

(joy) is a product of consistency and uniformity. This is why the verse states, "*Yismechu haShamayim v'sagel haaretz*—The heavens will be glad and the earth will rejoice,"[4] for the Heavens are a place of *chiddush*, and therefore *simchah*, but the earth is a place of consistency as it states, "*Ein kol chadash tachas ha'shamesh*—There is nothing new under the sun."[5] Since *chassan* and *kallah* are bestowed with a brand new *neshamah*, they are mentioned in the *berachah* immediately after the word "*simchah*" which denotes the joy of *chiddush*.[6] In this way the *berachah* concerns itself not just with the general *simchah* shared by the *chassan* and *kallah*, but with a specific facet of that *simchah*, namely a new *neshamah*.

This notion is also alluded to in the conclusion of the *berachah*, "*Mesame'ach chassan im hakallah*—Who gladdens the heart of the *chassan* with his *kallah*." *Rashi* explains[7] that with these words we thank Hashem for having created the concept of marriage and the joyous union between man and wife. Ostensibly this concept does not appear in the main body of the *berachah*. Since the conclusion of a *berachah* is meant to reflect and encapsulate the main body of the *berachah* ("*chasimah me'ein ha'pesichah*"), it is strange that this *berachah* appears to reference ideas that were not previously mentioned. However, in light of the above, this problem can be resolved.

The great joy that the *chassan* has with his *kallah*, and indeed the *kallah* has with her *chassan*, is due to the new *neshamah* that they receive together. This joy is alluded to in the placement of the *chassan* and *kallah* after the word "*simchah*" in the main body of the *berachah* as explained above. Therefore, the conclusion of the *berachah* dovetails beautifully with the main body of the *berachah*, for both call upon the glorious feelings of *hischadshus* (novelty) of the new *neshamah* of *chassan* and *kallah*.

The source for this idea can be found in *Parashas Bereishis* where the Torah relates that "G-d created man...male and female he created

---

4   *Tehillim* 96:11.

5   Ecclesiastes 1:9.

6   The reference to *gilah* immediately after *chassan v'kallah* alludes to the **constant**, unremitting joy of marriage for the rest of their lives.

7   *Kesubos* 8a, *s.v.* "*Mesame'ach chassan v'kallah*."

them,"[8] implying that man and woman were created separately. *Rashi* notes[9] that this appears to contradict a later verse[10] which describes how G-d took one of Adam's ribs in order to form Chavah. To resolve the contradiction, *Rashi* cites a *Midrash Aggadah* which explains that Adam and Chavah were originally attached to one another, back-to-back, but G-d later separated them.

If G-d intended to separate Adam and Chavah why did he create them together? We may suggest that this was to reflect the fact that Adam and Chavah truly comprised one single *neshamah*. Therefore, even once they were separated, their mission was to find each other once again and reunite, and this is also the mission of every *chassan* and *kallah*. Chazal say[11] that forty days before a fetus develops in the womb, a heavenly voice announces its future mate—"*bas ploni l'ploni*," and although upon its birth it finds itself apart from its soul mate, on the day of its marriage it reunites with the partner for whom it was always destined.

This process is captured in the words of the sixth of the *sheva berachos*, "*Same'ach tesamach, rei'im ha'ahuvim, k'samechacha yetzircha b'Gan Eden mi'kedem*." With these words we beseech the Almighty to gladden the hearts of the *chassan* and the *kallah* just as He gladdened Adam and Chavah in Gan Eden in former times. The double expression of joy reflects both the *simchah* of the *chassan* and *kallah's* marriage today and the *simchah* akin to that of Gan Eden, namely, the joy of the reunion of the souls just like Adam and Chavah.

We have explained that the joy of *chassan* and *kallah* is due to their reunion and of each rediscovering their soul mate. But how can that be considered a *simchah* of *hischadshus*? Upon their marriage, *chassan* and *kallah* would appear to achieve *hisachdus* (unification) rather than *hischadshus*, for while their two souls are indeed reuniting, that surely does not constitute a new *neshamah*.

---

8   *Bereishis* 1:27.
9   Ad loc., s.v. "*Zachar u'nekeivah bara osam.*"
10   2:21.
11   *Sotah* 2a.

The answer is that rediscovering a lost world, or a lost partner, is the biggest manifestation of *chiddush* there can be! The verse states, "*Hashivenu Hashem Eilecha v'nashuvah, chadesh yameinu k'kedem*— Return us, G-d to You, and we will return, renew our days of old."[12] What do we mean by asking G-d to "renew our days of old"—do we want renewal or a return to the past? The answer is that the "days of old" are the utopian days of Gan Eden when man was unsullied by sin and could rejoice with his soul mate. Those days were of a world gone by—a world that is surely beyond us, yet we beseech G-d to return us to those times, and indeed He acquiesces. In granting us atonement for our sins and in uniting every man and wife, He takes His people back in time to the days of old. This is an expression of utter *chiddush*, for returning to those glorious times is as miraculous as *techiyas ha'meisim* (the revival of the dead) itself. Would one claim that *techiyas ha'meisim* is not a *chiddush* because the dead were once alive?

The joy of *chassan* and *kallah* is therefore not only over their union but of the great *hischadshus* of their *neshamah*. On the day of their marriage, *chadesh yameinu k'kedem*, "Their days are renewed as old," and they follow in the steps of Adam and Chavah over whom G-d rejoiced, "*K'samechacha yetzircha b'Gan Eden mi'kedem.*"

2

Shabbos Sheva Berachos

At every *sheva berachos* event there is a requirement to have *panim chadashos*—people who haven't attended any of the preceding days' festivities.[13] These new attendees purportedly add a new level of joy to each day's event.

It seems obvious that if the *panim chadashos* sit glumly in their seats and do not joyfully participate in the *simchah* then they will hardly have

---

12   *Eichah* 5:21.
13   *Kesubos* 7b.

contributed to the event. The joy that a *chassan* and *kallah* experience due to their guests, and particularly their *panim chadashos*, is seeing how their *simchah* has affected other people and how others are sharing and delighting in it with them.[14]

In fact, a *chassan* and *kallah* are uniquely attuned to the state of being of their guests. We have already described how they are the recent recipients of a new, unified *neshamah*, and this grants them sensitive antennae to perceive the sincere joy of others. When a person is struck by a sense of joy, or when his soul or mind are suddenly taken by a *chiddush* of some sort, his face lights up, and thus the faces of the attendees at a wedding who truly feel the *simchah* of the moment will exude joy. This will be immediately sensed by the *chassan* and *kallah* whose faces are similarly alit with *chiddush* and *simchah*.

On Shabbos there is no requirement of *panim chadashos*. Tosafos cites[15] a fascinating Midrash which states, "*Mizmor shir l'yom haShabbos, panim chadashos ba'u l'kan, nomar shirah*—The song of Shabbos, *panim chadashos* have arrived, let us sing." In other words, Shabbos itself apparently fulfills the requirement of *panim chadashos*—how so?[16]

Perhaps we may suggest the following.

The Midrash states,[17] "*Va'yevarech Elokim es yom ha'shevi'i, bircho bi'meor panav shel Adam*—And G-d blessed the seventh day, He blessed it with the shining countenance of man." On Shabbos, man is bestowed with a *neshamah yeseirah* (an extra soul) that imbues him with *simchah* and *chiddush*, which has the potential to make his face shine. The word "*panim*," meaning face, is related to the word "*penim*," meaning internal, for the face (and particularly the eyes) reflects a person's deepest essence. On Shabbos, as his *neshamah yeseirah* helps him overcome the

---

14   This flies in the face of the popular view that the mitzvah is to make the *chassan* and *kallah* happy. That would be unnecessary—they are already happy! The same is true of the mitzvah of *nichum avelim*. Its purpose is not to cheer up the mourners and make them happy—they are not allowed to be happy! To the contrary, the mitzvah is to commiserate with them by showing that their pain affects you.

15   *Kesubos* 7b, s.v. "*V'hu she'ba'u panim chadashos.*"

16   See *Tosafos's* own explanation of this Midrash.

17   *Bereishis Rabbah* 11:2.

boundaries set by his earthly body, his *panim* shines with the light of his *penim*.

At a *sheva berachos* on Shabbos, there may not be any new attendees, but the people in attendance are bearing *panim chadashos*—new, shining, and joyous faces. And due to their sparkling new *neshamah*, the *chassan* and *kallah* are themselves the greatest *panim chadashos* of them all, and can very much perceive it in others. The *panim chadashos* of Shabbos therefore especially enhance their *simchah*.

Shomer Shabbos

1

The Gemara in *Pesachim* cites the sages of Pumpedisa[1] who hold that there is a marked difference between the composition of Kiddush in the *Amidah* of Shabbos and that of Yom Tov. On Shabbos, the *berachah* should conclude simply with the words "*Mekadesh haShabbos*." On Yom Tov, a reference to the Jewish people should be interpolated—"*Mekadesh Yisrael v'ha'zemanim*."

The reason for this is that the *kedushah* of Shabbos is not dependent upon the Jewish people, rather it is "*kevi'i v'kaymi*"—fixed in place since the days of creation and not dependent upon *kiddush ha'chodesh* (the Jewish people's sanctification of the moon).[2] For this reason, the Jewish people are not invoked by the *berachah* before the reference to Shabbos. Yom Tov, however, depends on *kiddush ha'chodesh* which determines when it will take place. Therefore, the *berachah* makes reference to the Jewish people (represented by *beis din*) before it references Yom Tov, because the *kedushah* of Yom Tov depends upon them.

This also sheds light on another difference between the *tefillos* of Shabbos and those of Yom Tov. During *Musaf* of Shabbos we reference

---

1   117b.
2   *Rashbam*, ad loc.

Eretz Yisrael—"*Shetaalenu b'simchah l'Artzenu*," but on Yom Tov we focus upon Yerushalayim—"*V'li'Yerushalayim Beis Mikdashecha.*" The reason for this may be that Eretz Yisrael, like Shabbos, is *kevi'i v'kaymi*, and it is thus referenced in the *Musaf*. Yom Tov, which is not *kevi'i v'kaymi*, does not focus on Eretz Yisrael but on Yerushalayim, which was the location of the *aliyah la'regel*.

Why does the *berachah* on Shabbos not make mention of Am Yisrael at all? Chazal, in *Maseches Sofrim*, address this question and explain that this is because "Shabbos preceded the Jewish people."[3] However, this doesn't appear to answer why Yisrael could not be mentioned **after** Shabbos. Why can the *berachah* not conclude, "*Mekadesh haShabbos v'Yisrael*," which would clearly indicate that Shabbos preceded Yisrael?

Perhaps we may suggest the following.

Kedushas Shabbos and Kedushas Yisrael

The *kedushah* of Shabbos and the *kedushah* of Yisrael have something very important in common, namely that they are both *kevi'i v'kaymi*. Shabbos is, as stated, fixed in place as a timeless remembrance of creation, immovable and impervious to change. Yisrael is similarly timeless, for the *kedushah* of the Jewish people is eternal and not subject to *bechirah* (choice) or change. No Jew can renounce his membership of the Jewish people and neither can his many sins sever him from his eternal heritage. "*Yisrael, af al pi she'chata, Yisrael hu*—A Jew, even though he sins, remains a Jew."[4]

(I once heard Rav Hutner use this concept to explain the *berachah* we bestow upon a child at his *bris milah*—*K'shem she'nichnas la'bris, kein yikaneis l'Torah, l'chuppah, u'l'maasim tovim*, "Just as he has entered into the covenant, so shall he enter [the world of] Torah, the *chuppah*, and [the world of] good deeds." Our blessing to the child, he said, is that his service of G-d throughout his life should resemble that of his *bris milah*. Just as he made no conscious decision to undergo *bris milah*, for he was a mere infant at the time, so shall all of his Torah and mitzvos

---

3   13:14, cited by the *Iyun Tefillah* in the *siddur Otzar HaTefillos*.
4   *Sanhedrin* 44a.

be performed by instinct, as if he had no *bechirah* whatsoever—a state of *kevi'i v'kaymi*.[5])

Nonetheless, the *kedushah* of Yisrael is not entirely equivalent to that of Shabbos. The *kedushah* of Shabbos not only stems directly from *Hashem* but also serves as a weekly reenactment of Creation when Hashem was the very first "*shomer Shabbos*." The permanent and undying status of Shabbos is thus borne out of the "*shavas va'yinafash*" (He stopped and rested) of the Creator of the world, the quintessential *Kevi'i v'Kaymi*. A person who is a *shomer Shabbos* thereby emulates Him.

This same concept can not be applied to the Jewish people, for there is no element of Creation whose *kedushah* can truly emulate G-d's. Any finite being, no matter how elevated, cannot assume a state of *kevi'i v'kaymi* that approaches that of the infinite One.[6]

Rather, the *kedushah* of Yisrael is in fact a product of the *kedushah* of Shabbos—an "*av*" and "*toldah*."[7] Rabbi Yehoshua Leib Diskin would say[8] that the Torah's first reference to any concept is the source for all later manifestations of that concept in the Torah; and since the Torah's first reference to *kedushah* is in the context of Shabbos (*Bereishis* 2:3, "*Va'yekadesh oso*"), Shabbos must be the source of all other facets of *kedushah*.

Perhaps this was the intent of Chazal in *Maseches Sofrim*. Their statement that "Shabbos preceded Yisrael" means that the *kedushah* of Shabbos is the source of the *kedushah* of Yisrael, and therefore must precede it.

Moreover, since Yisrael, in one sense, is also *kevi'i v'kaymi* as stated above, a person could mistakenly believe that the *kedushah* of Yisrael is equivalent to that of Shabbos, which emanates directly from G-d. It was therefore imperative that the *nusach* of the *berachah* not give that impression. Had Chazal used the expression "*Mekadesh haShabbos v'Yisrael*," though their intent would have been that "G-d sanctifies Shabbos

---

5   See *Maamar* "Sanctify Us with Your Mitzvos," where we elaborate upon this idea.
6   See the *Rambam, Hilchos Yesodei HaTorah* 1:1–4.
7   See Rabbeinu Yonah to *Berachos* 49a, in the name of the *Rif.*
8   Cited by Rav Hutner.

and **by means of Shabbos also sanctifies Yisrael**," it would also have allowed for an erroneous interpretation that **G-d sanctifies Shabbos and Yisrael equally**. They therefore declined to mention Yisrael at all.

2

The *Magen Avraham* notes[9] that although the text of the *Amidos* of *Maariv*, *Shacharis*, and *Minchah* of Shabbos all contain the *tefillah* of "*Elokeinu v'Elokei avoseinu, retzei v'menuchaseinu*," there is a slight difference between them. At *Maariv* we use the word "*vah*"—"*v'yanuchu* **vah** *Yisrael mekdashei Shemecha*." At *Shacharis* we switch the "*vah*" with "*vo*"—"*v'yanuchu* **vo** *Yisrael*." Finally, at *Minchah* we replace "*vah*" and "*vo*" with "*vam*"—"*v'yanuchu* **vam** *Yisrael*."

In light of all of the aforementioned principles we can offer the following explanation of these discrepancies.

There are three facets of the joy beheld at every wedding: the joy of the *chassan*, the joy of the *kallah*, and the joy they feel together as a unit. On Shabbos all three facets are referred to—the *chassan* (*Hakadosh Baruch Hu* or variably, Am Yisrael), the *kallah* (Shabbos), and their unity. This is illustrated by the opening words of *Lechah Dodi* which read, "*Lechah dodi likras kallah p'nei Shabbos nekabelah*." *Lechah Dodi* (Go my beloved) refers to the *chassan*. *Likras kallah* clearly references the *kallah*. *P'nei Shabbos nekabelah* (Let us together welcome Shabbos) depicts their unification and mutual joy.

At *Maariv* on Friday night we refer to Shabbos with a *lashon nekeivah* (a feminine expression) for we are then greeting Shabbos as a *kallah*. "*V'yanuchu* **vah** *Yisrael mekadshei Shemecha*—Yisrael will find tranquility in Shabbos like a *chassan* in his *kallah*."[10] This notion is inextricably linked to the Shabbos of Creation, which is *kevi'i v'kaymi*, and thus represents the notion of perfection and contentment, which transcends *bechirah*. This is also indicative of the state of a *kallah* who waits for

---

9   *Orach Chaim* 268:3.
10   Without a wife, a person has no peace and no joy (*Yevamos* 62b).

her *chassan* to find her as his perfect mate—his *kevi'i v'kaymi*. Each morning, women recite the *berachah* "*She'asani kirtzono*—He created me, as He willed," which gives cause to their contentment with their life and mission. The Shabbos of Creation similarly expresses the eternal perfection and *ratzon* (will) of the Creator, the essence of *kevi'i v'kaymi*—the One who is **eternal** and **extant**. "He is because He is and nobody and nothing else is." The instant that He effected Creation preceded and anteceded the entire notion of *bechirah*.[11]

At *Shacharis*, we refer to Shabbos with the *lashon zachar* (a masculine expression) of "*V'yanuchu vo*." This places the focus on the *chassan* rather than the *kallah*, and reflects the commitment of the male to search for his *kallah*, like the commitment of the six hundred thousand Jews at Sinai to the 613 mitzvos, and specifically to the commitment of a person who observes Shabbos with all of its halachos. This is also depicted by the Shabbos of Matan Torah where the Jewish people accepted the yoke of the Torah and committed themselves to its laws. The theme is one of *bechirah*, the choice between right and wrong, and not the elevated *kedushah* of *kevi'i v'kaymi* in which *bechirah* is irrelevant.

Lastly, at *Minchah* we refer to Shabbos with the plural expression "*V'yanuchu vam*" alluding to the union between male and female. At this time, as we reference the Shabbos of the World to Come, we allude to the *chassan* rising above the world of *bechirah* and assuming the status of *kevi'i v'kaymi* just like the *kallah*. In so doing, he will unite the finite world of *bechirah* with the infinite world of *kevi'i v'kaymi*, the *middas ha'din* with the *middas ha'rachamim*, and the Jewish people with G-d, as it says "*Atah Echad v'Shimcha Echad u'mi k'amcha Yisrael, goy echad ba'aretz*—You are one and Your name is one and who is like your people Israel, a singular nation in the land."

---

11   See footnote 6 in Translator's Preface above.

Last in Deed, First in Thought

In the *berachah* of *Me'ein Sheva* recited at *Maariv* on Friday night, we state that G-d was "*Mekadesh haShabbos u'mevarech Shevi'i*—Sanctified the Shabbos and blessed the seventh day," referencing the *kedushah* (sanctity) of Shabbos before its blessing. Strangely, this is a reversal of the order of the verse in *Parashas Bereishis* which states, "*Va'yevarech Elokim es yom ha'shevi'i va'yekadesh oso*—And G-d blessed the seventh day and sanctified it."[1] Why did the author of *Me'ein Sheva* reverse the order?[2]

The *Ramban* explains the words "*Va'yevarech...Va'yekadesh*"[3] as follows: "*Ha'berachah b'yom haShabbos hi maayan ha'berachos...ki yimshoch min ha'kodesh*—The blessing of the Shabbos day is the source of all

---

1   2:3.

2   The *Amidah* of *Maariv* on Friday night presents a similar dilemma. The middle *berachah* begins with "*Atah kidashta es yom ha'shevi'i*—You sanctified the seventh day," but then states, "*U'veirachto mi'kol ha'yamim*—And You blessed it, of all the days" thereby referencing *kedushah* before *berachah*. To confound the issue, the *berachah* then states, "*V'kidashto mi'kol ha'zemanim*—And you sanctified it, of all the seasons," reverting again to *kedushah*.

    Perhaps the second mention of *kedushah* does not mean to compare Shabbos with the days of the week, like "*U'veirachto mi'kol ha'yamim*" but to compare it with other holy days such as the festivals.

3   Ad loc.

blessing...for it is drawn from holiness."[4] In other words, the *berachah* of Shabbos **stems from its** *kedushah* with the words "*Va'yevarech Elokim es yom ha'shevi'i va'yekadesh oso*," meaning "G-d blessed the seventh day **because** He sanctified it." Put simply, the verse first references the product, and then traces it back to its source.

The text of *Me'ein Sheva*, by contrast, runs in chronological order and therefore first references the source, namely the *kedushah* of Shabbos, and then the product, namely the blessing that follows. In this way, Chazal (as they often did) sought to explain the meaning of verses of the Torah within the prayer liturgy.

Why does the verse not describe the *kedushah* and *berachah* of Shabbos chronologically as is *Me'ein Sheva*? Perhaps it means to allude to a fundamental element of Shabbos explicated by Rav Hutner in his *sefer Pachad Yitzchok*.[5]

Teva and Kedushah

Rav Hutner would say that the entire concept of Shabbos is captured in the pithy words of *Lechah Dodi*, "*Sof maaseh b'machashavah techilah*—Last in deed but first in thought." The *teva* (natural world) is *tafel* (subservient) to the spiritual world[6] (represented by Shabbos), and although *teva* was created before Shabbos, Shabbos had been "*B'machashavah techilah*—First in G-d's thoughts." The reason for this is that Shabbos was the very goal of creation, and had therefore been considered long before anything else. A goal must always be determined at the outset of a project even if many stages must take place before it is achieved.

The reason that Shabbos was the goal of Creation is because it serves to imbue *teva* with *kedushah* which is the purpose of the world's existence. And since it was the first instance of *kedushah* in the world, it is the basis for all aspects of sanctity.

---

4   The idea is also referenced in *Lechah Dodi*, in the words "*Likras Shabbos lechu v'nelcha ki hi mekor ha'berachah*—To welcome the Shabbos, come let us go, for it is the source of blessing."

5   *Shabbos* 1:4.

6   See *Maamar* "*Kah Ribon*" and "*Shabbos Chanukah*" where we discuss this notion at length.

Zecher L'yetzias Mitzrayim

Rav Hutner noted that G-d employed the same model in creating the Jewish people whose true birth was at the time of *yetzias Mitzrayim* (the Egyptian exodus)[7] long after the other seventy nations had come into being. Since the Jews help the world fulfill its purpose, they are considered to be the goal of Creation and are thus, similarly, "last in deed but first in thought." This is summed up in the famous words of Chazal who say[8] that the word "*Bereishis*," the word with which creation began, means "*Bishvil Yisrael she'nikreu reishis*—[Creation was] on account of Israel who are called *reishis*."[9]

Thus, Shabbos, which was the goal of Creation, and *yetzias Mitzrayim*, which formed the nation that would help this goal be realized, were in mind at the onset of Creation. This may be why the Kiddush of Shabbos must make mention of *yetzias Mitzrayim*—"*Ki hu yom techilah l'mikraei kodesh, zecher l'yetzias Mitzrayim*—For that day is the first of the holy convocations, a remembrance of the exodus from Egypt." In fact, as we have mentioned on other occasions,[10] *yetzias Mitzrayim* and the Revelation at Sinai that followed, **were a second version of Creation itself,** thus they were certainly an integral part of the "*Sof maaseh b'machashavah techilah*" of Creation.

Perhaps the Torah references the *kedushah* and *berachah* of Shabbos in non-chronological order to allude to the idea of "*Sof maaseh b'machashavah techilah*." For although *kedushah* does indeed precede *berachah*, it is only invoked at the end because it is the goal—the very purpose of Creation.

---

7   *Maharal, Gevuros Hashem* 5:36.

8   *Bereishis Rabbah* 1:1, cited by *Rashi* to *Bereishis* 1:1.

9   *Yirmiyahu* 2:3. Correspondingly, Moshe Rabbenu's first warning to Pharaoh (see *Shemos* 4:22–23) referenced *Makas Bechoros* (the killing of the Egyptian firstborn), though chronologically it was the last of the plagues. This is also an example of "*Sof maaseh b'machashavah techilah*."

10   See the *Maamar* on Kiddush.

Blessing the Children

1

The Torah relates[1] that Yaakov blessed his grandchildren, Ephraim and Menasheh, that they should become a source of blessing. When fathers of the future would bless their children they would cite Ephraim and Menasheh as the prototype toward whom their children could aspire.[2]

Yaakov's blessing is the basis for the almost universal Jewish custom for parents to bless their children before the Shabbos meal on Friday night. Daughters are blessed that they should resemble the four Imahos (Matriarchs), Sarah, Rivkah, Rachel, and Leah; but curiously, as predicted by the verse above, the blessing we afford our sons is not that they should resemble the Avos (Patriarchs), Avraham, Yitzchak, and Yaakov, but that they should follow the ways of Ephraim and Menasheh, the two sons of Yosef. Why do we not similarly bless our sons that they resemble the Avos? And why, of all the Shevatim (twelve tribes), Ephraim and Menasheh?

---

1   *Bereishis* 48:20.

2   *Rashi* ad loc. A more precise reading of *Rashi* may be that the children of the future **shall in turn serve as models for their children**. Indeed, serving as a prototype is itself the greatest blessing one can bestow.

Eretz Yisrael

Rav Chaim Soloveitchik contends[3] that there were two aspects to the inheritance of the Land of Israel. First, there was a *yerushah pratis* (individual inheritance) of each of the Shevatim and the families that they comprised. Second, there was a *yerushah klalis* (inheritance by the Jewish people as a whole). This was particularly manifested in Jerusalem, which is why it was forbidden for the residents of the city to charge a rental fee to other Jews who sought accommodation there.[4]

Women do not have a share in the *yerushah pratis* of the Land of Israel for it is dependent upon *kibush* (conquering the land militarily), something in which women do not traditionally play a role.[5] But they do have a share in the *yerushah klalis*, bequeathed to them by their forefathers.

Rav Chaim used this distinction to explain a seeming inconsistency between the laws of *bikkurim* (the first fruits that are brought to the Temple), and those of *maaser sheni* (the second tithe, brought to Jerusalem). The *Rambam* rules[6] that if a woman brings *bikkurim* she does not recite the verses that are generally a part of the ritual. However, he does not rule as such regarding *maaser sheni*.[7] Rav Chaim explained that this distinction is due to a subtle difference between the verses that describe the ritual of the *bikkurim* and those of *maaser sheni*. When bringing *bikkurim*, a person is commanded to thank G-d "for the land that You have given **me**,"[8] a reference to his individual *yerushah pratis*. Since a woman has no *yerushah pratis*, she cannot recite this verse. But when bringing *maaser sheni*, a person is expected to thank G-d "for the land that you have given **us**,"[9] a reference to the *yerushah*

---

3   Cited in the *sefer Bad Kodesh* of Rabbi Baruch Dov Povarski *Shlita*.
4   *Megillah* 26a.
5   One could challenge this assumption as the Mishnah (*Sotah* 8:7) rules explicitly that in the case of a *milchemes mitzvah* (a war that began due to a command of G-d) "even a newly-wedded bride is taken out to battle." See also *sefer Marcheshes* (26:6) for a possible solution.
6   *Hilchos Bikkurim* 4:2.
7   See *Hilchos Maaser Sheni* 11:17.
8   *Devarim* 26:10.
9   Ibid., 15.

klalis of the land. A woman, who as stated, has a part in the *yerushah klalis*, is certainly able to recite these words.

Perhaps the reason that we bless our daughters that they should resemble Sarah, Rivkah, Rachel and Leah is that their connection with the Avos and Imahos is what affords them a connection with the *yerushah klalis* of the Land of Israel. The *yerushah klalis* is derived from the promise of the land to the Avos in *Sefer Bereishis*, the very *sefer* of the Avos.

However, our sons enjoy an additional, more individualized inheritance of the land—a *yerushah pratis*. This inheritance was bequeathed to them due to the covenant made by G-d with the Shevatim in *Sefer Shemos*, the *sefer* of the *banim*.[10] The Brisker Rav explains[11] that this covenant is implied by the verse, which states,[12] "...and all of this land I will grant to your children, an eternal grant," for the promise of the land is the very covenant of the Shevatim among whom the land was divided.[13] For this reason we bless our sons that they resemble two of the Shevatim, Ephraim and Menasheh—rather than the Avos—for Ephraim and Menasheh represent the transmission of both *yerushah pratis* and *yerushah klalis*.

How is the inheritance of the Land of Israel germane to blessing the children on Friday night? The answer is that the aspirations we have for our children are not that they enjoy the ephemeral pleasures of the world, but rather that they be attached to *nitzchiyus* (matters of eternal value). Inheriting the Land of Israel is crucial to the ongoing survival of the Jewish nation, as Rav Hutner said,[14] "The *nitzchiyus*, the eternity, of the Jewish People comes by way of the inheritance of the land of Israel."[15]

---

10   See *Maamarei Pachad Yitzchok: Pesach*, 69:5.

11   *Chiddushei HaGriz, Parashas Vayechi.*

12   32:13.

13   It therefore follows, and herein lies the proof, that the Shevatim will exist forever—"*v'nachalu l'olam*" (eternally theirs).

14   See *Pachad Yitzchok: Igros U'Kesavim* Letter 39. This supports the *Maharal's* thesis that the Aseres HaShevatim (the ten lost tribes) will eventually return and unite with the tribes of Yehudah and Binyamin prior to the building of the third Beis Hamikdash despite the decree that they are lost to us and lost to themselves. See *Bava Basra* 115b, *Gemiri d'lo kalu Shivta*, "The Shevatim will exist forever." See *Maharal Netzach Yisrael* 2:34.

15   For witness to this principle, see the beginning of *Perek Chelek* in *Maseches Sanhedrin* which

The Land of Israel is the embodiment of *nitzchiyus*; in fact, both its *yerushah klalis* and *yerushah pratis* are eternal. The eternal nature of its *yerushah klalis* is exemplified by the city of Jerusalem, the eternal heritage of every Jew. The *yerushah pratis* of the land is enshrined by the mitzvah of *yovel*, which dictates that each Shevet, and the members thereof, retained the ownership of their ancestral land eternally.

Our children are the key to our immortality, the vehicle by which we, and all of the Jewish people, live forever. We therefore bless them that they retain their connection to *nitzchiyus* by assuming their status of heirs to the Land of Israel.

2

We have explained that when we bless our children on Friday night, we reference both the *yerushah klalis* and *yerushah pratis* of the land of Israel, which signifies *nitzchiyus*. But there may be a deeper element to this too. Perhaps, rather than focusing outward on our children's part in the holy land, we really mean to bless our children that they access the *yerushah pratis* and *yerushah klalis* of *kedushah* that exist **within their very souls**.

Each person's *neshamah* is imbued with the **holiness of the individual**—a form of *kedushah* specific to him, akin to a *yerushah pratis*. Additionally, it is imbued by the **holiness of the entire nation**, akin to a *yerusha klalis*. When we bless our children each week, we pray that they tap these fountains of *kedushah*, stemming both from their status as individuals and as an integral part of the Jewish nation as a whole.

But in fact, there may be another aspect of *yerushah pratis* and *yerushah klalis* within the purview of the soul. The *neshamah* is a pure and unadulterated emanation of *kedushah*, a *yerushah klalis* of holiness,

---

states, "All of Israel have a portion in the World to Come, as the verse states, 'Forever they shall inherit the land.'" The words "the land" would seem to refer to this world; how then does it prove that every Jew has a portion in the World to Come? It must be that the land of Israel is the guarantor of the eternity of Israel.

carved from beneath the Divine throne. It represents *guf ha'kedushah*, "the essence of holiness itself."

But it also has a specific mission in this world, namely, to impress *kedushah* upon the earthly body in which it is housed. This mission could be described as a *yerushah pratis*, for it is specific to each and every individual, or as *kedushas ha'guf*, "the impression of holiness upon the earth." A soul's innate holiness, its *guf ha'kedushah*, is integral and a given. But its success in effecting *kedushas ha'guf* depends upon each individual's efforts in acquiring it.

One might have thought that man should be named for his G-dly and lofty soul—his attachment to *guf ha'hedusha*—but, as the *Maharal* notes,[16] it isn't so. Man was dubbed "Adam" which is related to the word "*adamah*" (earth), a hint to his earthliness rather than his G-dliness. This is because man's name is meant to define his life mission: to allow his *neshamah* to influence his earthly *guf* **and** to transform the *adamah* into a spiritual entity. In fact, in his name Adam we may detect a trace of the deepest yearning of his soul which cries out, *Adameh l'Elyon*, "I long to emulate the Almighty."

When we bless our children, who are the next link in the chain of our eternal nation, we bless them that they should connect with the Land of Israel and the notion of eternity that it represents, for this is the very key to their own eternal status. But more importantly, we bless them that they live up to their status of heirs to the *yerushah klalis* and *yerushah pratis* of *guf ha'kedushah* and *kedushas ha'guf*. For while we want our children to be blessed with physical comforts, that isn't what life is all about.

Jewish mothers shed copious tears as they light their Shabbos candles hoping that their children become *b'nei Torah*, *talmidei chachamim*, and *ehrliche Yidden*. The blessings afforded to the children after the father returns from shul are no different. Both mean to impart the blessings of eternity inherited from the Avos and the Imahos.

---

16   *Maharal, Derush al haTorah,* at the back of *sefer Be'er Hagolah.*

3

Yosef HaTzaddik

L et us return to the question with which we began. Why of all the Shevatim do we bless our sons that they resemble Ephraim and Menasheh? We have explained that our blessing is that they should attain not only a *yerushah klalis*, but also a *yerushah pratis* in the Land of Israel. However, this does not explain why Ephraim and Menasheh were selected over any of the Shevatim who were also included in the *bris* of the *yerushah pratis* of the land.

The answer is that while all of the Shevatim were equal in their status of heirs to the *yerushah pratis* of the Land, this was not the case with regard to the *yerusha pratis* of the soul and life-mission of the Jewish people. In this regard, Yosef was the one Shevet who would ensure that the lofty, eternal charge of the Jewish people to imbue the *adamah* with *kedushah* would be realized.

The complete devotion of the Avos to Hashem, as exemplified by Yaakov Avinu, could not by itself secure the eternal future and mission of the Jewish people. The nation's existence would be threatened by intermarriage, by the faith of heathen mothers determining the faith of the next generation. This would cut the nation away from its hallowed roots, unable to return.

It was Yosef who implanted the nation with the ability to arrest such a decline. With his act of supreme self-control in fleeing from the unimaginable test presented by the nefarious wife of *Potiphar*, he showed the way for all those tested by intermarriage, and thus solidified the structure of *kedushah* and *nitzchiyus* erected by his father Yaakov.[17] Yaakov, with Yosef's aid, was able to bequeath the qualities of *kedushah*, *nitzchiyus*, and self-control to his descendants, allowing them to become a part of their identity.[18]

---

17   See *Pachad Yitzchok: Sukkos* 12:3.
18   It is noted that Yosef, in this regard, had a dual status of "*av*" (one of the *Avos*) and "*ben*" (one of the Shevatim). This is alluded to in his own blessing from Yaakov in which he was dubbed

As a reward for Yosef's role in preserving the *nitzchiyus* of the Jewish people, Yaakov granted the status of Shevatim to his two sons, Ephraim and Menasheh. This signified the vital role that their father, Yosef, played in ensuring the eternity of the Jewish people and their eternal mission.

When Yaakov blessed Ephraim and Menasheh, he uttered the words, "By you, Yisrael shall bless, saying, May G-d make you like Ephraim and Menasheh."[19] *Rashi* explains[20] that Yaakov was addressing the words "by you" to Ephraim and Menasheh, but the *Targum Yonasan* maintains that these words were in fact addressed to Yosef. This alludes to the fact that the blessing of Ephraim and Menasheh, and the awarding them with the status of Shevatim, was a nod to Yosef himself and his seminal importance in the scheme of *nitzchiyus*.

These are the qualities that are in the heart and mind of every Jewish mother and father when they bless their children on Friday night. As their children stand before them, they long to imbue them not only with a sense of the *yerushah klalis* of *guf ha'kedushah*, but also of the legacy of Yosef, which is the *yerushah pratis* of *kedushas ha'guf*. This, they hope, will grant them the ability to tap into the *kedushah* and *nitzchiyus* bequeathed to them by the Avos, and also to hold fast to their values in a sea of trials and tribulations like their forebearer Yosef.

"*even Yisrael*" (Bereishis 49:24). The word "*even*", as *Rashi* (ad loc., s.v. "*Even Yisrael*") notes, is an abbreviation of the two words "*av*" and "*ben*."

19   *Bereishis* 48:20.

20   Ad loc., s.v. "*Becha yevarech Yisrael.*"

Kiddush

1

Rav Yitzchok Hutner in his *sefer Pachad Yitzchok* discusses[1] why the Torah in *Parashas Ki Sisa* outlines the commandment of Shabbos after that of the festival of Pesach, when in other places it discusses Shabbos first. He explains that the answer lies in an important distinction between Shabbos standing as a remembrance of the world's Creation, and Shabbos as a remembrance of the Exodus from Egypt.

In *Parashas Ki Sisa*, the Torah relates to Shabbos as a remembrance of the Exodus, for it is mentioned in the context of the *Luchos Sh'niyos* (the second set of Tablets of stone),[2] which state, "And you shall remember that you were a slave in the land of Egypt, and Hashem your G-d has taken you out from there with a strong hand and an outstretched arm; **therefore Hashem your G-d has commanded you to observe the Shabbos day.**"[3] It is therefore logical that in this *parashah*, the festival of Pesach, the time when the Exodus from Egypt actually took place, is mentioned before Shabbos which commemorates the Exodus.

---

1   *Pesach, Maamar* 25.

2   Moshe brought these down from Mount Sinai, following the mass repentance for the sin of the golden calf and the forgiveness that was achieved on Yom Kippur.

3   *Devarim* 5:15.

However, in other places the Torah relates to Shabbos as it is described by the *Luchos Rishonos* (first set of Tablets), "For in six days **Hashem made the Heavens and the earth**, the seas and all that is in them, and He rested on the seventh day. **Therefore, Hashem**[4] **blessed the Shabbos day and sanctified it.**" In this context, Shabbos is described as a remembrance of Creation and thus clearly precedes any of the festivals.

In light of Rav Hutner's observation, the text of Kiddush of Friday night is particularly apt. First, we make mention of Shabbos as a remembrance of Creation, as it appears on the *Luchos Rishonos*, and after that Shabbos is referenced as a remembrance of the Egyptian Exodus as it appears on the *Luchos Shniyos*.

2

First Person Relationship

E very blessing that precedes a mitzvah switches from *lashon nochach* (first person) to *lashon nistar* (third person). It begins with "*Baruch Atah Hashem…*—Blessed are **You** Hashem," speaking in the first person, but then states, "*Asher Kideshanu b'mitzvosav*—That **He** has sanctified us[5] with **His** Mitzvos…" The *Rashba* famously explains[6] that this is designed to reflect the notion that G-d is "**revealed** in terms of His existence but **hidden** in terms of His essence."

However, the text of Kiddush, unlike any other blessing, strangely **reverts to the first tense** in the middle of the blessing. It begins, as does every blessing with the words "Blessed are **you**"—in the first person. It then states that Hashem "Has sanctified us with **His** commandments, took pleasure in us, and with love and favor gave us **His** holy Shabbos as a heritage, a remembrance of Creation"—speaking in the third person.

---

4   *Shemos* 20:11.
5   If it had continued in the first person, it would have written "*Asher Kidashtanu*—"You sanctified us with Your mitzvos."
6   Responsa 5:52.

It then states, "For that day is the prologue to the *chagim*, a reminder of the Exodus from Egypt. For **You** chose us and **You** sanctified us from all the nations. And **Your** holy Shabbos, with love and favor, did **You** give us as a heritage"—reverting to the first person.

Perhaps, the reason for this is that Kiddush, as stated, makes mention of Shabbos in two different contexts—that of Creation and that of the Exodus from Egypt. When discussing Shabbos as a remembrance of Creation, the text utilizes the third person, for at that time G-d was **hidden**. But when discussing Shabbos as commemorating the Exodus, it reverts to the first person, as the miracles of the Exodus, which were performed before mankind, **revealed** G-d to the world. In fact, it was the very Exodus that granted the Jewish people the right to speak to G-d in the first person.

3

Chessed Mishpat

From the time of Creation and until the Egyptian Exodus, G-d was unable to reveal Himself to the world for there was no vessel—no people who could appreciate or understand the Torah. The generation that experienced the Exodus and went on to receive the Torah was thoroughly unique for they had been fashioned in the *"kur ha'barzel"* (the iron furnace) of the exile, helping them become a vehicle of G-d's revelation to the world.

The twenty-six previous generations of the world had been sustained only by G-d's benevolence (alluded to by the twenty-six declarations of *"Ki l'olam chasdo*—His **kindness** endures forever,"* [*Tehillim* 136]). This was *chessed vittur* (unearned kindness). But the generation that experienced the Exodus helped usher in a new system called *chessed mishpat* (kindness that is earned), which created a dramatically different dynamic in the relationship between man and G-d. Henceforth, man could no longer rely on handouts from G-d—he had to earn His kindness and benevolence through the system of reward and punishment.[7]

This new system of *chessed mishpat* served to unify all of the following generations in the sense that they would all be guaranteed reward for their adherence to Torah and mitzvos. Previously, the kindness bestowed upon one generation had not guaranteed kindness to the next one. *Chessed mishpat* dictated that each generation could earn G-d's benevolence.

This idea is alluded to in the first blessing of the *Amidah*. The blessing begins by stating that G-d "bestows beneficial **kindnesses** and **creates** everything." Then it states how He "recalls the **kindnesses** of the Patriarchs and brings a **Redeemer** to their children's children." Perhaps these two phrases hint at the two forms of G-d's kindness, *chessed vittur* and *chessed mishpat*, as follows:

The first phrase references **Creation** and asserts that it was based on **chessed**, as per the verse in *Tehillim*, "*Olam chessed yibaneh.*"[8] It thus describes how our world was created by virtue of G-d's kindness, the work of the *Tov V'Ha'Meitiv*. The second phrase mentions **redemption** and attributes it to the merit of the **chessed** of the Patriarchs. This may hint at a switch that took place between *chessed vittur* following Creation, to *chessed mishpat* at the time of the Exodus. Initially, G-d is described as a bestower of "beneficial kindnesses", a purveyor of all forms of *chessed*. But later, at the time of the redemption, and in preparation for Matan Torah, the children of Israel, due to the merit of their forefathers, were deemed worthy of beginning a new era of *chessed mishpat*. Of course, this transition was always the plan, but it was only realized upon the Exodus and Matan Torah, which, as we have discussed elsewhere,[9] was a second version of Creation.

And just as this world was built with *chessed*, and just as its purpose was realized due to the merit of the Patriarchs and *chessed mishpat*, so will the World to Come be built on these same tenets. In the merit of

---

7   *Pachad Yitzchok: Pesach, Maamar* 22:8.
8   89:3.
9   See *Maamar "Nishmas Kol Chai."*

the *chasdei Avos*, and their bequeathal of that *chessed* to their children, the World to Come will take shape—"*U'Meivi go'el li'v'nei v'neihem.*"

The text of Kiddush and its switch from the third to the first person now takes on added meaning. G-d's honor, post Creation was **concealed**, for the world was only the recipient of His *chessed vittur*—in effect a charitable handout. However, upon the Exodus from Egypt and the establishing of *chessed mishpat*, His honor could be **displayed** to the entire world, as those who earn their *chessed* are far greater beneficiaries than those who receive *chessed vittur*.[10] The Jewish people at that time thus honored G-d with the immortal phrase, "This is my G-d and I will honor him,"[11] and from that point on it was possible to refer to G-d in the first person.

G-d had always intended to introduce *chessed mishpat* to Creation. The Torah relates[12] that G-d completed Creation on "**the** sixth day" unusually employing the definite article (*yom ha'shishi*). The Sages say that it alluded to a certain other singular "sixth day"—the sixth of Sivan on which the Torah was given **and when the purpose of Creation was realized**. Thus, from the time of creation until the Exodus, G-d was biding His time, waiting for the chance to dispense with *chessed vittur*, and crown a nation who could switch from speaking to Him in the third person and address Him directly in the first person.

---

10 Rav Hutner would offer a parable to explain this. If a person gives a poor man a dollar each day, he will, by the end of the year, have given a large sum of charity. If he instead offers him a job and the chance to earn a living, while he will no longer perform a charitable act each day, he will have given him something far greater in value—the chance to earn money for himself. For this, the poor man will be far more grateful.

11 *Shemos* 15:2.

12 *Bereishis* 1:31.

Matanah Tovah

The middle *berachah* of the Yom Tov *Amidah (Shemoneh Esreh)* begins with the *tefillah* of *"Atah bechartanu mikol ha'amim."* This *tefillah* delineates how G-d chose the Jewish people to be his nation, loves them, elevates them, and draws them close. It seems strange, therefore, that this *tefillah* does not form a part of the *Amidah* of Shabbos; are these themes not relevant to Shabbos too?

Possibly the reason that this *tefillah* is not suitable for Shabbos is because the *kedushah* of Shabbos preceded that of the Jewish people. The Gemara explains[1] that Shabbos is *kevi'i v'kaymi*, whereas Yom Tov is only set in place by the Jewish people who establish Rosh Chodesh and thereby the schedule of the Yamim Tovim. It is therefore incongruous to elaborate upon the "chosen nation" on Shabbos, for its *kedushah* preceded them.

This answer requires further explanation. True, the *kedushah* of Shabbbos preceded that of the Jewish people, but the Torah does stress that Shabbos is a special covenant between the Jewish people and G-d—*"Beini u'vein B'nei Yisrael os hi l'olam ki sheshes yamim asah Hashem es haShamayim v'es haaretz*—Between Me and the children of Israel it is a sign forever that in a six-day period Hashem made Heaven and earth."[2] Furthermore, the text of the Kiddush of Shabbos explicitly states that

---

1   *Pesachim* 117b.
2   *Shemos* 31:17.

G-d chose us as a nation, "*Ki vanu vacharta v'osanu kidashta*—For us did you choose and us did you sanctify." Why then is it not appropriate to recite *Atah Bechartanu* in the *Amidah*?

The Gemara describes[3] Shabbos as a *matanah tovah*—a wonderful gift that was bestowed upon the Jewish people. Chazal relate that G-d said to Moshe, "I have a wonderful gift in my treasure houses, Shabbos is its name, and I seek to bestow it upon the Jewish people—go and inform them!"

Sending a gift to one's friend is certainly a **sign** of a dear friendship, but paying a visit to his home is an **act of friendship in and of itself**. In spending time together, two dear friends enjoy their *yedidus* (their mutual friendship) and rejoice in the very fact that they are *yedidim*.

This may be the distinction between Shabbos and Yom Tov.

Shabbos is essentially a day which belongs to G-d; the day on which He rested from Creation and on which the people of the world reinforce their *emunah* that He created the world in seven days. Nevertheless, G-d benevolently gifted this day to the Jewish people as an eternal gift and as a sign of their *yedidus*. And while this is certainly an indication of their status as the chosen nation, it is no more than a gift dispatched from one *yedid* to another.

The Yamim Tovim, by contrast, are days on which the Jewish people celebrate the experience of *yedidus*. The pilgrimage to Yerushalayim was a chance to meet with G-d in the Beis Hamikdash and rejoice together[4]—*liros v'leiraos*, "to see and be seen," an experience immortalized by the loving words of *Shir Hashirim* in which King Shlomo, the architect of the Beis Hamikdash—the meeting place with G-d—extolled the loving relationship between Him and His chosen nation.

It follows that the Yamim Tovim are a time of **celebration of the yedidus that was brought about by G-d having chosen us as His nation**. At other times, we invoke our status as chosen nation only as a means to an end. For example, prior to *k'rias Shema* each day, we declare that G-d chose the Jewish people out of love—"*ha'bocher b'amo*

---

3   *Shabbos* 10b.
4   As I heard from Rav Hutner.

Yisrael b'ahavah"—but this only serves as an introduction to *kabbalas ol Malchus Shamayim* (accepting the yoke of Heaven upon ourselves). *Atah Bechartanu* on the Yamim Tovim is no introduction, no means to an end—but the end itself.

The joy of the Yamim Tovim is over the very *bechirah*—the choice of the Jewish people as the chosen nation, the *Am HaNivchar*. We rejoice over this together with G-d, the *Melech HaNivchar*, in the *Makom HaNivchar*—the Beis Hamikdash, where G-d chose to rest his presence. In the words of Hillel HaZaken as he danced at the *simchas beis hashoevah*, "If you [the Jewish people] visit My house [the Beis Hamikdash] I, in turn, will visit yours."[5]

If it is only the Yamim Tovim which truly celebrate our election as *Am HaNivchar*, why do we also mention this fact in the text of Kiddush of Shabbos? The answer is that this also serves as a means to an end. The text of Kiddush is designed to mention the Exodus from Egypt—*"Techilah l'mikraei kodesh, zecher l'yetzias Mitzrayim,"* and therefore must describe how the Jews were chosen to be the people who would ultimately receive the Torah upon the Exodus—*"Ki vanu vacharta v'osanu kidashta mi'kol ha'amim."* This is not the case with the *Amidah* of Shabbos, in which there is no obligation to detail the Egyptian Exodus.

This distinction between Shabbos and Yom Tov may also be alluded to in the conclusion of the middle *berachos* of the *Amidah* of Shabbos and Yom Tov, respectively. On Shabbos, we conclude with the words *"V'yanuchu vah*[6] *Yisrael mekadshei Shemecha*—"Yisrael, the sanctifiers of Your name, rest on it," where the "it" refers to Shabbos. In these words, we stress **the wonderful gift** of Shabbos and the *menuchah* (tranquility) that it bestows upon us. However, on Yom Tov we conclude with the words *"V'yismechu vecha Yisrael mekadshei Shemecha*—And may Yisrael, the sanctifiers of your name, rejoice in You," placing the focus on G-d. This is because the joy of Yom Tov is over G-d and our convening with Him.

---

5   *Sukkah* 53a.

6   At *Maariv* the text is *"v'yanuchu* **vah**," at *Shacharis* and *Musaf "v'yanuchu* **vo**," and at *Minchah,* *"v'yanuchu* **vam**."

Mekadesh Yisrael V'HaShabbos

Kiddush

The Gemara records[1] two opinions as to the composition of Kiddush and the *Amidah* on Shabbos and Yom Tov. On Shabbos the Sages of Pumpedisa would conclude both Kiddush and the middle *berachah* of the *Amidah* with the words "*Mekadesh haShabbos*," whereas on Yom Tov they would conclude both with the words "*Mekadesh Yisrael v'hazemanim*." According to Rava, for the purposes of *tefillah*, a person should always say *Mekadesh Yisrael* and only make a distinction between Shabbos and Yom Tov in Kiddush.

Rava explained his reasoning as follows: Since *tefillah* takes place together with a *tzibbur* (congregation), it is appropriate to mention Yisrael in order to accord honor to the *rabbim*.[2] Kiddush that does not require a *tzibbur* needn't mention Yisrael on Shabbos.

The *Yerushalmi* rules[3] that if the *tzibbur* has no wine with which to make Kiddush on a Friday night they should conclude the *berachah* of "*Me'ein sheva*" (the blessing at the conclusion of *Magen Avos* following the *Amidah* on a Friday night) with the words "*Mekadesh Yisrael*

---

1   *Pesachim* 117b.
2   See *Rashbam*, ad loc.
3   *Pesachim* 10.

v'haShabbos." At first glance this appears to be inconsonant with both the opinions of the sages of Pumpedisa and Rava. According to the sages of Pumpedisa, both Kiddush and *tefillah* (of which *Me'ein Sheva* is a part) conclude with the words *"Mekadesh haShabbos."* Why then would one add the word "Yisrael" when no wine for Kiddush is available? According to Rava, Kiddush concludes with the words *"Mekadesh haShabbos";* it would thus certainly seem incongruous to add the word "Yisrael" to cover for the lack of Kiddush!

Perhaps we may suggest the following answer. The *Yerushalmi* never intended to say that when wine is unavailable for Kiddush the word "Yisrael" should be added to *Me'ein Sheva*. In fact, the reverse is true—when there is no wine available, **the word Shabbos should be added**! In this, the *Yerushalmi* follows the opinion of Rava who holds that in *tefillah* only *Mekadesh Yisrael* is recited. Therefore, in the circumstances that the *tzibbur* have been unable to fulfill the mitzvah of Kiddush, they should **add the word "Shabbos," which is supposed to be recited in Kiddush, into the** *tefillah*, in order to fulfill them both simultaneously.

Rav Chaim Yitzchak Kaplan noted that although the *berachah* of *Me'ein Sheva* is an abbreviation of the Friday night *Amidah*, there is a marked difference between them. *Me'ein Sheva* states that G-d "grants rest to His people," that "He was pleased with them to grant them rest," and that they are a "people who are saturated with delight," focusing upon the praises of the Jewish people. The *Amidah* contains no such references and focuses exclusively on lauding the day of Shabbos.

Perhaps the reason for this is that, unlike the *Amidah, Me'ein Sheva* is only recited with a *tzibbur*. Therefore, just as Rava contended that when a *tzibbur* is present they should be honored by the words of the *tefillah Me'ein Sheva*, which can only be recited by a *tzibbur,* it similarly honors the *tzibbur* by delineating the praises of the Jewish people.

In fact, perhaps even the sages of Pumpedisa would agree with this reasoning. Though they hold that *Me'ein Sheva* is concluded with the words *"Mekadesh haShabbos,"* and do not agree that the word "Yisrael" should be added, that is only because the *berachah* should reflect the text of the *Amidah*, which in their view concludes with the words *"Mekadesh haShabbos.*" However, as far as the **content** of the *berachah* is concerned, they could well agree that the praises of Yisrael should be referenced given that the obligation of *Me'ein Sheva* rests only upon a *tzibbur*.

In addition, the very institution of the *berachah* of *Me'ein Sheva* demonstrates Chazal's concern for the needs of the *tzibbur*. Since there were those who arrived late to the shul and who missed the *Amidah*, Chazal inserted *Me'ein Sheva* to allow them to hear at least a synopsis of the *tefillah*. We see that the underlying theme of *Me'ein Sheva* is a concern for the honor and needs of the *tzibbur*.

Kah Ribon

1

Kaddish

Rav Chaim Volozhiner in his *sefer Nefesh Hachaim* explores the meaning[1] of the seminal words of Kaddish, "*Yehei Shemeih Rabba mevorach l'alam u'l'almei almaya*—May His great Name be blessed forever and ever." The words "*alam*," "*almei*," and "*almaya*" are related to the word "*olam*" meaning "world," thus the intent of these words is that there should be "an intensification of blessing and an outpouring of supernal light *(or ha'Elyon)* affecting and influencing the four worlds of *Atzilus, Bri'ah, Yetzirah,* and *Asiyah.*"

First, we pray that the supernal light reach *l'alam*—the world of *Atzilus,* which is the most abstract and celestial of the worlds of creation and the source of it all. Then it spreads to "*l'almei*"—two further worlds of *Bri'ah* and *Yetzirah,* the former representing the world that is purely spiritual (the world of "*ha'neshamah she'nasata bi tehorah hi*"), and the latter the aspect of Creation that ties the spiritual to the physical (the world which demonstrates the "*u'mafli laasos*"[2]). Lastly, we pray that the

---

1   1:20, footnote.
2   See the *Rama, O.C.* 6:1.

light reach "*almaya*"—the world of *Asiyah*, the components of creation that are purely physical.[3]

Rav Chaim explains that the four worlds of creation are also found within man. His *shoresh neshamah* (root of his soul) corresponds to the world of *Atzilus*. His *neshamah* itself corresponds to *Bri'ah*. The combination of his *neshamah* and his physical body corresponds to *Yetzirah*. Lastly, his *nefesh* (purely physical self[4]) corresponds to the world of *Asiyah*.

When a person recites *Yehei Shemeih Rabba* and intends to inspire supernal light to permeate his *shoresh neshamah, neshamah, ruach,* and *nefesh*, he wipes away any sin he has committed on each of those levels. In fact, this is what underlies true repentance and is why Chazal state[5] that if a person recites *Yehei Shemeih Rabba* with all of his strength,[6] "his verdict is torn up and even if he has a smirch of idol worship upon his soul, it is forgiven."

Shabbos is a weekly, miniature version of the World to Come,[7] a world of *Bri'ah*, when even the physical is transformed into the spiritual. A person who observes Shabbos transcends the world of *Yetzirah* and *Asiyah*, and experiences in miniature the glories of a world that is purely spiritual.

It follows that during the regular days of the week man must pray that the supernal light descend through four worlds, for he stands in the world of *Asiyah*. However, on Shabbos, where he frequents the world of *Bri'ah*, and stands that much closer to the eternal light, he need only pray that it descend through two worlds—*Atzilus* and *Bri'ah*.

This may be alluded to in the words of the famous *zemer* (song) of Friday night, *Kah Ribbon Alam V'almaya* (Master of this world and the next). Unlike *Yehei Shemeih Rabba*, which invokes *alam, almei,* and *almaya* (which represent the four worlds of *Atzilus, Bri'ah, Yetzirah,* and

---

3   See *Bereishis* 1:1 et al.
4   *Nefesh* in this context refers to the physical. An animal, although devoid of a *neshamah*, is nevertheless described as a *nefesh*.
5   *Shabbos* 119b.
6   In the view of the *Nefesh Hachaim*, "his strength" means his "*kavanah*" (intention).
7   *Berachos* 57b.

Asiyah, as stated), the author of this song (the great Rav Yisrael Najara) only references *alam* and *almaya*, thus referencing just two of the worlds. This may be because he means to allude to Shabbos when man occupies the world of *Bri'ah* and hopes for the celestial light to permeate the two worlds of *Atzilus* and *Bri'ah*.

If *Kah Ribbon* is a song about Shabbos, why does it not reference Shabbos directly? The answer is that since Shabbos is a miniature version of the World to Come, its true nature is concealed and hidden from view.[8] Therefore, the notion that man stands on Shabbos in the rarefied air of the world of *Bri'ah* and of the World to Come, is not something that would be overtly referenced by one of the *zemiros*.

The *Chasam Sofer* was known to have refrained from singing *Kah Ribbon* on Shabbos, and Rav Hutner posited that the *Chasam Sofer* likely felt that the song was too elevated to be sung. Perhaps the reason for this is that the vehicle of song is meant to be engaged when a person is visibly rewarded in the physical world of *Asiyah*, as the verse states, "I will sing to G-d for he dealt kindly with me."[9] Therefore, the *zemiros* of Shabbos should comprise only the obvious and palpable benefits of Shabbos, not the veiled and lofty ones.

Alternatively, the *zemiros* of Shabbos are devoted to describing the mitzvah of *oneg Shabbos*, the command to experience physical pleasure on Shabbos.[10] Man's transcendence to the world of *Bri'ah*, while of seminal importance, is therefore not a topic for the *zemiros*.

---

8   This is the reason that *"Mizmor shir l'yom haShabbos*—The Song of the Day of Shabbos" (*Tehillim* 92) makes no mention of Shabbos in the text of the *perek* itself. Instead, it references the state of unity that can be appreciated by the Jewish People on this day (see above, "The Song of Shabbos" where we discuss this notion at length). This alludes to the notion that the sublime nature of Shabbos is not experienced overtly.

9   *Tehillim* 13:6.

10   This helps to explain some curious words in the *zemer* "Baruch Keil Elyon." The *zemer* states that whoever observes Shabbos should find favor in the eyes of G-d "**like a meal-offering in a sacred pan.**" Why is the observing of Shabbos akin to offering a meal-offering rather than another type of sacrifice such as a *Korban Olah*, the elevation offering (which is also offered as part of the *Musaf* offering of Shabbos)? The answer may be that the *zemiros* focus on the concept of *oneg Shabbos*, and the only offering in the Beis Hamikdash that could be said to contribute towards *oneg Shabbos* is the *Lechem Hapanim* (the showbread), which was a form of meal-offering, whereas the *Korban Olah* was entirely burned on the *Mizbei'ach*.

2

W e have said that on Shabbos man occupies the rarefied world of *Bri'ah*—in miniature. If so, how are we to understand the mitzvah of *oneg Shabbos*? This mitzvah would surely seem to belong only in the world of *Asiyah*.

The answer is that the true nature of *oneg Shabbos* is not mere physical enjoyment. Since man has a foot in the world of *Bri'ah*, he experiences the subjugation of the physical to the spiritual, the mortal to the immortal. His partaking of *oneg Shabbos* is a celebration of this experience, as he **brings the world of *Asiyah* into the world of *Bri'ah*.**

It follows that rather than escaping the worlds of *Asiyah* and *Yetzirah*, man finds through the vehicle of *oneg Shabbos* that his four worlds are integrated—the physicality of *Asiyah* and *Yetzirah* is subsumed by the spirituality of *Bri'ah*. This is why *Kah Ribon* only references *alam* and *almaya*—for the four worlds of the regular weekday are, so to speak, combined into the two higher worlds of *Atzilus* and *Bri'ah* ("*shtayim she'heim arbah*").

On the days of the week man must plead with G-d that the supernal light descend and give meaning to his daily chores and the travails of the world of *Asiyah*. On Shabbos he is in a position to raise his mundane, physical existence and to find his way back to his source in the world of *Atzilus*.

The first of the *berachos* of *Shema* in the weekday *Shacharis* relates the praises of Hashem in the order of *aleph* to *tav* ("*Keil, Baruch, Gadol, De'ah*"). On Shabbos, the *Musaf* prayer is arranged in the order of *tav* to *aleph* ("*Tikanta Shabbos ratzisa korbanoseha*"). The reason for this is that in our daily supplications we ask for inspiration from above, from the source of our *neshamos*—the *aleph* of our existence—and that it be filtered down to our daily physical lives—*aleph* to *tav*. But on Shabbos, as we cross the threshold of the world of *Bri'ah* and introduce the spiritual into the mundane through *oneg Shabbos*, we are in a position to proceed from the physical world of *Asiyah* and approach the world of *Atzilus*—the *shoresh ha'neshamos*—*tav* to *aleph*.

Let us return to the text of *Kah Ribbon*. As stated, this *zemer* invokes *alam* and *almaya*, the elevated worlds of *Bri'ah* and *Atzilus*, but, as we have discovered, the worlds of *Asiyah* and *Yetzirah* are themselves elevated to join them. And in fact, a close examination of the four stanzas of *Kah Ribbon* reveals that the great Rabbi Yisrael Najarah left an allusion to each of those four worlds within the immortal words of the *zemer*:

The first stanza, "*Shevachin asadeir*" references "*Tzafra v'ramsha*" (morning and evening), as well as "*Cheivas bera v'ofei Shemaya*" (the beasts of the field and birds of the sky). This is a clear reference to physical Creation—the world of *Asiyah*.

The second stanza, "*Ravrevin ovdech*," declares that G-d is "*Macheich remaya v'zakeif kefifin*" (He humbles the haughty and straightens the bent). This is a manifestation of reward and punishment, a reflection of man's battle to serve G-d and avoid sin. The battle is fought between his *guf* and *neshamah*—the extraordinary synthesis of "*u'mafli laasos*" that was the product of the world of *Yetzirah*.

"*Elaka di lei*," the third stanza, describes redemption. "*Prok yas anach mipum aryevasa, v'apeik yas ameich mi'go galusa*" (Save your sheep from the mouth of lions, and bring your people out of its exile). Redemption is a moment of victory, the conclusion of the battle between *guf* and *neshamah*, and when the *neshamah* reigns supreme. This is reflective of the world of *Bri'ah*.

Finally, the *zemer* concludes with "*L'Mikdasheich tuv*," the return of the *Shechinah* to Jerusalem and the Beis Hamikdash. The *Shechinah* is a reflection of the world of *Atzilus*—the source of the "*Ruchin v'nafshin*" of the Jewish People. When they too return to Jerusalem they will finally rejoice and utter songs and praises, "*v'yezamrun Lach shirin v'rachashin*."

The Gra and the
Baal Shem Tov

The *kedushah* of Hashem and the *kedushah* of Am Yisrael together form an indivisible entity. *"Yisrael v'Orasya v'Kudsha Brich Hu chad hu*—Am Yisrael, the Torah, and G-d are one." I once heard Rav Hutner say that prior to the era of the Vilna Gaon and Baal Shem Tov, the focus of those who would give counsel in areas of *avodah* (service of Hashem), would emphasize the *kedushah* of Hashem Himself. However, from the times of the Vilna Gaon and the Baal Shem Tov and onwards, the focus switched to the *kedushah* of Am Yisrael. In the following paragraphs I would like to examine why that is so.

1

Galus Yavan

The Torah records that prior to Creation the earth was *"sohu va'vohu, v'choshech al p'nei s'hom*—astonishingly empty, with darkness upon the surface of the deep."[1] Chazal assert[2] that the four

---

1   *Bereishis* 1:2.
2   *Bereishis Rabbah* 2:4.

expressions in this verse, *sohu, vohu, choshech,* and *s'hom,* allude to the four exiles that would be experienced by the Jewish people, the third of which was *galus Yavan* (the exile of ancient Greece). Yavan corresponds to *choshech* (darkness), for the Greeks would darken our eyes with their decrees ("*hecheshichu eineihem shel Yisrael b'gezeroseihem*").

In contrast to Yavan, Am Yisrael is charged with ridding the world of darkness by being a "light unto the nations."[3] In preparation for receiving the Torah, they became the bearers of light ("*U'l'chol B'nei Yisrael hayah ohr b'moshvosam*—But for all of the Jewish people there was light in their dwelling places"[4]) and bid to spread that light to others. The Yevanim, who suppressed that light, were characterized as bearers of *choshech* for all eternity.

The darkness espoused by Yavan, and its fierce opposition to the light shed by Am Yisrael, stems from their deeply mistaken view of Creation. Ancient Greece, and the Roman and Western civilizations that were its natural heirs,[5] champion the notion that "seeing is believing," expressing fealty only to human accomplishment, science, or matters that are proven empirically, believing all else to be anathema.[6] This worldview, though ostensibly a product of "enlightenment," is in fact shrouded in utter darkness and folly.

But the Jewish people, who are dubbed as "backward" and unenlightened by Yavan, are in fact, the biggest promulgators of light, for they see the world through the lens of *kedushah*. Far from considering the created world to be an objective in and of itself (a perspective cloaked in *choshech*), they uncover the true secrets (the *he'elem*) of the world (the *olam*) through the understanding of holiness (*chochmas ha'kedushah*),

---

3   *Yeshayahu* 49:6.

4   *Shemos* 10:23. See the comments of the *Ohr Hachaim Hakadosh* to *Shemos* 13:21.

5   Though the Roman Empire and Western civilization, as we know it, stand at the helm of the last of the four exiles—*galus Edom* and not *galus Yavan*, the two are very much connected. According to the *Maharal* (*Netzach Yisrael* 18), *galus Edom* is a composite of each of the three preceding exiles, Bavel, Paras u'Madai, and Yavan, and therefore presents us with a composite challenge. In addition, Rav Hutner maintained (*Pachad Yitzchok: Pesach* 65) that according to the *Maharal, galus Edom* draws most directly from the *galus* that directly preceded it, namely *galus Yavan*, and its worldview is thus greatly influenced by that of Yavan.

6   See *Ramban* at the end of his comments to *Vayikra* 16:8.

and know that there isn't always the need for empirical proof or scientific verification. Through the unique *chochmah* of Yisrael, *emunah* assumes a new dimension—"believing is seeing."[7]

2
―――――

Torah She'baal Peh

What are the means by which the Jewish people enlighten the world and vanquish the worldview and legacy of Yavan? The answer is simple: *Torah She'baal Peh* (the Oral Law). The capacity of *Torah She'baal Peh* is to shed light upon that which is hidden, cryptic, or obscure, and is the only means of deciphering *Torah She'bichsav* (the Written Law). Am Yisrael can make use of the capacity of *Torah She'baal Peh* not only to understand the Torah, but also to understand Creation, which is a product of the Torah; "*Histakel b'Oraisa u'bara alma*—G-d looked at the Torah and created the world." For while *Torah She'bichsav* does delineate the form and the significance of Creation, *Torah She'baal Peh* reveals its purpose and essence.

Am Yisrael entered a covenant with Hashem, specifically regarding *Torah She'baal Peh*. The Torah states, "Hashem said to Moshe…according to these words I have sealed a covenant with you and Yisrael,"[8] and Chazal maintain[9] that "these words" refer to those of *Torah She'baal Peh*. This covenant gave Yisrael exclusive ability to divine the meaning behind Creation, perceive the light amidst the darkness, "*La'Yehudim haysah orah, zu Torah*—To the Jews there was light—this refers to the light of Torah."[10]

The leaders of the Jewish people, the Sanhedrin (members of the supreme *beis din*) were the prime exponents of *Torah She'baal Peh*. This

---

7   See *Maamar* "Shabbos Chanukah," where this topic is also discussed. See also *Pri Tzadik*, *Bereishis, Chanukah* 2 and *Derashos Haran* 1 and 11.
8   *Shemos* 34:27.
9   *Gittin* 60b.
10   *Megillah* 16b. See the comments of the *Ben Yehoyadah* ad loc.

is why they are dubbed by the Torah as *Einei Ha'Eidah*, "the eyes of the community," for the light of *Torah She'Baal Peh* guides their way and enlightens their eyes.[11]

3
___

Am Yisrael makes a vital contribution to *Torah She'baal Peh*. Unlike *Torah She'bichsav*, which is exclusively in the domain of Hashem, *Torah She'baal Peh* is subject to the decisions and understanding of the Chachamim (sages of Israel).[12]

Rabbi Chaim Volzhiner explains[13] why this is so. Since Hashem did not want His people to feel indebted for the entirety of Torah, He benevolently gave them the chance and the capacity to have their say and to assume a portion in *Torah She'bichsav*. He therefore allowed them to wield the thirteen rules of exposition of halachah[14] and the thirty-two rules of exposition of Aggadah.[15]

In exercising these rules of exposition, the Torah of Hashem becomes the Torah of the Jewish people. The verse states, *"Ki im b'Soras Hashem cheftzo u'v'Soraso yehegeh yomam va'laylah—*His desire is in the Torah of Hashem, and in His Torah, he meditates day and night."[16] Why does the verse first reference the "Torah of Hashem," and then "His Torah"? The answer is that in deliberating, reflecting, and toiling in Torah, man makes Hashem's Torah his own.[17]

The entirety of the Torah, including *Torah She'baal Peh,* and every exposition of the Chachamim, was of course already transmitted to Moshe

11   *Bamidbar* 15:24. See *Rashi* to *Taanis* 24a, s.v. *"Me'einei ha'eidah."* See also *Maamar "Kiddusha Rabba,"* where we discuss the special perception of the Chachamim—the gift of *re'iyah.*
12   See the *Ramban* to *Devarim* 17:11.
13   See *Sichos Mussar* of Rav Chaim Shmulevitz, *maamar* 72, "Hakaras Hatov."
14   Cited in the introduction to the *Sifra*, and recited each morning at *Shacharis*, "Rabbi Yishmael omer."
15   Of *Rabbi Elazar* the son of *Rabbi Yosi Hagelili.*
16   *Tehillim* 1:2.
17   *Rashi* ad loc., s.v. *"U'b'Soraso yehegeh."*

at Sinai.[18] Nevertheless, Hashem, in his great benevolence, sought to allow us the chance to determine halachah and the elucidation of *Torah Shebichsav* by our own efforts.

4

W e have stated that the Jewish people play a vital role in deciphering and explicating *Torah Shebichsav*. But it is even true to say that in so doing they **shine a light for Hashem Himself!**[19] For in granting them the right to determine halachah and clarify the perplexing words of *Torah Shebischsav*, Hashem became, so to speak, in need of His people's input into His Torah.

This notion is borne out by the Gemara[20] that discusses the purpose of the *Menorah* in the *Mishkan*. Essentially, as the Gemara notes, the idea of lighting a candelabra in the house of G-d appears to be counter-intuitive—"Does He have any need for light?" But the answer is that "it is a testimony to all of the inhabitants of the world that the Divine Presence rests upon Yisrael." In other words, while indeed Hashem has no need for the physical light produced by the *Menorah*, He sought by means of the miraculous properties of the *neir maaravi* (the middle lantern which would miraculously remain alight at all times) to demonstrate to the world that His Shechinah rests among the Jewish people.

Why did Hashem choose to disseminate this message precisely through the vehicle of the *Menorah*? There were numerous miracles that were observed daily in the *Mishkan*[21]—could they not have served as a demonstration that Hashem had rested his Shechinah among us?

---

18   *Yalkut Shimoni* 405. See the *Beis Halevi's* monumental thesis in this regard—printed at the end of Volume 2 of his Responsa, *Derush* 18.

19   See *Maamar "Kesser Yitnu Lecha,"* where we elaborate upon this idea and find reference to it in the *Kedushah* of *Musaf* of Shabbos and Yom Tov for *nusach sefard*, *"Kesser yitnu lecha."* See also *Maamar* "The *Berachos* of the *Haftarah."*

20   *Shabbos* 22b.

21   *Avos* 5:7.

We will return to this question presently, but first, let us examine a related statement of Chazal.[22]

> The verse states, "For it is you who will light my lamp."[23] The Jewish People say to Hashem: "Master of the World, are you instructing us to illuminate for You [by kindling the Menorah in the Beis Hamikdash]? Surely You are the light of the world—light dwells with You! But yet, You instruct us 'toward the face of the Menorah'?"
>
> Hashem replies: "It is not that I need you, but you should nevertheless illuminate for Me just as I illuminated for you. Why? So as to elevate you before the nations, for they will say, 'See how the Jewish People cause illumination for the One who is a light for the world.'"
>
> This may be compared to a pike'ach (person of vision) and a blind person who are journeying together. The pike'ach said to the blind person: "When we enter the house, light a candle for me so that I will have light." The blind person replied: "Pray tell, when I am traveling, you support me, escorting me to the house, and now you are instructing me to light the candle for you!?" The pike'ach replied: "I asked you to light the candle for me so that you wouldn't be beholden to me for having escorted you on your journey."
>
> The pike'ach represents Hashem, as the pasuk states, "The eyes of Hashem—they scan the entire world."[24] The blind person represents the Jewish People, as the pasuk states, "We grope the wall like the blind."[25] Hashem would lead the people, and light the way for them, as the pasuk states: "And Hashem traveled in front of them by day."[26] Once the Mishkan was erected,

---

22 *Bamidbar Rabbah,* 15:5.
23 *Tehillim* 18:29.
24 *Zechariah* 4:10.
25 *Yeshayahu* 59:10.
26 *Shemos* 13:21.

Hashem called to Moshe instructing him: "Illuminate for me!"
As the pasuk states, "When you kindle the lamps," in other
words, to exalt you.

According to the Midrash, Hashem asked the Jewish people to
"illuminate for Him" in the manner of a *pike'ach* asking a blind person to
light a lamp for him. However, at first sight, the comparison appears to
be flawed, for while a *pike'ach* does ultimately have the need for the light
of the lamp, Hashem has no need for the lights that we kindle in the
Mishkan—"does He have any need for light?" Why then do we have any
need to light the *Menorah*, and how does doing so confer honor upon us?

In light of the above, these questions may be resolved. The commentators explain that while the *Aron Hakodesh* is symbolic of *Torah
She'bichsav*,[27] the *Menorah* represents *Torah She'baal Peh*.[28] Our kindling of the *Menorah* may thus allude to our nation's enormous contribution to *Torah She'baal Peh*, which does indeed "illuminate for Him,"
as detailed above. The *pike'ach's* gesture of requesting that the blind
man light a lamp for him is symbolic of Hashem's generous gesture in
allowing us to determine the path of *Torah She'baal Peh*, as described by
Rav Chaim Volzhin, cited above.

5

Now we may also understand why it was precisely the miracle of the
neir ha'maaravi of the *Menorah* that demonstrated that Hashem
had rested His Shechinah upon the Jewish people. Kindling the *Menorah*
was, as stated, a symbol of the nation's contribution to *Torah She'baal
Peh*, an act of illumination for Hashem Himself. But true comprehension

---

27 See the aforementioned *Maamar*, "Keser Yitnu Lecha."

28 See, for example, *Rabbeinu Bachya* to *Shemos* 25:39; the *Chasam Sofer* (*Derush L'zayin Adar*,
end of paragraph "*V'Atah tetzaveh*"); *Haamek Davar* (*Shemos* 27:20); and the *Malbim* (*Rimzei
HaMishkan*). See also *Rabbeinu Chananel* to *Shemos* 25:39. Chazal (*Bava Basra* 25b) also state,
"*H'arotzeh she'yachkim yadrim*—A person who wishes to become wise shall turn toward the
south (in prayer—*Rashi* ad loc., s.v. "Yadrim")," for the *Menorah* was positioned on the
southern side of the *Heichal* in the *Mishkan*.

of *Torah She'baal Peh* is grasped only by means of *hashraas haShechinah* (the resting of the Divine Presence upon the people).

This, as noted by Rav Tzadok Hakohen,[29] is alluded to by Chazal. The *Tosefta* states,[30] "Said Rabbi Yosi, 'It would have been fitting for the Torah to have been given to Yisrael by means of Ezra, were it not for the fact that Moshe preceded him." The Gemara in *Sanhedrin*,[31] in a similar vein, relates that a *bas kol* (Heavenly voice) declared, "There is a person, who is worthy of the *Shechinah* resting upon him as it did upon Moshe Rabbeinu," referring to Hillel HaZaken. Why regarding Ezra do Chazal say that "the Torah could have been given through him," but with regard to Hillel HaZaken they say that "the *Shechinah* is worthy of resting upon him"?

Ezra and Hillel

The answer, avers Rav Tzadok, is that the greatness of these two men was that they restored Torah to Yisrael after it had almost been forgotten. They therefore resembled Moshe Rabbeinu, who brought the Torah to Am Yisrael in the first place. Ezra chiefly reinstated *Torah She'bichsav*, therefore Chazal focus on the notion that "the Torah could have been given through him." But Hillel HaZaken reinstated *Torah She'baal Peh*, therefore Chazal stress the fact that "the Shechinah was worthy of resting upon him," as the acquisition of *Torah She'baal Peh* is dependent upon *hashraas haShechinah*.

The miracle of the *neir ha'maaravi* was symbolic of the *hashraas haShechinah* granted by Hashem to His people to help them grasp the *emes*—the true and profound secrets of *Torah She'baal Peh*, and thereby bring illumination back to Him. The nations of the world perceive in the *Menorah* and in the dynamic of *hashraas haShechinah* and *Torah She'baal Peh* that it engenders that Hashem rests His Shechinah upon the Jewish people. The people's defining role in *Torah She'baal Peh*—the

---

29   *Takanas ha'Shavim* p. 26.
30   *Sanhedrin* 4:5.
31   11a.

wisdom of G-d Himself—is a deafening testimony to the Shechinah that must reside in their midst.

Thus, the "testimony" invoked by the Gemara that the Shechinah rests upon Yisrael, is one and the same with the declaration of the nations of the world invoked by the Midrash that "the Jewish people bring illumination to the One who illuminates the world." For, simply, *hashraas haShechinah* is the very source of the illumination that they bring to bear.

The awe that the nations of the world have toward the Jewish people is a fulfillment of an explicit verse in the Torah, "You shall safeguard and perform them, for it is your wisdom and discernment in the eyes of the peoples, who shall hear all these decrees and who shall say, "Surely a wise and discerning people is this great nation!"[32] The Gemara explains[33] that the wisdom and discernment perceived by the people of the world is that of *chishuv tekufos u'mazalos* (the aptitude of the Chachamim in discerning the progression of the seasons and the constellations). Since the nations also consider this to be a form of wisdom, they are astounded that the Chachamim are adept at it even without the help of contemporary scientific principles.[34]

At this point, the nations realize that the Torah of the Jewish people reveals the essence and workings of Creation. As they sit in their universities and halls of power, they slowly begin to realize that they are in fact engulfed by the thick, black clouds of Yavan, and that a quaint and ancient nation, swaying in its halls of study, is the one which can truly see "from one end of the world to another."

---

32   *Devarim* 4:6.
33   *Shabbos* 75a.
34   *Maharsha* ad loc., s.v. *"She'neemar ki hi."*

6

Neiros Chanukah

The days we celebrate the victory of the *chochmah* of Yisrael over the *choshech* of Yavan are, of course, those of the Yom Tov of Chanukah. The message that the Jewish people enlighten the world through the power of *Torah She'baal Peh* is transmitted through the Chanukah candles, which, as we will see, are an heir to those of the *Menorah* of the *Mishkan*.

The Gemara rules[35] that it is forbidden to make use of the light of the Chanukah candles. The *Rashba* and *Ran* explain[36] that this is because they are a remembrance of the lights of the *Menorah* of the Beis Hamikdash, from which it was prohibited to derive any benefit. At first glance, this statement appears incongruous—after all, the mitzvah of *neiros Chanukah* was enacted specifically to remind us of the miraculous flask of oil found by the Chashmona'im, which burned for eight days. What have they to do with the regular light of the *Menorah* of the Beis Hamikdash?

The answer is that the miracle of the oil of Chanukah symbolized the victory of the light of *Torah She'baal Peh* over the darkness of Yavan. The Yevanim tried to indoctrinate Yisrael and the world that the *teva* is of foremost importance; but in the victory of the Chashmona'im, and in the shining, miraculous lights of their *Menorah*, their position was repudiated and rejected. The vessel employed to teach this lesson was the *Menorah*—for it is the symbol of *Torah She'baal Peh* and of the light that the Jewish people cast out into the world and to the Almighty Himself.

This notion is also evident in the famous words of the *Ramban* in *Parashas Behaalosecha*.[37] The *Midrash Aggadah* relates[38] that when Aharon HaKohen saw that each of the heads of the tribes had offered

---

35   *Shabbos* 22a.
36   Ad. loc.
37   *Bamidbar* 8:2, s.v. *"Behaalosecha."*
38   Cited by *Rashi* ibid., s.v. *"Behaalosecha."*

a special set of offerings in honor of the inauguration of the *Mishkan*[39] and he hadn't participated, he was most dejected. Hashem therefore comforted him, "Your lot is greater than theirs, for you will kindle and prepare the lights of the *Menorah*."

The *Ramban* asks why Hashem chose to comfort Aharon specifically with the fact that he was to kindle the Menorah; after all there were other tasks that only he, as Kohen Gadol, would be privileged to perform. He answers by citing the *Megillas Setarim* and *Midrash Tanchuma*,[40] which reveal that Hashem comforted Aharon not only with the knowledge that he was to light the *Menorah* of the *Mishkan*, but also that his descendants, the Chashmona'im, would partake of another inauguration (*Chanukah acheres*) many years later when they would recapture the Beis Hamikdash from the hands of the nefarious Yevanim. Not only that, but the Chanukah candles, kindled in honor of the miracles witnessed by the valiant Chashmona'im, would continue to be lit for the entirety of the *galus*, long after the Beis Hamikdash had been destroyed, via the study of *Torah She'baal Peh*.

Why are the Chanukah candles lit in our homes centuries after the destruction of the Beis Hamikdash and the burial of its *Menorah* a comfort for Aharon HaKohen, and a fulfillment of the promise "your lot is greater than theirs"? One can only conclude, as did the *Rashba* above, that the Chanukah candles are an extension of those of the *Menorah* of the *Mishkan* and Beis Hamikdash, and continue to emit the light of *Torah She'baal Peh* throughout the dark exile.[41]

7

Neiros Shabbos

We have spoken at length of the distinction between Yisrael and Yavan and between light and darkness (*bein ohr l'choshech,*

---

39   Detailed in the preceding *parashah*, *Naso* (7:1–89).
40   Ibid., 5.
41   See *Pachad Yitzchok: Chanukah*, end of *Maamar 3*.

bein Yisrael la'amim). Now we will turn our attention to the distinction between Shabbos and the days of the week (*yom ha'shevi'i l'sheshes yemei ha'maaseh*). We will quickly see that the theme of the light of Torah illuminating Creation comes very much to the fore on Shabbos as well.

In several places in this *sefer* we have discussed the fact that Shabbos lends meaning and purpose to the rest of the week.[42] We have seen that Shabbos is the source of all *kedushah* in Creation, and that it therefore sheds light on a world that would otherwise be blanketed in darkness. Moreover, Shabbos reveals that all of Creation, including its most apparently mundane elements, are there to promote *kedushah* and help forward G-d's masterplan. Chazal relate[43] that during the first Shabbos of Creation there was no darkness, as the *ohr ha'ganuz* (the primeval light) shone for a full thirty-six hours. This reflects the fact that Shabbos negates darkness.

On the eight days of Chanukah, we light a total of thirty-six candles.[44] The *Arizal* says that these represent the thirty-six hours of the aforementioned reign of the *ohr ha'ganuz* on the first-ever Shabbos, for the light of Chanukah and the light of Shabbos are one and the same. Both upend the worldview of Yavan, illuminate the *choshech al p'nei s'hom*, and demonstrate that *teva* itself is nothing but a miracle. *Teva* itself cannot possibly cast illumination for it is lifeless and devoid of power. It is only the miraculous light of *kedushah* that powers Creation.

Rav C. Y. Kaplan noted that the *Zayis Raanan*, in his comments on the aforementioned Midrash, states that Hashem in His words of comfort to Aharon assured him that his lot was greater, for he was to have *neiros Chanukah* **and the** *neiros Shabbos*! What have the Shabbos candles of all generations have to do with Aharon HaKohen? The answer is that the Shabbos candles represent the *ohr ha'ganuz* and the illumination of the

---

42   See *Maamarim*, "The Song of Shabbos," "To Declare that Hashem is Just," "Good Shabbos," "Source of Blessing," "*Kah Ribon*," "Shabbos Chanukah," and "Sanctity and Blessing."
43   *Bereishis Rabbah* 12:6. See the *Sefas Emes* to *Bereishis, Chanukah* 5661; *B'nei Yissaschar Maamarei haShabbosos*, 3; *Leshem Shevo v'Achlomoh, sefer Hade'ah* 4:9:4.
44   Excluding the *shamash* which is lit on each night.

teva with the light of *kedushah*; precisely the message of the *Menorah* in the *Mishkan* and the candles of Chanukah.[45]

This is also apparent from the Gemara which attests, *"Ha'ragil b'ner havyan lo banim talmidei chachamim*—A person who is accustomed to lighting candles will have sons who are Torah scholars."[46] *Rashi* explains[47] that this refers to both the kindling of Shabbos and Chanukah candles, and, in light of all of the above, this is tremendously apt. The Shabbos and Chanukah candles represent the downing of *choshech* by means of the light of Torah; it is therefore most appropriate that a person who is dedicated to these mitzvos will be rewarded with sons who will fill the world with the light of their Torah.

8

We began with the observation of Rav Hutner that from the times of the Vilna Gaon and the Baal Shem Tov, the *Chachmei Avodah* (the *talmidim* of the *Gra*) and the *Chachmei Emes* (the *talmidim* of the Baal Shem Tov) focused more upon the *kedushah* of Am Yisrael. Considering all the above, perhaps we may explain why.[48]

Ever since the empire of Yavan was established, *kefirah* (heresy) descended upon the world[49] to an extent not previously known. Though Ancient Greece ultimately become ancient history, their legacy remains the beating heart of Western civilization,[50] and its influence has only strengthened over time. In the last several hundred years, particularly

---

45   See the *Baal Haturim* to *Shemos* 27:20, s.v. *"V'Atah tetzaveh."*

46   *Shabbos* 23b.

47   Ad loc., s.v. *"Banim."*

48   My dear friend Rabbi Shlomo Freifeld told me that the reason that the Baal Shem Tov merited the title of "Reb Yisrael Baal **Shem Tov**" (lit. "possessor of a good name") was because he lived in an era of great despair following the dreadful pogroms of *tach v'tat* and the disastrous affair of Shabtai Tzvi. His message to the nation was, "Do not despair, you are a Yisrael," encouraging those who flocked to him for comfort by reminding them of their name Yisrael. He thus merited to be known as "**Yisrael** Baal **Shem Tov**."

49   At the end of his comments to *Vayikra* 16:8.

50   See footnote 4 in Translator's Preface above.

following the Industrial Revolution, the French Revolution, and subsequently the Bolshevik Revolution, the *emunah* in the power of man has replaced the *emunah* in Hashem and in the Torah. Ironically, though, this has led to the absolute negation of man's worth due, in no small part, to the doctrines of Charles Darwin and Sigmund Freud; for Darwin sought to make an animal of man's body and Freud made an animal of man's mind.

This has also been accompanied by exponential advances in technology and science. With the astounding prowess of scientists across the world, the inner workings of Creation have become known to man, fueling the all-powerful *kochi v'otzem yadi* sentiment of Yavan.[51] By means of sophisticated equipment and apparatus, Western civilization has apparently conquered Creation, examining and probing the deepest secrets of the universe. *Chochmas Yavan*, it may be said, has become an inexorably potent force, proclaiming that man is omnipotent and Torah is obsolete, despite the denudement of man wrought by Darwin and Freud.

The Baal Shem Tov who passed away in 1760 (at the birth of the Industrial Revolution) and the *Gra* who passed away in 1797 foresaw the relentless growth of Yavan in the years that were to come. The seeds of the revolutions that were to come had already been sown, heralding a rising wave of *kefirah* and *apikorsus*, and the crushing of pure faith in Hashem.

Seeing that this philosophy would engulf the world, they prepared their students and all of Am Yisrael to fight for their lives. They knew that Am Yisrael would need to hold fast to their unique status as bearers of *Torah She'baal Peh*, and remain faithful to the notion that the true inner workings of Creation can only be found in Torah and not in the lens of a microscope or telescope or in the chemicals of a crucible or test tube. They, and the great sages who followed them, therefore pivoted to focusing on the glorious stature and eminence of Am Yisrael for this they understood to be the panacea for an ailing world.

---

51   *Devarim* 8:17: "And you may say in your heart, 'My strength and the might of my hand made me all this wealth.'"

The focus hitherto on the *kedushah* of Hashem would no longer be effective in combating the rising tide of Yavan. It would become necessary to counter Yavan directly by focusing on the power of man just as Yavan did. However, rather than extolling the accomplishments of his mind, the focus would be on the power of his *emunah*.

For while man certainly has the capacity for scientific accomplishments and dazzling logic, his power is derived from the Torah, not from his own mind. The true supremacy of the human race is measured only by the extent of its fealty to Torah and Hashem, and is a fact known only to Am Yisrael who "shine light for G-d Himself." A Jew is bid to illuminate Creation by providing it with purpose and a masterplan and reveal the true power of man. In the words of Chazal, "*Atem keruyim Adam v'ein umos ha'olam keruyim Adam*—You are called Man, but the nations of the world are not called Man."[52]

Ultimately, Western civilizations, and the doyens of science and technology will have to bow their heads to the Creator of the World and to the philosophy and Torah of the Jews. For with all their prowess in discerning and harnessing the forces of the universe, they can do no more than transform *yesh l'yesh* (one thing to another) and remain perplexed as to the notion of *yesh me'ayin* (ex nihilo*).

Yesh me'ayin is manifested by two elements of Creation—the tiniest and the vastest; the cells that comprise a human being, and the outermost reaches of space. Despite the astonishing powers of the microscope that traces the pathways and essential makeup of human cells, and the magnificent vista provided by the telescope of the universe and galaxies millions of light years away, there is a point of infinity at which the grandest and most advanced machinery is defeated.

Amidst sparkling laboratories, powerful computers, volumes of research of sub-atomic particles, cells and DNA, the greatest experts of the world will eventually come to the recognition that they are in the dark. For in the infinitesimal workings of the tiniest of cells, which cannot

---

52   *Yevamos* 61a and *Bava Metzia* 114b.

be duplicated, and in the unreachable, immeasurable outer reaches of space (the point of infinity), science ultimately meets its match.

At this moment as the Western world gropes in the dark, it will turn to the Jewish people who are as enlightened as they ever were. The Jew knows that in the infinite depths of Creation, humankind **does not meet its match, but meets its Maker,** an idea captured by David HaMelech who wrote, "*Mi'ktzei haShamayim motza'o*—From the farthest point in space, He is found."[53] There is simply no need for new-generation telescopes that may perhaps even attempt to capture infinity, for with the supremely powerful eyes of the intellect and the light of *Torah She'baal Peh* and our *emunah*, the Jewish people can point to infinity and help the world understand, "*Hinei Elokeinu zeh*—Behold this is our G-d."

We allude to this idea in the Kedushah we recite each day. First, we state, "*Kadosh, kadosh, kadosh Hashem Tzevakos, m'lo chol haaretz kevodo*—Holy, holy, holy is Hashem, Master of Legions, the entire world is filled with His glory,"[54] stating the simple fact that G-d can be found behind all aspects of Creation. But then we state that "*Baruch kevod Hashem mi'mekomo*—"Blessed is the glory of Hashem from His place,"[55] acknowledging that His glory emanates particularly from one special "*makom*" in Creation. This perhaps refers to the *makom* of infinity of outer space[56] and the infinitely tiny elements of the cell, for although those imbued with true faith know intuitively that "the entire world is filled with His glory," the non-believers will only discover that glory in the "*makom*" that the human mind cannot penetrate. For in the very places that humankind cannot reach, there G-d can be found by all who are open to see Him.

The legacy of the *Gra* and Baal Shem Tov is that the glory of the Jewish people and their relationship with *Torah She'baal Peh* should enlighten

53 *Tehillim* 19:7.
54 *Yeshayahu* 6:3.
55 *Yechezkel* 3:12.
56 Rav Hutner would say that the word "*shamayim*" is a plural of the word "*sham*" meaning "there," for the Heavens, which are the resting place of G-d ("*ha'shamayim, shamayim la-Hashem*"—*Tehillim* 115:15), are ever further away—"there, there."

the eyes of the world even as it reaches the peak of human attainment.[57] For in spite of the knowledge and wisdom that abounds among the nations, they ultimately still walk in the darkness of Yavan, and it is the Jews who will guide them towards the infinite light of the Almighty.

---

57 Rabbi Chaim Segal, the *Menahel* of the Mesivta of Rabbeinu Chaim Berlin, once asked Rav Hutner what the defining message of the *chinuch* of the Mesivta should be. Rav Hutner answered him that he should place the focus on "*Atah bechartanu*"—the chosenness and importance of Am Yisrael.

The Soul of a
Talmid Chacham

The *Maharal* explains[1] that unlike the nations of the world, the Jewish nation is a single unified entity, and each individual Jew is hewn from one composite soul called *K'nesses Yisrael*. Therefore, even when a national census is taken, the result is a collection of **fractions** rather than individual integers. Rav Hutner added[2] that, in fact, the soul of a *talmid chacham* comprises a larger fraction of this unified composite soul, which is why there is a greater obligation of *v'ahavta l'rei'acha kamocha*, "love your fellow as yourself" to a *talmid chacham*, who is a greater *rei'a* than those not of the same stature.

The etymological source of the root *"rei'a"* (spelled *reish*, *ayin*) is identical to that of the word *"ra"* (evil). Rav Hutner would explain that both represent the notion of something that is "a part of something greater than itself." *Ra* is a break-off—a fraction of the greater good with which G-d created the world—for without *ra* there cannot be *tov* (good), and without *din* (strict judgment) there cannot be *chessed* (loving-kindness). Likewise, each individual person—each *rei'a* of the

---

1   *Gur Aryeh, Ki Sisa* 30:12.
2   *Pachad Yitzchok: Shavuos* 15:13.

Jewish nation—is another fraction of the master plan, and the soaring soul of a *talmid chacham* comprises a greater fraction yet.[3]

Perhaps this is why one must treat a budding Torah scholar as though he were already a full-fledged *talmid chacham,* and treat him with the acts of deference referenced by the Gemara[4] as soon as he shows signs of promise. The proof for this is the Gemara[5] which relates that Rabbi Yehoshua ben Chananyah redeemed Rabbi Yishmael ben Elisha from captivity when he was but a child for more than his true value, explaining that "I am certain that this child is destined to issue rulings for the Jewish people."[6]

Why should a person be treated as a *talmid chacham* before he has become one? Surely, the state of *talmid chacham* is only reached upon achieving a certain degree of erudition and spiritual standing!

In light of the above, we may suggest that when a person succeeds in becoming a *talmid chacham*, he reveals that he was endowed with a more elevated soul from the very start. Therefore, as soon as he shows signs of fulfilling his potential, he should already be treated in a manner befitting someone with a soul as elevated as he.

Chazal say that a *talmid chacham* represents the *bechinah* (quality) of Shabbos. On Shabbos each Jewish person is endowed with a *neshamah yeseirah* which seeks to attach itself to his physical body and imbue it with spirituality.[7] Thus, on some level, on Shabbos, each Jew assumes the status of *talmid chacham*—each individual transformed into a greater *rei'a*, a greater fraction of *K'nesses Yisrael*.

---

3 See *Horayos* ibid. for the practical applications of this idea.
4 *Horayos* 12b–14a.
5 *Gittin* 58a.
6 *Pachad Yitzchok: Sefer HaZikaron* p. 107.
7 See *Maamar* "*Nishmas Kol Chai*," where we discuss this notion.

Sanctify Us with Your Mitzvos

1

Torah and Mitzvos

"*Kadesheinu b'mitzvosecha v'sein chelkeinu b'Sorasecha*—Sanctify us with Your commandments and grant our share in Your Torah." These oft-recited words are a staple of the Shabbos and Yom Tov *tefillos* but curiously they appear to give precedence to mitzvos over Torah, unlike many of the other *tefillos*.

For example, in *Birchos Ha'shachar* we state, "*She'targilenu b'Sorasecha v'dabkeinu b'mitzvosecha*—That you accustom us to study Your Torah and attach us to Your commandments," placing Torah before mitzvos. Similarly, at the conclusion of the *Amidah* we say, "*P'sach libi b'Sorasecha, u'v'mitzvosecha tirdof nafshi*—Open my heart to your Torah, then my soul will pursue Your commandments." In *Birkas K'rias Shema* we say, "*V'ha'eir einenu b'Sorasecha, v'dabek libenu b'mitzvosecha*—Enlighten our eyes in Your Torah, attach our hearts to Your commandments." Lastly, in *U'va L'Tzion* we daven, "*Hu yiftach libenu b'Soraso v'yasem b'libenu ahavaso v'yiraso*—May He open our heart through His Torah and imbue our hearts with love and awe of Him." Why of all the *tefillos* does the

Amidah of Shabbos and Yom Tov reverse the order, mentioning *mitzvos* before Torah?

There is, moreover, a good reason for Torah to precede mitzvos. The *Rambam* (*Hilchos Talmud Torah* 3:3) explains that "*Talmud*" (Torah) is always found to precede "*maaseh*" (the performance of *mitzvos*) "because *Talmud* leads to *maaseh* but *maaseh* does not lead to *Talmud*."

Perhaps we could suggest the following.

The *Sefas Emes* explains the words of the *tefillah* as follows:

> "*Retzei v'menuchaseinu*" refers to Shabbos, "*Kadsheinu b'mitzvosecha*" refers to Pesach, "*V'sein chelkeinu b'Sorasecha*" refers to Shavuos, "*Sabeinu mi'tuvecha*" refers to Sukkos, and "*Samcheinu b'yeshuasecha*" refers to Shemini Atzeres.

The connection between "*Retzei V'menuchaseinu*—May you be pleased with our rest," and Shabbos is clear—for Shabbos is a day of rest, *baah Shabbos, baah menuchah*."

The allusion to Pesach in the words "*Kadsheinu b'mitzvosecha*" may be in the fact that the Jewish people were commanded to perform several mitzvos upon the Exodus from Egypt, prior to the giving of the Torah. This is referenced by a verse of the Ten Commandments which states that the people were to observe Shabbos "*Ka'asher tzivcha Hashem Elokecha*—As Hashem your G-d commanded,"[1] which *Rashi* says[2] refers to the mitzvos that were given in Marah prior to the giving of the Torah.

The connection between "*V'sein chelkeinu b'Sorasecha*" and Shavuos is self-evident.

The *tefillah* of Shabbos and Yom Tov thus alludes to Shabbos and the Yamim Tovim in chronological order, first referencing Shabbos (*menuchah*), then Pesach (by means of the commandments that were given upon the Exodus), then Shavuos (by means of the giving of the Torah) and so on. But the regular *tefillos* of the week (listed above) speak in conceptual order, thus Torah (*Talmud*) precedes *mitzvos* (*maaseh*).

---

1   *Devarim* 5:12.
2   Ad loc.

This approach also helps explain another notable exception to the model of "Torah before mitzvos." In the *berachah* of *Emes v'yatziv* immediately following the *Shema*, we state, "Praiseworthy is the person who obeys Your commandments and takes to his heart Your teaching and Your word," invoking mitzvos before Torah. Considering the above, this can easily be explained, as *Emes v'yatziv* was instituted as a means of remembering and mentioning the Exodus from Egypt each day. Therefore, we invoke the mitzvos, which, as stated, were first given upon the Exodus, before we invoke the Torah that was only given on Shavuos.

2

———

Yetzias Mitzrayim

We have seen that regarding *yetzias Mitzrayim*, mitzvos are invoked before Torah. This we said alludes to the chronology of events in which mitzvos were issued prior to the Torah, but there may be a deeper aspect to this too. Rav Hutner would cite the verse, "*Zacharti lach chessed ne'urayich ahavas kelulosayich lectech acharai ba'midbar*—I recall for you the kindness of your youth the love of your nuptials, your following Me into the wilderness,[3] and explain that these words praise the Jewish people for utterly nullifying their judgment and blindly going out to the wilderness like a flock following their master.

The nullification of their judgment brought to fore their natural instincts which were to attach themselves to G-d and to flock into the barren, frightening desert in His wake. Rav Hutner would explain that the instinct of a Jew is *emunah*—simple faith, or, as he put it, "If you were to dissect a Jewish heart you would find *emunah*." And this *emunah* is a higher, purer form of faith than that engendered by logical argumentation, for it can never be shaken, no matter how logical the counterargument.

———

3   *Yirmiyahu* 2:2.

The Jewish people's purest instincts were manifested before the giving of the Torah. This was a stage of their development in which they had not yet been invested with *daas* (wisdom) and could therefore completely nullify their judgment in the face of G-d's, resembling a trusting flock (which similarly has no *daas*) that nullifies itself to its master, or a suckling infant, which is totally reliant on its mother. This may be the stage that Chazal referred to when they stated, *"Derech eretz kadma l'Torah."*[4]

These instincts are passed down from one generation to another. Chazal therefore relate[5] that the Jewish people are characterized as *"Rachmanim, bayshanim, v'gomlei chassadim*—People who are merciful, bashful, and purveyors of loving-kindness." These traits, which form the fabric of the Jewish soul, the Jewish instinct, have been bequeathed by Jewish parents to their children, since the birth of our nation.

Avos HaKedoshim

This began with the Avos—Avraham, Yitzchak, and Yaakov—who conferred to their descendants not only the promise of Eretz Yisrael but also their *middos tovos* (their exemplary character traits and instincts). These traits and instincts formed the original DNA of Am Yisrael, and each generation that followed simultaneously became heirs to this precious heritage and *"manchilin"* (those who bequeath their instincts and traits to the generations that followed).

Before Matan Torah (the revelation at Sinai) the nation had not been invested with the *daas* of Torah and could thus transmit these instincts in their purest form. Rav Hutner once explained[6] that the reason we teach the *Shema* to a *tinok* (a child of three) is not so that he should be fluent in the recitation as he gets older. If that were to be the case, we could very well wait until he is older and understands its meaning. To the contrary, we want the *Shema* to form the basis for his instinctive

---

4   *Vayikra Rabbah* 19:8.

5   *Yevamos* 79a.

6   Based on *Shulchan Aruch, Yoreh Deah* 245:8, *Rama* citing the *Abarbanel* (*Avos* 5:24).

emunah, and therefore we teach it to him when he is but an infant, when only instinct is his purview and not *daas*.

This notion exists among the animals too, proving that the sphere of instinct is a more basic, and therefore more truthful element of Creation extending beyond human logic and reason. Chazal note[7] that numerous character traits can be detected among animals, each of which pass these traits to their offspring. Therefore, at the stage where the Jewish people were lacking in *daas* like the animal kingdom, they could pass their traits to the next generation. Character and *middos* can be transmitted, *daas*, intellectual achievement, cannot.

For this reason, the land of Israel was divided among the people who left Egypt even though many of them did not live to enter the land.[8] For as of the Exodus, the people became "*manchilin*," not only of the purest essence of a Jewish soul, but also of the purest of lands—Eretz Yisrael.

This process is alluded to by the *tefillos* of Shabbos and Yom Tov and the *berachah* of *Emes V'yatziv*. *Kadsheinu b'mitzvosecha* refers to the stage of mitzvos—basic commands and subjugation to the will of G-d, "*Ashrei ha'ish she'yishma l'mitzvosecha*—Praiseworthy is the person who obeys Your commandments." After that there is the stage of *V'sein chelkeinu b'Sorasecha*, the phase of *daas* and of "*V'Sorascha u'dvarcha yasim al libo*—And takes to his heart Your teaching and Your word.'"

3

Neir Mitzvah V'Torah Ohr

We may suggest another approach as to why the *tefillos* of Shabbos invoke mitzvos before Torah. The verse states, "*Ki neir mitzvah v'Torah ohr*—For a commandment is a candle, and the Torah is light."[9] Rav Hutner would explain[10] that the intent of the verse

---

7   *Eruvin* 100b.
8   *Bava Basra* 117a.
9   *Mishlei* 6:23.
10   *Pachad Yitzchok: Chanukah* 10:9.

is that the mitzvos are kindled by the Torah, for the Torah is the very source of all the mitzvos. This is the basis for the aforementioned tenet of the *Rambam* that "Talmud leads to *maaseh*," and also why a person who interrupts his Torah study in order to perform a mitzvah receives reward as though he had studied Torah during that time. In fact, according to Rav Hutner, the same is true if he interrupts his Torah study to attend to his essential needs.[11]

The *tefillos* of the week proceed in the order of *aleph* to *tav* (from A to Z), which is why the first letters of the words of the first *berachah* of *K'rias Shema* are "*Ei-l, Baruch, Gadol, De'ah*" which begin with *aleph, beis, gimmel* and so on. This connotes a gradual and sequential buildup of the six days of Creation through to the seventh day—the day of *kedushah*, which teaches mankind that the goal and purpose of the natural world of Creation and of the mundane is *kedushah* and meaning. For this reason, they also invoke Torah before mitzvos, for Torah is the source of the mitzvos—the light to their candle. The source—the "*aleph*," therefore precedes the product—the "*beis*."

However, on Shabbos the *Musaf* prayer is arranged in the order of *tav* to *aleph*—"*Tikanta Shabbos ratzisa korbanoseha*," alluding to the fact that on Shabbos everything returns to its source and we are therefore enjoined to contemplate the source and purpose of Creation. Therefore, the *tefillos* also invoke mitzvos before Torah, for in contemplating the mitzvos, notably the mitzvah of Shabbos, we cast our minds back to their source, namely, the Torah that is not only the source of the mitzvos, but of all Creation and all elements of holiness and blessing.

4

Neshamah Yeseirah

The words "*Retzei v'menuchaseinu, kadsheinu b'mitzvosecha, v'sein chelkeinu b'Sorasecha, sabeinu mi'tuvecha v'samcheinu*

---

11 See *Pachad Yitzchok: Shavuos* 13.

b'yeshuasecha" are brought into sharper focus by the following excerpt from the *Pachad Yitzchok:*[12]

> *In mundane matters, the various physical pleasures are consigned in accordance with the capacity of the various physical senses that are the receptacles for the pleasure. For example, the enjoyment of sounds or music are felt through the ears, the enjoyment of sights through the eyes, and so on and so forth.*
>
> *The enjoyment and pleasure that is the reward for the performance of a mitzvah also require a receptacle with the capacity to receive it. The name of this receptacle is the "neshamah yeseirah." Though the soul was brought into being and revealed in a general sense on the sixth day of Creation as explicitly stated by the Torah, the capacity to receive the pleasure of the reward of a mitzvah was not revealed until the seventh day. These reflect the words of the Ramban, who explains that the words va'yekadesh oso, "and He sanctified it" [that are stated with regard to Shabbos] refer to the Creation of the neshamah yeseirah.*

Shabbos is a day on which the capacity for experiencing spiritual pleasure is granted to us by dint of the *neshamah yeseirah.*

Shabbos is the *zeman ha'sechar* (the time for reward); but reward is only conferred upon a person at the conclusion of a period of labor, effort, and toil. The Jewish people, for instance, only received their portion in the Land of Israel after an arduous seven years of conquest; they could only receive their *nachalah* (inheritance) after the onset of *menuchah* (rest from the strains of conquest).[13]

The Torah states in *Parashas Va'eschanan,* "You shall observe the commandment, and the decrees and the ordinances that I command you today, to perform them."[14] *Rashi* adds,[15] "Today, to perform

---

12   *Shabbos* 3:4.

13   Based on *Devarim* 12:9.

14   *Devarim* 7:11.

15   S.v. *"Ha'yom."*

them—and tomorrow, in the World to Come, to receive their reward." This world—**today**—is a place of performance, a place of labor, effort, and toil, and the World to Come—**tomorrow**—is a place of reward.

But on Shabbos, after six days of toil, this world also becomes a place of reward by dint of the *neshamah yeseirah*. With the newfound capacity to experience spiritual bliss, man is able to turn this world into the World to Come—"*me'ein Olam Haba.*" In fact, this is the notion that underpins the mitzvah of *oneg Shabbos*, for by delighting and imbibing the pleasures of Shabbos, man alludes to the extraordinary pleasures felt by his soul on this day.

Let us return to the *Amidah* of Shabbos.

The *berachah* begins with a reference to *menuchah*—"*Retzei vi'me-nuchaseinu*"—for *menuchah* is a prerequisite of reward. And if there is *menuchah* we may be hopeful of *nachalah*—the reward for our efforts, and so we immediately ask that G-d sanctify our souls as a product of our performance of mitzvos, "*Kadsheinu b'mitzvosecha.*"[16]

We then ask to each receive our *nachalah*, our portion in Torah, "*V'sein chelkeinu b'Sorasecha*" just like we received our portion in Eretz Yisrael after seven years of conquest. Chazal say that the word "Yisrael" is an acronym for "*Yesh shishim ribo osiyos laTorah*—There are six hundred thousand words in the Torah," which alludes to the fact that each person has their own portion—their own letter—in the Torah. After all our toil, we ask that our letter in the Torah be revealed to us; we ask to receive our individual *nachalah* in the "*Morashah kehillas Yaakov.*"

The next words of the *tefillah* are "*Sabeinu mi'tuvecha v'samcheinu b'Yeshuasecha.*" According to the aforementioned *Sefas Emes*, they re-fer to Sukkos and Shemini Atzeres respectively, which are also times of *nachalah* and reward. At this time man is rewarded for his intense efforts during the Yamim Nora'im (the Days of Awe) that preceded it and gathers in his fruits after all of his efforts in sowing, planting, and harvesting.

---

16 This is the intent of the Chazal (*Avos* 4:2) that states, "*S'char* mitzvah, mitzvah—the reward of a mitzvah is a mitzvah." In other words, "the reward for a mitzvah is the sanctity of that very mitzvah which envelops his soul."

Thus, the middle *berachah* of the *Amidah* of Shabbos and Yom Tov—the centerpiece of the *tefillah*—contains a litany of reward—an inundation of *nachalah* that is the bequest of the *neshamah Yeseirah* of Shabbos and Yom Tov.

Nishmas Kol Chai

1

Seder Night

The Mishnah states[1] that on Seder night a person recites *Birkas Ha'shir* over the fourth cup of wine. Rabbi Yochanan explains[2] that *Birkas Ha'shir* refers to the prayer of *Nishmas* that is otherwise only recited during *Shacharis* on Shabbos and Yom Tov. Why is *Nishmas* particularly pertinent to Shabbos and Yom Tov and to the Seder night?

Adam, the first man, was warned not to eat from the Tree of Knowledge in the Garden of Eden, "On the day you eat of it, you shall surely die."[3] The *Ramban* notes[4] that although scientists maintain that man was always destined to die, according to Chazal, if Adam had not ultimately eaten from the Tree of Knowledge he would never have died. This is because "the supernal soul [that he was endowed] would provide him with eternal life. The Divine favor to him at the time of Creation would have always remained with him and would have preserved him forever."

---

1   *Pesachim* 117b.
2   Ibid., 118a.
3   *Bereishis* 2:17.
4   Ad loc.

In other words, just as G-d's desire to maintain the world helps preserve it forever, so would His desire to maintain Adam have granted man immortality if only he wouldn't sin. The opening words of the *Nishmas* prayer, "*Nishmas kol chai*—the soul of every living being," in fact allude to this very concept, for life enjoyed by every "living being" is provided by its soul.[5]

Nishmas continues with the following famous words:

> Were our mouth as full of song as the sea, and our tongue as full
> of joyous song as its multitude of waves, and our lips as full of
> praise as the breadth of the heavens, and our eyes as brilliant
> as the sun and the moon, and our hands as outspread as eagles
> of the sky, and our feet as swift as gazelles—we still could not
> thank You sufficiently.

These words are difficult to understand. What role could a person's eyes, hands or feet play in thanking G-d? Further, what is the purpose of stating that had our mouths or tongues etc. had a different capacity we would have theoretically been able to thank G-d in a different way?

A few sentences later we read the following:

> Therefore, the organs that You set within us, and the spirit and
> soul that You breathed into our nostrils, and the tongue that
> you placed in our mouth—all of them shall thank and bless...

Having stated earlier that even if our organs resembled the sea, waves, or heavens we would not be capable of suitably praising Hashem, how can we now say "therefore" our organs will thank and bless Hashem? In addition, the words "all of them" appear in the original Hebrew as "*hein, heim*" utilizing the feminine and masculine form. To what does this allude?

---

5   Perhaps this is the reason for the phenomenon observed in the medical world that the will to survive can often impact greatly upon a patient's chances of recovery from illness. His *neshamah* is the provider of his life force, as the *Ramban* explained, and to the degree that it wills that he survive, he will indeed do so. When he summons up the will from the deepest part of his soul to battle his illness, he stands a greater chance of survival.

It appears to me that when we invoke the image of a human being filled with praise like the sea, waves, or heavens, we are not imagining a theoretical being that never existed, for this would be a thoroughly pointless statement. Rather, we allude to *Adam HaRishon kodem ha'chet* (Adam, the first man in the glorious state that he occupied before he sinned). He was indeed capable of singing a praise of G-d with his entire being, for his soul and spirit were utterly united with every element of his physical body. According to the aforementioned *Ramban*, in this state, his soul and body were in such harmony that they could never be separated—he was to be immortal.

The day of Shabbos is a weekly, miniature version of the World to Come.[6] On this day, by dint of his *neshamah yeseirah* (the "additional soul" granted on Shabbos) that seeks to attach itself strongly to the physical body, man somewhat resembles *Adam HaRishon kodem ha'chet*, and it's as though his body and soul were inseparable. The Torah alludes to this notion in *Parashas Bereishis*, as it describes G-d's creation of Shabbos before relating the episode of the sin of Adam and Chavah, which is in non-chronological order. This intimates that Shabbos has the power to return a person to the state of Adam **before he sinned**.[7]

Thus, on Shabbos, man is capable of singing G-d's praises not only with his spiritual faculties but with his physical body too. That which during the week is only recognized by his soul, on Shabbos is felt by his hands and feet as well. Therefore, we recite *Nishmas* only on Shabbos and Yom Tov for it is then that we are granted a *neshamah yeseirah*,[8] which helps achieve the union between the body and the soul.[9]

But in spite of that, we are still incapable of thanking G-d sufficiently. Though our bodies and soul join as one, we can never praise G-d enough, in fact, even *Adam HaRishon kodem ha'chet* could not do Him justice.

---

6   *Berachos* 57b.

7   *Pachad Yitzchok: Shabbos*, Chap. 8—*Reshimos*, §1–5.

8   *Bi'ur HaGRA* O.C. 664.

9   In fact, when a person avails himself of physical pleasures for the purposes of *oneg Shabbos* he infuses his body with the holiness of the *neshamah yeseirah*. This grants his body a taste of the eternity of the soul. For if the soul always seeks to attach itself to the body and render it immortal, as the *Ramban* stated, the *neshamah yeseirah* seeks to do so even more strongly.

What then is the meaning of the continuation of *Nishmas*—"Therefore, the organs that You set within us…all of them shall thank and bless…"? Have we not already confessed our inability to praise Him sufficiently?

The answer is that our inability to praise Him sufficiently does not deter us from attempting to do so. By means of Shabbos and assuming the status, in miniature, of *Adam HaRishon kodem ha'chet*, we can at least try and include all of our earthly faculties to praise Him.

2

Man Recreated

L et us return to the text of *Nishmas*.

"You redeemed us from Egypt, Hashem our G-d, and liberated us from the house of bondage." How does the redemption from Egypt fit into the context of *Nishmas* and *"Kol atzmosai"*?

The answer is that the Exodus from Egypt was also a time in which the Jewish people returned to the state of *Adam HaRishon kodem ha'chet*, and were granted a path to do so again in the future. Rav Hutner explained that the Exodus should be considered a second version of man's creation;[10] a version whereby *K'nesses Yisrael*, the unified soul of the Jewish people, was formed. This was followed by Matan Torah, when the people assumed an almost godly status—*"Ani amarti Elokim atem, u'vnei Elyon kulchem."*[11]

Second Creation of Man

The second version of man necessitated a second version of Shabbos which is why the mitzvah of Shabbos was given to the Jewish people soon after the Exodus (detailed in *Parashas Beshalach* in the *Parashas*

---

10   Based on the *Ramchal* (Rabbi Moshe Chaim Luzzatto), cited in *Maamarei Pachad Yitzchok: Pesach, Maamar* 104; the *Ramchal* postulates that the Exodus from Egypt represents the beginning of a long process by which the world returns to its pristine state of *Adam HaRishon kodem ha'chet*.

11   *Tehillim* 82:6.

Ha'Mann—the section that discusses the *mann*). At that time, Shabbos became a day that did not only commemorate Creation ("*Zecher l'maaseh Bereishis*") but also the Exodus ("*Zecher l'yetzias Mitzrayim*").[12]

Thus, Shabbos and the Egyptian Exodus, which return man to the ideal world, represent the notion so gloriously expressed by the *Ramban* above, that the human soul seeks to bestow life upon the physical body and form an unbreakable bond with it. And thus, even though we can never appreciate G-d enough, "*Ein anachnu maspikin*," on Shabbos and upon the occasion of the Exodus we are able in some way to move body and soul to the rhythm of His majesty, "*Kol atzmosai tomarnah Hashem mi Kamocha*—All my bones shall proclaim: G-d, who is like You?"

Let us now return to the text of *Nishmas*.

Nishmas begins with a series of praises of G-d uttered by man's spiritual elements—his soul and his spirit, "*Nishmas kol chai...v'ruach kol basar*—The soul of every living being...the spirit of all flesh." He does not yet have the capability to praise G-d with his physical elements as Adam HaRishon could, as he ruefully notes, "Were our mouth as full of song as the sea, and our tongue as full of joyous song as its multitude of waves etc."

However, with the Egyptian Exodus man underwent a transformation. "You redeemed us from Egypt, Hashem our G-d, and liberated us from the house of bondage," thus allowing us to ascend the pantheon of *Adam HaRishon kodem ha'chet* once more. You allowed us to touch eternal life with the bond between our body and soul unbreakable—"*Al titsheinu la'netzach*—Do not abandon us forever." And "Therefore, the organs that You set within us, and the spirit and soul that You breathed into our nostrils, and the tongue that You placed in our mouth—all of them shall thank and bless..." With the wind of the Egyptian Exodus in our sails we are capable of praising Hashem with the totality of our physical existence once again.

When do we assume something akin to this glorious state? Only on Shabbos and Yom Tov. Then we experience, in miniature, the wondrous

---

12   See the *Maamar* "*Kiddush*," where we discuss this concept at length.

bliss of *Adam HaRishon kodem ha'chet* and the dizzying heights of the plateau of the Exodus and Matan Torah.

And even if "we still could not thank You sufficiently," for even Adam HaRishon could never do Him justice, we will thank G-d to the greatest possible degree and with every faculty that we can—"All my bones shall proclaim: G-d, who is like You?" The two words *"hein, heim"* refer to the spirit and soul—**which are feminine nouns**, and the *"eivarim"* (organs)—**a masculine noun**. Both shall unite in the praise of the L-rd.[13]

This is why *Nishmas* is pertinent to Shabbos and to the Seder night. At these times we commemorate the Exodus from Egypt which allows us, in a small way, to experience the unanimity of body and soul. And although we can never thank G-d sufficiently, we can at least, during these rarefied times, do the very best we can.

---

13   Correspondingly, the mitzvah of *"shamor"* (observing Shabbos) represents the power of the female—*"kochos d'nukvin*," and the mitzvah of *"zachor"* (commemorating Shabbos) represents the power of the male—*"koach d'guvrin*." We seek to connect with both elements of Shabbos—both the *"hein"* and the *"heim*."

K'rias HaTorah
and Birkas Kohanim

1

On Mondays and Thursdays we call three people to the Torah to receive *aliyos*. On Yom Tov we call up five, and on Shabbos seven. The Gemara explains[1] that the various numbers of *aliyos* correspond to the number of words of the three *berachos* of *Birkas Kohanim* (the priestly blessing). Thus, the three *aliyos* of a weekday correspond to the *berachah* of "*Yevarechecha*," which is comprised of three words; the five *aliyos* of Yom Tov correspond to the five-word *berachah* of "*Ya'er*"; and the seven *aliyos* of Shabbos correspond to the seven words of "*Yisah*."

What is the connection between the *aliyos* of the Torah reading and *Birkas Kohanim*?

Perhaps we may suggest the following.

Weekdays are the time when a person seeks to earn a living. Chazal therefore instituted three *aliyos* to the Torah to correspond to the *berachah* of *Yevarechecha*, **which refers to material blessing** (finances and progeny).

---

1   *Megillah* 23a.

Yom Tov is a time of *"he'aras panim,"* a time when G-d shows his shining countenance to the Jewish people who ascend to the Beis Hamikdash—*liros v'leira'os,* "to see and be seen." For this reason Chazal instituted five *aliyos* in order to correspond with the *berachah* of Ya'er—a blessing that G-d should "illuminate His countenance" on the Jewish people.

Rav C. Y. Kaplan noted that this is also supported by a comment of the *Baal Haturim* who contends[2] that the three *berachos* of *Birkas Kohanim* correspond to the three primary forms of sacrifice—*Chatas* (sin offering), *Olah* (elevation offering), and *Shelamim* (peace offering). The connection between the *berachah* of Ya'er and the *Olah* offering is established by a verse[3] describing the *olei regel* (the pilgrims who would come to Jerusalem on Yom Tov) and invokes the phrase *"Ba'alosecha leira'os*—When you go up to appear." The word *"ba'alosecha"* shares the same root as the word *"olah,"* and the word *"leira'os"* is the same root as the word *"Ya'er."* This, explained the *Baal Haturim,* alludes to the fact that the *berachah* of *"ya'er"* corresponds to the *Olah* offering.

It therefore appears to be most fitting that the five *aliyos* of a Yom Tov, on which the **olei regel would each offer an** *Olah* **offering, correspond to the *berachah* of Ya'er, which represents the** *Olah* **offering.**

The seven *aliyos* of Shabbos correspond to the final *berachah* of *"Yisah,"* which closes with the words *"V'yaseim lecha shalom*—And He shall establish for you peace." This is an apt blessing for Shabbos when the entire world is at *shalom* (peace), culminating with the *shleimus* (perfection) of the world. The number seven, moreover, alludes to the *shleimus* of Creation that was completed in seven days.

---

2   *Vayikra* 9:22.
3   *Shemos* 34:24.

2

Shalom

The Gemara explains[4] that the reason Chazal placed the final *berachah* of the *Amidah*, *Sim shalom*, after *Birkas Kohanim* is that immediately following the *berachah* of *Birkas Kohanim* in the Torah, the verse states "Let them place My name upon the Children of Israel, **and I shall bless them**." Since G-d's primary blessing is one of peace, Chazal instituted the *berachah* of *Sim Shalom* (establish peace) to follow *Birkas Kohanim*.

Fascinatingly, the text of the *berachah* of *Sim Shalom* actually appears to allude to the three *berachos* of *Birkas Kohanim*:

- "*Barcheinu Avinu*—Bless us, our father" corresponds to the *berachah* of "*Yevarechecha*—May He bless you."
- "*Kulanu k'echad b'ohr panecha*—All of us as one, with the light of Your countenance" corresponds to "*Ya'er Hashem Panav eilecha*—May Hashem illuminate His countenance to You."
- "*V'tov b'einecha l'varech es amcha Yisrael*—And may it be good in Your eyes to bless Your people Israel" references the special favor conferred upon Am Yisrael by G-d and therefore corresponds to the *berachah* of "*Yisa Hashem Panav eilecha*—May Hashem lift His countenance to you."[5]
- "*Bi'shlomecha*—"With Your peace" corresponds to the words "*V'yaseim lecha shalom*—"And He shall establish for you peace."

Lastly, the *berachah* concludes by reiterating "*Ha'mevarech es amo Yisrael ba'shalom*—Who blesses His people Israel with peace," for G-d's primary blessing is one of peace.[6]

---

4   *Megillah* 18a.
5   See *Berachos* 20b, "*Yisah Hashem Panav eilecha*—How can I not show them favor?"
6   *Megillah* 18a.

The Berachos
of the Haftarah

Blessed are You, Hashem, our G-d, King of the universe, Who has chosen good prophets and was pleased with their words that were uttered with truth. Blessed are You, Hashem, Who chooses the Torah; Moshe, His servant; Israel, His nation; and the prophets of truth and righteousness.

The *berachah* recited before the *haftarah* appears to contain some peculiarities. First, it states that G-d "chose good prophets"—a strange statement considering that He would surely not choose **bad** prophets! Furthermore, the conclusion of the *berachah*, the *chasimah*, unusually makes mention of certain entities that are not mentioned in the main body of the *berachah*, namely, Torah, Moshe, and Yisrael. Lastly, the *berachah* states that G-d "chose the Torah" when it usually refers to Him as having "given" or "taught" us the Torah.

The *Rambam* rules[1] that prophecy is only granted to a person who is supremely wise, of exemplary character traits, in utter control of his inclinations, and of broad and true intelligence. These traits were found among all of the prophets of the *Tanach*, with one exception—the

---

1   *Hilchos Yesodei HaTorah* 7:1.

wicked Bilaam. Chazal famously assert[2] that although there was no Jewish prophet who was the equal of Moshe Rabbeinu, there was one non-Jewish prophet who was, namely Bilaam. In fact, in some ways Bilaam's perception of prophecy was superior to Moshe's![3]

How could Bilaam, a depraved and degenerate individual,[4] be said to be the equal of Moshe Rabbeinu? The comparison appears utterly preposterous!

Prophecy

Rav Yehoshua Leib Diskin offered the following explanation[5] to resolve this statement of Chazal, and to clarify the nature of prophecy in general.

Prophecy, he writes, is a vision that the prophet must interpret. But that interpretation will depend on the character traits and perception of the prophet in question. The Gemara explains[6] that while Moshe saw his prophetic visions through a "clear lens," other prophets saw their visions through a "cloudy lens." This means that in order to understand a prophecy, a prophet must apply himself to understanding the vision that is granted, and his success will depend upon his grasp of the ways of G-d. Moshe, who was utterly attuned to the ways of G-d and who

---

2   *Sifri, Devarim, V'zos Hamitzvah* 34:10.

3   According to the *Midrash Tanchuma* (*Balak* 1, cited by *Rashi* to *Bamidbar* 22:5), the reason that G-d granted prophecy to *Bilaam* was so that the nations of the world could not claim that had they had prophets to guide them they would not have been so sinful. But there may be a deeper idea at play as well. Rav Hutner would explain that the reason Chazal (*Berachos* 34b and *Sanhedrin* 99a) say that a person who has repented (a *baal teshuvah*) "occupies a place [in Heaven] that even a completely righteous person does not" is because the honor of Heaven that is brought about by a *baal teshuvah* is greater, in some ways, than that brought about by a completely righteous person **for he has come from far away to draw close to G-d.** See *Pachad Yitzchok: Pesach*, 37:3, and see also 37:2. See also *Sefer HaZikaron, Maamarim* section, no. 7.

   Perhaps the same could be said of the prophecy of Bilaam. G-d granting prophecy to a person so far removed from Him brought honor to Him that was exponentially greater than the honor that would have been brought about by granting prophecy to a person who wasn't as far removed.

4   See *Avos* 5:19.

5   End of *Yeshuos Malko, Maamar "L'siyum HaTorah,"* based on the *Abarbanel.*

6   *Yevamos* 49b.

absolutely subordinated himself to the Divine will, perceived his visions with pristine clarity—"through a clear lens." Other prophets, of lesser stature, saw them through the murkier lens of their slightly less than pristine characters.

Intriguingly, this means that a prophet impacts upon the prophecy that he has been granted;[7] the more pristine his character, the clearer will be his vision of the prophecy. His clarity of thought and deed will ultimately enable him to decipher the purpose of the vision. In the words of Rabbi Yehoshua Leib Diskin, "prophecy is the impression on the soul of that prophet. The prophet peers into his soul to comprehend the solution to the impression."

This fact was known to the wicked Bilaam and was precisely the method by which he sought to curse the Jewish people. Though he knew that he could not utter any prophecy that had not been granted to him by G-d (for G-d had explicitly told him so[8]), he believed that his perverted character traits and hatred for the Jewish people would distort the prophecy to the extent that the repercussions would be negative for them.

To counteract this, G-d granted a prophecy to Bilaam that was so clear, it was akin to that perceived by Moshe Rabbeinu. His prophecy needed no deciphering whatsoever—the words were relayed to him with great clarity, and he had no choice but to relay them verbatim. Put simply, his prophecy needed no human input at all.[9]

According to Rav Yehoshua Leib Diskin, regular prophecy **depends upon the interpretation of the prophet in question.** Therefore, we may suggest, that the words of the prophets in *Tanach*, though certainly

---

7   The *Malbim* (Introduction to *Sefer Yirmiyahu*) dismisses this notion out of hand. He argues that it simply cannot be true that a *sefer* of *Tanach* would have been subject to the interpretation of any particular person. Rather, prophets differ only in their style and rendition of prophecy, not in their perception of the word of G-d, which they disseminate in its pure and unadulterated original form.

8   *Bamidbar* 22:20 and 35.

9   This may be the reason that the Torah describes G-d's appearance to Bilaam with the words "*Vayikar Hashem el Bilaam*" (*Bamidbar* 23:4 and 16), which literally means "and G-d chanced upon Bilaam." This implies that Bilaam was practically selected at random; there was no reason in terms of his character why he should have been deserving of prophetic insight.

an essential component of *Torah She'bichsav*, **have an element of *Torah She'baal Peh* in them too, for both depend on human interpretation**.

Chamishah Chumshei Torah

A similar idea is expressed by the *Maharal*, who discusses[10] the difference between the first four books of *Chumash* and the book of *Devarim*, known as *Mishneh Torah*. He explains that the Torah that G-d gave to the Jewish people has two aspects—one from the perspective of the giver (G-d), and the other from the perspective of the recipients (the Jewish people). When a giver and recipient are on equal footing and their perspectives are alike, any transaction between them is simple and momentary. However, where giver and recipient are unequal (as in this case), any transaction will naturally be protracted because the party that is on a lower footing must apply itself to understanding the nature of the transaction, and be given time to understand its complexities and profundities.

This was the case with G-d's bestowing of the Torah upon the Jewish people. Since they could never truly fathom absolute Divine wisdom, the transaction between them and G-d was protracted and complex. The first four *Chumashim* reflect G-d's own wisdom—a wisdom that is barely intelligible to the human mind. *Mishneh Torah* reflects the engagement of the recipients with the Torah in a manner that is intelligible to them. For this reason, the book of *Devarim* begins by stating[11] that Moshe **explained** the Torah to the Jewish people, for they, as recipients, needed it to be explained and elucidated.

This is all the more true of *Torah She'baal Peh*. The *Ramban* states[12] that "The Torah was given based on the understanding of the Chachamim," in other words, G-d expects and awaits the input of the Chachamim into His Torah. For this reason, the Midrash relates[13] that when the Jewish people kindle the *Menorah* in the Beis Hamikdash, they "shine a light for the One who shines light onto the entire world." Since the

---

10   *Tiferes Yisrael* 43.
11   1:5.
12   *Devarim*, end of his comments to 17:11.
13   *Bamidbar Rabbah* 15:5.

Menorah represents *Torah She'baal Peh*, its kindling by the Jewish people symbolizes their input into the Torah, and the light that they shine then shines a light for G-d himself.

Let us return to the *berachah* of the *haftarah*.

In light of Rabbi Yehoshua Leib Diskin's approach to prophecy, the phrase "good prophets" is readily understood. Since a prophecy may be affected by the malevolent intentions or foul traits of its promulgator, G-d specifically chose "good prophets" whose exemplary traits and grasp of the Divine will ensure that they interpret their prophecy in line with His intentions and in a manner that benefits the Jewish people. The *chasimah* of the *berachah* similarly reiterates that G-d chose "prophets of truth and righteousness."

And the reason that G-d did so is because He "chose the Torah," in other words, **He chose the Torah of his people**. He did not merely "give them the Torah" or "teach them the Torah," he allowed them as recipients of his Torah to contribute to it and illuminate it for Him. He therefore granted them the *Mishneh Torah*, and a defining role in *Torah She'baal Peh*. He also granted their prophets the chance to engage in perceiving and ultimately defining the prophecies that they were to confer to the Jewish people—"*V'ratzah b'divreihem*, He was pleased with their words."[14]

This makes the *chasimah* of the *berachah* wonderfully apt and most certainly linked with the main body of the *berachah*. G-d's selection of "good prophets" **is due to His choice of the Torah of His people**—*Mishneh Torah, Torah She'baal Peh*, and therefore prophecy. This is why it also mentions Moshe Rabbeinu who was the father of *Torah She'baal Peh* and makes mention of Yisrael who light the *Menorah* of *Torah She'baal Peh* to illuminate for G-d Himself.

Kesser Yitnu Lecha

According to the above, the words of the *Kedushah* recited at *Musaf* (according to *nusach Sefard*), "*Kesser yitnu lecha*—They will place

---

14   The mitzvah stresses the "words" of the prophets since their prophecies are dependent on their interpretations—**their words**, not just the words of G-d.

a crown for You" come alive. The crown that we set upon G-d's "head," so to speak, is the same as the *Menorah* we light in the Beis Hamikdash. The *kesser* of His Torah is our Torah—*Torah She'baal Peh*—and that is why this *kedushah* deviates from all other *kedushos* that state, "*ka'davar ha'kasuv*—as the matter is written," to "*ka'davar ha'amur*—as the matter is said" (for further extrapolation see the *Maamar* in this *sefer* titled "*Kesser*").

Our Heartfelt Requests

Birkas HaChodesh

"May G-d fulfill all of your requests."[1] This verse is invoked by the *tefillah* of *Birkas HaChodesh* in which we beseech G-d for a month of "life in which our heartfelt requests will be fulfilled for the good." Noticeably, the verse itself does not add that our requests shall be fulfilled "for the good," however, that may be because it refers to those who are seeking spiritual success, those who yearn to "sing for joy at your salvation, and raise our banner in the name of our G-d." Since they ask for spiritual success, the fulfillment of their requests will inevitably be "for the good."

However, *Birkas HaChodesh* focuses on material, in addition to spiritual, success, soliciting a month of "peace, goodness, blessing, and sustenance." Therefore, it is important to append the words "for the good," for a person must set aside his own interests and ask for material success for the sake of the greater good, namely the service of G-d.

This idea may help answer another question. Given that a person may not ask for his material needs on Shabbos, why is it permissible to do so in *Birkas HaChodesh*? Some would in fact refrain from reciting this *tefillah* at all due to this question. Others offer the solution to add the words *b'zechus tefillas rabbim*, "in the merit of the prayers of the *tzibur*"

---

1   *Tehillim* 20:6.

to the *tefillah*, since one may ask for the material needs of an entire community on Shabbos.[2]

Considering the above, this problem can be resolved. Although *Birkas HaChodesh* deals ostensibly with material success, those who recite it should intend to dedicate that success to their spiritual pursuits—"for the good." The *tefillos* of Shabbos are replete with requests for spiritual success such as "*Kadsheinu b'mitzvosecha v'sein chelkeinu b'Sorasecha*—Sanctify us with Your commandments and grant us our share in Your Torah." By asking G-d to grant us life in which our heartfelt requests will be fulfilled "for the good," *Birkas HaChodesh* also becomes a *tefillah* for spiritual success and thus may take its rightful place in the Shabbos liturgy.

---

2   *Siddur HaGra on Birkas HaChodesh.*

Shabbos and Yom Tov

When Yom Tov coincides with Shabbos, the *tefillos* of Shabbos are replaced by those of Yom Tov. This appears to be a somewhat surprising halachah, since after all, the holiness of Shabbos is greater than that of Yom Tov.[1] Why then is the *tefillah* of Yom Tov given precedence?

Rav Hutner suggested the following answer. Yom Tov, he said, should be considered a "disciple" of Shabbos because Shabbos is the source of the *kedushah* of the Yamim Tovim—"*Techilah l'mikra'ei kodesh.*" It is customary that a teacher suppresses his honor in favor of the honor of his student—in fact the honor to his student is itself a form of honor to him. Therefore, when Yom Tov coincides with Shabbos, the teacher, namely Shabbos, stands aside so that Yom Tov can be extolled in the *tefillah*.

Chiddush and Pashtus

I would like to elaborate on the words of the Rosh Yeshiva by citing another of his comments contrasting Shabbbos and Yom Tov.[2] Yom Tov, he would say, affords us a glimpse of *Olam Haba*, the *yom she'kulo tov*, and is a time of *chiddush* (novelty) as we are granted a sudden vista

---

1   Somebody who desecrates Shabbos is deserving of capital punishment, whereas for desecrating Yom Tov he is only given lashes.

2   *Pachad Yitzchok: Shabbos* 3:16.

of the astounding World to Come. In fact, each of the Yamim Tovim uniquely portend *Olam Haba*. On Pesach we celebrate the Exodus, the harbinger of the ultimate redemption. On Shavuos, we celebrate Matan Torah which hints to the Torah of Mashiach. Finally, on Sukkos, we remember the Clouds of Glory which depict the eternal protection and salvation of Am Yisrael—"*U'fros aleinu sukkas shlomecha.*" On Yom Tov, *Olam HaBa* is a **perception.**

Shabbos, however, grants us an actual miniature experience of **the World to Come**, "*me'ein Olam Haba,*" and a time of *pashtus* (utter simplicity and unity) which is what abounds in *Olam Haba* itself. The *chiddush* of *Olam Haba*, as perceived intellectually on Yom Tov, morphs into the *pashtus* of an actual experience.

Pashtus is the stage after a *chiddush* has been internalized and become a part of reality. If a *chiddush* is true, it ultimately settles in the mind and soul of its originator such that it no longer appears to be a *chiddush* at all. In the World to Come, *chiddush* itself becomes the norm and is therefore a place of *pashtus*. Shabbos, which is *me'ein Olam Haba*, allows us to partake of that even now.

The Vilna Gaon notes[3] that *simchah* (gladness) is a product of *chiddush*, whereas *gilah* (joy) is a product of consistency and uniformity. This is why the verse states, "*Yismechu ha'Shamayim v'sagel ha'aretz*—The heavens will be glad, and the earth will rejoice,"[4] for the Heavens are a place of *chiddush*, and therefore *simchah*, but the earth is a place of consistency as "*Ein kol chadash tachas ha'shamesh*—There is nothing new under the sun."[5]

Since Yom Tov is a time of *chiddush*, it is also a time of *simchah*, hence the injunction to be joyous on the festivals—"*V'samachta b'chagecha v'hayisa ach same'ach.*"[6] This commandment enjoins us to eat meat and drink wine, both of which confer an experience of *chiddush*, for it is in their nature to bring about a physical manifestation of *simchas halev*—

---

3   In his commentary to *Mishlei* (23:24).
4   *Tehillim* 96:11.
5   *Koheles* 1:9.
6   *Devarim* 16:14 and 15.

"*Ein simchah ela b'basar v'yayin.*" But Shabbos is a time of *pashtus*, thus there is no commandment of *simchah*. Instead, we experience *oneg* (delight) that is the product of *pashtus*—an otherworldly feeling of tranquility and peace.[7]

The Gemara states[8] that a teacher of Torah gains more from his students than he does from his contemporaries or teachers, "*Mi'talmidai yoser mi'kulam.*" Simply understood, this is because the presence of students compels a *rebbi* to plumb the depths of the Torah over and over again in order to answer their questions and thereby fashion more *chiddushim* to teach them. But there may be a deeper idea at play.

When a *rebbi* has already formulated *chiddushim* in Torah, they may no longer appear to him to be *chiddushim* at all. But when he teaches them to his students, he will find that he begins to appreciate their *chiddush* once again, suddenly able to taste the sweetness of *chiddushim* for which every Torah scholar yearns. His students thus enable him to retain the semblance of *chiddush* in his Torah even after it has become *pashtus* to him.

Rebbi and Talmid

The notion of "*Mi'talmidai yoser mi'kulam,*" is thus that students not only compel a teacher to formulate **new** *chiddushim*, but also help him retain the *chiddush* in the Torah **that he already has**.

Rav C. Y. Kaplan added that this notion may be alluded to by the juxtaposition of the verse "*V'hayu ha'devarim ha'eileh...ha'yom al levavecha,*"[9] from which Chazal derive[10] that on each day the words of Torah should appear to a person as though they were brand new, and the verse "*V'shinantam l'vanecha,*"[11] which is the source of the commandment to teach Torah to our disciples.[12] The reason for their juxtaposition is that

---

7   *Pachad Yitzchok*, ibid.

8   *Taanis* 7a and *Makkos* 10a.

9   *Devarim* 6:6.

10   *Berachos* 17a.

11   *Devarim* 6:7.

12   *Berachos* 14b and *Kiddushin* 30a.

by teaching Torah to our disciples, who are like our sons,[13] we retain the *chiddush* in our Torah, and thus the ability to consider the Torah "as new" on each and every day.

This is why the *tefillos* of Shabbos step aside when Yom Tov coincides with Shabbos. Since Yom Tov is the student of Shabbos it enables Shabbos to retain the notion of *chiddush* amidst its overwhelming *pashtus*. In the same way that a *rebbi* always yearns for the feeling of *chiddush*, so does Shabbos—the fountain of *pashtus* of *kedushah* yearn for the *chiddush* of *kedushah*. When Yom Tov and Shabbos come together, the *pashtus* of Shabbos is coupled with *chiddush* just like the experience of a *rebbi* with his students, prompting Shabbos to pay homage to Yom Tov in appreciation.

And this *chiddush* ultimately permeates every Shabbos of the year. As mentioned, a *rebbi* who steps aside to allow his student to be accorded honor, is himself honored, and in a sense becomes a student of his student as stated above. The same can be said of Shabbos. By stepping aside for Yom Tov, it also acquires for itself the honor of the "student" and therefore becomes not only a time of *pashtus* and *oneg* but also one of *chiddush* and *simchah*.

This is why *Chazal* also invoke *simchah* with regard to Shabbos. The Torah relates that the Jewish people were to sound the trumpets in the desert on "*Yom simchaschem u'moadechem*—A day of your gladness, and on your festivals."[14] *Ibn Ezra* asserts[15] that "*yom simchaschem*" refers to Shabbos, and the *Baal Haturim* notes[16] that the *gematria* of these words is identical to that of "*gam b'yom haShabbos*" (also on the day of Shabbos). Additionally, the Shabbos *Musaf* contains the famous phrase "*Yismechu b'malchuscha shomrei Shabbos v'korei oneg*—They shall rejoice in your kingship, those who observe the Shabbos and call it a delight."

Curiously, these sources also seem to indicate that Shabbos is **primarily** a time of *simchah* and that *oneg* comes secondary. The aforementioned

---

13 *Sanhedrin* 19b.
14 *Bamidbar* 10:10.
15 Ad loc.
16 Ad loc.

verse, according to Chazal, hails Shabbos as a day of *simchah*—"a day of your gladness," not a day of *oneg*. The *tefillah*, moreover, first describes the *simchah* of Shabbos—"*Yismechu b'malchuscha*," and only after that refers to the *oneg*—"*V'korei oneg*." Surely *oneg*, which connotes *pashtus* and *me'ein Olam Haba* as stated, is a more elevated concept than *simchah*, which is just the product of the *chiddush* experienced in a fleeting glance at *Olam Haba*. Why then do Chazal imply that *simchah* is primary?

The answer is that a sense of the *pashtus* of Shabbos can only be attained through **grasping and subsequently internalizing** its *chiddush*. Therefore, Chazal place *simchah* before *oneg* because chronologically *simchah* must precede *oneg*. Only by dint of *simchah* that comes from *chiddush* may a person ultimately attain the prodigious *oneg* of the *pashtus* of *me'ein Olam Haba*, which is the essence of Shabbos. Shabbos demands the understanding that *Olam Haba* is in fact a *chiddush*.

Rav Hutner would often say that while a person should aspire to *seviah min ha'kedushah*, "a state where he is filled with holiness," he should never lose the *tzipiyah l'kedushah*, "the yearning to become still more holy." For while *seviah* (satiation) and *tzipiyah* (the desire for more) are diametrically opposed, we still pray that we should experience both. This is the intent of the words of the *tefillah*, "*Sabeinu mi'tuvecha v'samcheinu bi'yeshuasecha*—Grant us satiation from Your goodness and gladden us with Your salvation." We pray that in spite of our satiation of goodness, in spite of our tranquil feelings of *pashtus*, G-d should still grant us the *simchah* of *chiddush* once again.

Contentment or Satiation

The Shabbos *Musaf* contains the words *"Kulam yisbe'u v'yisangu mi'tuvecha*—They will all reach a state of satiation and enjoyment from Your goodness." Generally, a person experiences enjoyment from his food before he reaches satiation—why do they appear here in reverse order?

The Torah describes Avraham as having been content at the time of his death—"And Avraham expired and died at a good old age, mature and content, and he was gathered to his people."[1] The *Ramban* explains[2] that the notion of satiation is not an objective state but a character trait possessed by the righteous who have no wish for any more than they have or need, and who are satisfied with their lot. In fact, fulfillment of one's physical desires is an impossibility, for "He who has a hundred wishes he had two hundred"—never reaching total satisfaction.

Pose'ach Es Yadecha

This notion may be alluded to in the verse, *"Pose'ach es yadecha u'masbia l'chol chai ratzon*—You open your hand and satisfy the desire (*ratzon*) of every living being."[3] The verse describes a satisfaction of the *ratzon* rather than a satisfaction of the stomach—a satisfaction of the drive to

---

1   *Bereishis* 25:8.
2   Ad loc.
3   *Tehillim* 145:16.

physical desire rather than its fulfillment, for a person will only be truly content when he is in control of his desires and not when he fulfills them. This is also why the verse implies that contentment is granted to humankind merely by G-d "opening His hand," for the smallest opening through which man receives precisely what he needs is sufficient. As Chazal aver,[4] "Who is wealthy? He who is happy with his lot. Who is the conquerer? He who conquers his desires." Rav Hutner would cite[5] one of the *chachmei ha'avodah* who declared, "He who has not attempted to rule over his physical desires has not sensed the feel of his *nefesh*."

However, those who are not counted among the righteous do not experience the glorious sensation of true contentment. They are alluded to in the previous verse, "*Einei chol Eilecha yesabeiru v'Atah nosen la'hem es achlam b'ito*—The eyes of all look to You with hope, and You give them their food in its proper time." Rather than merely "satisfying their desire," those of lesser faith hope to be actually granted ample sustenance by G-d and are only reassured by Him "giving them their food in its proper time." To them, G-d merely "opening His hand" would not be sufficient. *Rashi* notes[6] that the enormously wealthy Eisav, when reflecting upon his material wealth, declared "*Yesh li rav*—I have plenty."[7] Yaakov, by contrast, said simply "*Yesh li kol*—I have all I need."[8]

Oneg Shabbos

On Shabbos, the partaking of gastronomic delights takes on a different dimension. Rav Hutner would say that the mitzvah of *oneg Shabbos* (delighting in Shabbos) enjoins a person to enjoy his food and not just eat to absolve his pangs of hunger—in fact, a person may well be expected to eat to satiation on Shabbos. This is in keeping with Rav Hutner's own dictum that the mitzvah of *oneg Shabbos* is designed to

---

4   *Avos* 4:1.
5   *Pachad Yitzchok: Purim* 26:1.
6   *Bereishis* 33:11.
7   Ibid., 33:9.
8   Ibid., 33:11.

replicate the original *oneg Shabbos* of Hashem, who upon the conclusion of the sixth day of Creation, took pleasure in "all that he had created."[9]

This may be the reason that the *tefillah* references "satisfaction" before "delight." During the week, the righteous experience a "satiation of their desires"—a state in which they needn't fill their stomachs in order to feel satisfaction. But on Shabbos they need to go a step further—they need to delight in their food and eat to actual satiation. And in truth, it is not only the righteous—on Shabbos all Jewish people assume that lofty position.

Rav C. Y. Kaplan added that this same idea is emphasized by the *tefillah* itself, which states, "**The people** that sanctify the seventh—they will **all** be satisfied and delighted from Your goodness." On Shabbos, all may join the ranks of the righteous and eat to satiation to fulfill the *mitzvah* of *oneg Shabbos*.

---

9   Ibid., 1:31.

Kesser Yitnu Lecha

1

Mishkan

The *Ramban* notes[1] that the defining concept of the *Mishkan* was that it **captured the glories of the Revelation at Sinai**. He cites numerous verses that demonstrate the correlation between Sinai and the *Mishkan*, and which depict how Hashem would speak to Moshe from within the *Mishkan* as He did from atop Mount Sinai.

Interestingly, the Gemara implies[2] that the defining concept of the *Mishkan* was something else. It cites a verse regarding the family of Kehas, which states, "The Kehasites, the bearers of the *Mikdash*, would carry it, and the *Mishkan* would be erected before they arrived,"[3] and explains that the word *Mikdash*, in this context, refers to the *Aron Hakodesh*. This implies that the central feature of the *Mishkan* was the *Aron Kodesh*.[4] In fact, none other than the *Ramban* makes note of

---

1 Introduction to *Parashas Terumah*.
2 *Eruvin* 2a.
3 *Bamidbar* 10:21.
4 The Gemara attempts to adduce proof that the *Mishkan* was also identified by the term "*Mikdash*", and to that end it cites the verse regarding the family of Kehas, cited in the main text. Since the verse states that the family of Kehas would carry the *Mikdash*—when it in fact refers to the *Mishkan*—we see that the terms *Mishkan* and *Mikdash* are interchangeable.

124

this concept in an earlier paragraph, despite later contending that the essential characteristic of the *Mishkan* was that it captured the glories of Sinai. So, which was the *Mishkan*—a place which reenacted the revelation, or a place which housed the *Aron Kodesh*?

Aron Hakodesh

The answer is that both are true. Certainly, the *Aron Kodesh* was the *ikar* of the *Mishkan*. However, Hashem wished to imbue the *Mishkan* with His Shechinah precisely as it had rested on Sinai and **this revolved primarily around the *Aron Kodesh*.** The primary manifestation of *kavod* (glory) that was manifested at Sinai was **that Hashem spoke to Moshe Rabbeinu in full view of the Jewish people.** This continued in the *Mishkan* by means of the *Aron Kodesh*, for Moshe would hear G-d's voice emanating from between the *Keruvim* which were atop the *Kapores* (the lid of the *Aron*).

The *Kapores* was considered the *"makom pegishah bein ha'dodim*—the meeting place of the beloved friends" (Hashem and the Jewish people).[5] It was thus a place of reenactment of that which occurred at Sinai when *"ha'elyonim yardu v'hatachtonim alu*—the upper heavens descended and the lower world ascended [to meet them]."[6] However, as the *Ramban*

However, the Gemara immediately dismisses this proof. When the verse references "the *Mikdash*," the Gemara argues, it refers to the *Aron Kodesh* that was carried by the family of Kehas, and not to the *Mishkan* as a whole.

In the context of the verse, it seems obvious that the word "*Mikdash*" refers to the *Aron Kodesh*. Why did the Gemara even entertain the thought that it may refer to the *Mishkan* as a whole?

The answer may be that the Gemara knew that the most important and defining aspect of the *Mishkan* was the *Aron Kodesh*. Therefore, if the verse describes the family of Kehas as bearers of the "*Mikdash*," meaning the *Aron Kodesh*, it could well be that the entire *Mishkan* would be identified by the term *Mikdash* as well.

5   See *Pachad Yitchak: Pesach, Reshima* 1, 6:2–3 who cites the assertion of the *Gra* that the *kedushah* of *Shir Hashirim* is rooted in the *kedushah* of the *Keruvim* (the two angelic figures that sat atop the *Aron Hakodesh*). When the *Keruvim* were facing one another, they reflected the love that exists between Hashem and Yisrael (see *Bava Basra* 99a and *Nefesh Hachaim* 1:8). He also cites the Gemara in *Yoma* (54a) that relates that when the Jewish people came to the Beis Hamikdash on the *Shalosh Regalim* the Kohanim drew open the curtain of the *Kodesh Hakodashim* revealing the *keruvim* in an embrace. At that time, they would be told, *Re'u chibaschem lifnei HaMakom,* "See the love that Hashem has for you."

6   *Pachad Yitzchok: Shavuos* 15:10.

notes, the *kavod* was only manifested in the *Mishkan* in a concealed manner (*b'nistar*); for unlike at Sinai when G-d spoke to Moshe in front of the nation, in the *Mishkan* the people were only privileged to witness the cloud of the Shechinah descending upon the *Ohel Mo'ed*[7] and not the exchanges between Moshe and Hashem.

2

Maamad Har Sinai

We have explained that the *Aron Kodesh* was the central facet of the *Mishkan* and that it was the magnet for the Shechinah. It is also known that the *Aron Kodesh* is representative of Torah, thus it can be said that there were two powerful elements to the *Mishkan*: Torah (represented by the *Aron Kodesh*) and Shechinah (the attendance of Divine presence, echoing that of Sinai).

The element of Torah could exist even without a *Mishkan*. The Jewish people were granted the Torah before they were ordered to fashion a *Mishkan,* and it has remained their eternal gift long after the eras of *Mishkan* and *Mikdash*. The *kavod* of the revelation of Sinai, however, could only be truly captured in the *Mishkan*.

Rav Hutner explained[8] that the *kavod* of the Torah witnessed at the revelation at Sinai was a goal in and of itself. The *Haggadah shel Pesach* famously states, "*Ilu kervanu lifnei Har Sinai v'lo nassan lanu es haTorah, Dayeinu*—Had He drawn us close to Mount Sinai and not given us the Torah, it would have been enough." What purpose would have been served by approaching Har Sinai and not receiving the Torah? The answer is that it would have been worthwhile to witness the revelation and realize the *kavod* of Torah even if they were not to receive the Torah itself.

---

7   *Shemos* 33:10.
8   *Pachad Yitzchok: Shavuos* 8.

The two components comprised by the *Mishkan*, namely Torah and Shechinah, are in fact inseparable. Chazal say, *"Ein kavod ela Torah*—There is no honor other than that of Torah," for Torah is inextricably related to the unparalleled *kavod* that was witnessed at Sinai, and which was encapsulated by the *Mishkan*.

In fact, it is imperative that man grants the Torah the honor that is due to it. Just as rain did not fall upon the earth until man was created and could appreciate its goodness,[9] so does Torah demand that man recognize its blessing and accord it honor. Learning Torah without an appreciation of the greatness of Torah is valueless.

This may be why recalling the Revelation at Sinai is one of the *shesh zechiros* (the six events one must recall each day), as the Torah states, "Only beware, and guard your souls, lest you forget the matters that your eyes witnessed, and lest you remove them from your heart all of the days of your life, and you shall transmit them to your sons and your grandsons. The day on which you stood before Hashem your G-d at Chorev."[10]

3

Nevuah and Chochmah

We have seen how Torah and Shechinah are inextricably related and how they are centered around the *Mishkan*. Throughout the era of the *Mishkan*, and indeed the first Beis Hamikdash which replaced it, the glory of Sinai lived and *nevuah* (as manifested in *Torah She'bichsav*) abounded.

This period of revelation is captured in the words of the verse, "Behold He [G-d] is standing behind our walls, watching from the windows."[11] At that time, G-d was, so to speak, in full view, standing at the window, and availing us of open miracles. He could then be likened to a general

---

9   See *Bereishis* 2:5 and *Rashi* ad loc., s.v. *"Terem."*

10   *Devarim* 4:9-10.

11   *Shir Hashirim* 2:9.

in battle who stands in full view of his soldiers who are inspired by his presence.

But upon the destruction of the first Beis Hamikdash, things began to change. Though it was later replaced by the second Beis Hamikdash, the Shechinah never returned in quite the same measure. Open miracles therefore dwindled, and *nevuah* was curtailed.

The nature of this period is captured by the end of the aforementioned verse, "Behold He [G-d] is standing behind our walls...peering through the cracks." While Hashem was certainly present, He had retreated behind the scenes, observing but not observable. He could be compared to a general who surveys the battle from behind a wall, peering through a slit. His soldiers know that he is there but are fearful when they see that he has retreated behind the wall.

The second Beis Hamikdash never housed the *Aron Hakodesh*, which had been buried following the destruction. This appears to portray the correlation between Shechinah and Torah detailed above. Since the Shechinah did not return to rest upon the Beis Hamikdash as in previous times, neither did the *Aron Hakodesh* and the Torah that it represented. This is also why *Tanach*—the body of *Torah She'bichsav*—was sealed at this time, for the conduits of the Divine inspiration of *nevuah* had been closed.

However, this heralded a new era of Torah and of Divine revelation. The era of *nevuah* was replaced with the era of *chochmah*—the wisdom of the Sages and their formation and transmission of *Torah She'baal Peh*. Though *Tanach* could no longer be furthered, it could be elucidated by those who devoted themselves to understanding its profundity and revealing its secrets. The Shechinah, rather than speaking through its faithful prophets, would now emerge through the mouths of the Sages of the Mishnah and the Talmud.

Ultimately, as the second Beis Hamikdash was also destroyed, the presence of the Shechinah was further concealed, and the force of Torah weakened again. With each passing year of exile, the nation was cast further into confusion and uncertainty, bereft of the Divine clarity of old. In fact, the Sages of Yavneh were concerned that *"asidah Torah she'tishtakach mi'Yisrael*—ultimately the Torah would be forgotten by the Jewish people."[12] However, Rabbi Shimon bar Yochai famously asserted, "*Ki lo sishachach mi'pi zaro*—The Torah shall never be forgotten." Though *halachah berurah* (clear-cut halachic rulings) and *mishnah berurah* (a clear rendition of the Mishnah and Gemara) would not be found in one place, the Torah would remain eternally in the hearts and minds of the Jewish people. By means of an intensification of *ameilus baTorah* (toil in understanding the Torah) they would be expected to unify every aspect of the halachos that are found in the Mishnah.

Why will the Torah never be forgotten? The answer is that although in the absence of the Beis Hamikdash the Shechinah is greatly concealed, it never left the Jewish people, even during their exile, as exemplified by "*Shechinta b'galusa*." To this day, the Shechinah rests at the *Kosel Maaravi* (the Western Wall) and grants us inspiration in Torah.

4

Kesser Torah

The transition between the era of *Torah She'bichsav* and that of *Torah She'baal Peh* granted the Jewish people a newfound status. Previously, the Torah *She'bichsav* had been purely in the domain of Hashem, but now the Sages of Israel were to decipher and determine the meaning of *Torah She'bichsav* through *Torah She'baal Peh*.

The Gemara relates[13] that when Moshe Rabbeinu ascended to Heaven he found Hashem attaching crowns to the letters of the Torah.[14] Moshe queried why this was necessary—did the letters and words themselves not represent the word of Hashem adequately? Hashem replied, "There is destined to be one man, following many generations, named Akiva ben Yosef, who will expound mounds of halachos from every spike of the crowns of the letters of the Torah."

---

12   *Shabbos* 138b.
13   *Menachos* 29b.
14   These are the "*tagin*," the crown-like markings on top of the letters in a *Sefer Torah*.

Rabbi Akiva played the most prominent role in establishing *Torah She'baal Peh*. His five main students are the authors of the preponderance of the Mishnah, and many anonymous statements in *Torah She'baal Peh* are attributed to him (thus he was known as "*Rabbi Akiva stimtaah*—Rabbi Akiva the anonymous one"). His expounding upon the crowns of the letters of the Torah represents the honored and treasured status of those who are devoted to *Torah She'baal Peh*, **who are considered to be placing a crown upon the Torah, and therefore a crown upon the head of Hashem Himself.**

This idea is invoked in the *Kedushah* of *Musaf* of *nusach sefard*: "*Kesser yitnu lecha hamonei maalah, im amcha Yisrael kevutzei matah*—The supernal legions will bestow upon You a crown, alongside your people Israel, who are gathered below." The crown bestowed by the Jewish people—the *kevutzei matah*—is that of *Torah She'baal Peh*, with which the Sages adorned *Torah She'bichsav*: the mounds of halachos expounded from the crowns of the letters. In fact, as Rav C. Y. Kaplan noted, it is known that the word "*kesser*" whose *gematria* (numerical equivalent) is 620, alludes to the 613 mitzvos and *sheva mitzvos B'nei Noach* that are derived, elucidated, and expounded by *Torah She'baal Peh*.

Torah She'Baal Peh

This notion is further alluded to in the continuation of the *Kedushah* of *Kesser* by the words, "*Ka'davar ha'amur al yad neviecha*—Like that which was stated by means of your prophets." The *Kedushos* of *Shacharis*, both of a regular weekday and of Shabbos, reference the verses that were **written** by the prophets, "*Ka'kasuv al yad neviecha*." Why does the *Kedushah* of *Musaf* focus on the words that they uttered? The answer is that the *Kedushah* of *Musaf* means to describe the crown fashioned by Am Yisrael for Hashem by means of *Torah She'baal Peh*. It therefore focuses upon the **oral** tradition of the Neviim, rather than their contribution to *Torah She'bichsav*.

In fact, as we have noted elsewhere,[15] the books of the prophets in *Tanach* serve as a bridge between *Torah She'bichsav* and *Torah*

---

15   See our *Maamar*, "The *Berachos* of the *Haftarah*."

She'baal Peh. The *Chamishei Chumshei Torah* (the Pentateuch) reflect the unparalleled wisdom of the *Nosein HaTorah* (the giver of the Torah), namely Hashem.[16] The books of the prophets reflect the engagement of the *mekablei haTorah* (the recipients of the Torah), because each of the Neviim (other than Moshe Rabbeinu) needed to employ their own wisdom to deciphering the vision that they were granted by Hashem.[17] This stage was a bridge combining the Divinity of *Torah She'bichsav* with the Divinely inspired *Torah She'baal Peh.*

5

At a regular weekday *Shacharis* we recite a form of *Kedushah* three times. First, during the *berachos* of *K'rias Shema* we invoke the praises offered by the Malachim (angels)—the "*Ahuvim, Berurim, Gibborim, Ofanim and Chayos Hakodesh.*" Then during the repetition of the *Amidah*, we declare that we too may join the Malachim in their praises, "*Nekadesh es Shimchah ba'olam kesheim she'makdishim oso b'shmei marom*—We will sanctify Your name in the world, just as they sanctify it in the heavenly realms." But following the *Amidah*, in *U'va L'Tzion*, we stand alone and recite "*Kedushah D'Sidra*" sans Malachim, for Hashem the "*Yosheiv tehillos Yisrael*" desires our praises most of all.

The same pattern can be seen in the *Kedushos* of Shabbos. Having referenced the praises of the Malachim in the *berachos* of *K'rias Shema*, and joined the Malachim in the *Kedushah* of *Shacharis*, at *Musaf* the focus is switched to the "*Kesser*," the crown of Hashem, and the "*Davar ha'amur al yad neviecha*," which honors Am Yisrael whose dedication to *Torah She'baal Peh* crowns Hashem in glory.[18] The *Musaf* prayer, thus

---

16   According to the *Maharal* (*Tiferes Yisrael* 43), *Sefer Devarim* (*Mishneh Torah*) is also part of the framework of "*mekablei haTorah*" rather than "*Nosein HaTorah.*"

17   *Maharil Diskin*, cited in our *Maamar* "The *Berachos* of the *Haftarah.*"

18   In fact, at this time, the Malachim themselves are in need of Am Yisrael. *Tosafos* (*Sanhedrin* 37b, s.v. "*Mi'kenaf ha'aretz*" in the name of the *Teshuvos HaGeonim*), cited by the *Siddur Otzar Ha'tefillos*, relates that every Malach is affixed with six wings, each of which correspond to a song of praise that it offers to Hashem on the six weekdays. On Shabbos the angels say to

makes a *hosofah* (an addition), for it alludes to the *Torah She'baal Peh* which is the essential addition to *Torah She'bichsav*. The *Kedushah* of *Musaf* is therefore the climax of the praises of Hashem, uttered by His treasured people, the "*Maangeha*," "*To'ameha*," and "*Ohavim Devareha*," on the holiest day of the week.

Hashem, "I have no wing for Shabbos" but He replies, "I have one wing in the world that says *shirah*, which is Yisrael." The Midrash thus clearly indicates that the praises of the Malachim are insufficient—there is need for the input of Am Yisrael and the unique praises that they impart which form the *kesser* of Hashem.

Kiddusha Rabba

The Gemara relates[1] that Rav Ashi was once paying a visit to the town of Mechuza. On Shabbos morning the townsfolk asked if he would recite *"Kiddusha Rabba,"* but Rav Ashi was unsure what this meant. He therefore recited *Borei Pri Hagafen* and paused to see whether he should continue with the second *berachah* of Kiddush which is recited on a Friday night. Noticing that a certain elderly man had already bent over to drink, Rav Ashi deduced that he was not expected to recite any further *berachos*. Pleased with his quick-wittedness, Rav Ashi exclaimed that *he'chacham einav b'rosho*, "a wise person plans ahead, anticipating what will transpire in the future."

Why is the Kiddush of Shabbos morning dubbed *"Kiddusha Rabba"*—literally, "The great Kiddush"? The simple explanation is that it is a euphemistic turn of phrase for the Kiddush of Shabbos morning, which is inferior to that of Friday night. However, Rav Hutner would say[2] that in some sense the Shabbos morning Kiddush is greater than that of Friday night. For nighttime is a time of *yediah*, as the verse states regarding the *mann*, "In the **evening** and you will **know**."[3] But daytime is a time of *re'iyah*, as the verse states regarding the *mann*, "In

---

1 *Pesachim* 106a.
2 See *Pachad Yitzchok: Shabbos* 13.
3 *Shemos* 16:6.

the **morning** you will **see.**[4] Sight avails a person of a clearer perception than knowledge. Thus, the Shabbos morning Kiddush has no need for verbosity, for a picture is worth a thousand words. The Friday night Kiddush, by contrast, is an expression of *yediah*, thus it is more verbose.

The experience of Shabbos through *re'iyah* is attainable only to the Chachamim. For this reason the Kiddush of Shabbos morning, which, as stated, reflects a condition of *re'iyah*, is a *mitzvah d'Rabbanan* (Rabbinic enactment). A *mitzvah d'Rabbanan* has an advantage over a *mitzvah d'Oraisa*, as evident in the words of Chazal[5] who cite the verse in *Shir Hashirim*, "*Tovim dodecha mi'yayin*—Your love is greater to me than wine," and explain that it alludes to the notion that "*Chavivin divrei sofrim mi'yeino shel Torah*—The words of the Sages are more beloved than the wine of the Torah itself." This is because it is Chazal, and only Chazal, who perceive the depths of the Written Law—only they who truly possess the trait of "in the morning you will see." This was alluded to by none other than Rav Ashi in that very episode, who dubbed himself a far-**sighted** *chacham* (*he'chacham einav b'rosho*) when he managed to ascertain the nature of *Kiddusha Rabba*—the Kiddush of "*boker u're'issem.*"

---

4   Ibid., 7.

5   *Yerushalmi, Berachos* 1:4 and *Avodah Zarah* 2:7.

Source of Blessing

Baruch Hashem Yom Yom

The first *zemer* of the Shabbos morning *seudah* is that of *"Baruch Hashem Yom Yom*—Blessed is G-d for every single day." At first glance, these words[1] appear ill-suited to Shabbos, for they serve as the source for Hillel HaZaken to rule that if a person procures a fine animal during the week, **he should eat it that day, rather than save it for Shabbos.**[2]

In the *tefillah* of *Retzei V'hachalitzenu* that we insert into the bentching on Shabbos, we pray that "there be no distress, grief, or lament on this day of our contentment." At first sight this would appear incongruous, for on Shabbos we do not usually make mention of any form of distress. This is why, in the view of the Arizal, the *tefillah* of *Hashkivenu* in the *Maariv* of Shabbos omits any mention of "foe, plague, sword, famine, and woe" that are all referenced during the week.

When I posed this question to Rav Yonasan David, he brought my attention to a comment of *"Echad min Ha'Rishonim"* who offers a different explanation of these words. Rather than praying that no distress or grief blight our Shabbos, he explains that we are asking that, "No

---

1   Whose source is *Tehillim* 68:20.
2   *Beitzah* 16a.

distress, grief, or lament **affect the other days of the week in the merit of** our day of contentment."

Mekor Ha'berachah

Perhaps this is the reason that the words *"Baruch Hashem Yom Yom"* are indeed pertinent to Shabbos. For while the words *"Yom Yom"* do indeed refer to the other days of the week, those days are only "blessed" and saved from "distress, grief, or lament" due to Shabbos, the *"mekor ha'berachah"* (the source of all blessing). In fact, the very declaration of the words *"Baruch Hashem Yom Yom"* on Shabbos may help convey blessing to the days of the week. This may be the reason that the *Ramban* concludes his comments on the words *"Asher bara Elokim laasos"* (the final words of the *parashah* of Shabbos) with the following statement: "Shabbos alludes to the World to Come when every day will be Shabbos and tranquil. G-d should watch over us on all days (in this world) and may our lot be cast together with that of his loyal servants."

The *Ramban* also notes that a person fulfills the mitzvah of invoking Shabbos (*"Zachor es yom haShabbos l'kadsho"*) when he states during the week, *"Ha'yom yom echad b'Shabbos*—Today is the first day of the week." In so doing, he creates a bond between Shabbos and the week and recognizes that Shabbos serves as the conduit for blessing.

In truth, Hillel HaZaken ultimately retracted his position, agreeing with Shammai that a person should save his finest food for Shabbos. Nevertheless, the words *"Baruch Hashem yom yom"* are still pertinent to Shabbos, for the lesson that Shabbos is the *mekor ha'berachah* remains as true as ever. Hillel came to realize that the words *"Baruch Hashem yom yom"* in fact contain a message that Shabbos is the source of all blessing. Therefore, to the contrary, a person should express *hakaras hatov* (gratitude) to Shabbos for its role in conveying blessing to the week and put aside their finest food to partake of on Shabbos.

Singing *"Baruch Hashem Yom Yom"* on Shabbos lends deeper expression to the principle mentioned elsewhere in this *sefer*:[3] *Lo l'lamed al atzmo yatza* (the novelty of Shabbos is not in how it itself should be

---

3   See *Maamar* "Shabbos Chanukah," where we discuss this idea at length.

perceived), *ela l'lamed al acherim yatza* (but in how it reflects on the other six days of the week). Through Shabbos, we may appreciate the true definition of Creation, which is that *kedushah* is *ikar* (of foremost importance) and *teva* is *tafel* (of secondary importance).

A Pleasant Fragrance

1

"A burnt offering, a fire offering, a pleasant fragrance to Hashem." (*Vayikra* 1:9)

The verse describes the *Korban Olah* (elevation offering) and declares that it generates a *rei'ach nicho'ach*, a pleasant fragrance, to Hashem. *Rashi*,[1] citing the *Sifri*,[2] explains:

> It is a cause of nachas ruach to Me, for I said [that the offering should be brought], and My will was fulfilled ("naaseh retzoni").

The *Sifri* continues:

> And likewise the verse states, "When you offer a thanksgiving sacrifice to Hashem, you shall sacrifice it to gain favor for you ("li'retzonchem tizbachuhu").[3]

This seems incongruous. Rather than proving that the purpose of a *korban* is to cause contentment to Hashem, these words seem

---

1   Ad loc., s.v. "Nicho'ach."
2   *Pinchas* 143.
3   *Vayikra* 22:29.

to indicate that its purpose is to fulfill the aspirations of the person offering it!

(We should point out that "*ratzon*" in the context of *rei'ach nicho'ach* means "aspiration" or "contentment." It does not mean the "will" of Hashem, for every mitzvah is the will of Hashem. *Rei'ach nicho'ach* implies a **higher** form of will, namely, contentment or *nachas ruach*. *Rei'ach* is equal to *ruach*, and *nicho'ach* is equal to *nachas*. The very special pleasant fragrance implies a very real pleasure that Hashem derives from our *korbanos*.)

This is compounded by a similar statement made by the Gemara in *Menachos*:[4]

> It is not due to My Ratzon that you are sacrificing, but it is due to your ratzon that you are sacrificing, as the verse states, "You shall slaughter it to find favor for yourselves."

The Gemara explicitly dismisses the notion that the idea of a *korban* is to fulfill Hashem's *ratzon*, asserting instead that it is to fulfill the aspirations of the person offering it. Moreover, the *Ramban*[5] appears to equate the comments of the *Sifri* and those of the Gemara in spite of the fact that the Gemara states that the purpose of a *korban* is to fulfill the aspirations of man, and the *Sifri* states that it is to fulfill the *ratzon* of Hashem!

2

The inconsistency in the words of the *Sifri* appears to have troubled Rav David Pardo in his eminent commentary, "*Sifri d'bei rav*." He explains that the *Sifri's* intent is that Hashem's contentment and our contentment are intimately connected. The message from Hashem is thus:

---

4   110a.

5   *Vayikra* 1:9, "*V'al derech ha'emes*."

What is My contentment? Li'retzonchem, l'hispashet ratzon haElyon ba'chem; in other words, li'retzonchem, in this case, does not mean to gain favor for you but that My contentment should extend to include your contentment. My contentment is dependent on yours; your wishes are My wishes, retzoni and retzonchem are one and the same. My will is to ensure that My people find favor in My eyes.

The *Netziv* in his commentary to the *Sifri* offers a similar explanation:

Why did I command that you shall offer sacrifices to Me? In order to fulfill My ratzon, so that you will be pleasant and agreeable to Me like a pleasant fragrance."

In other words, a *korban* is indeed offered to fulfill the *ratzon* of Hashem—*l'hispashet ha'ratzon haElyon ba'chem,* "but His very *ratzon* is to ensure that His people find favor in His eyes."

This was the intent of Rav David Pardo. By offering a korban to fulfill the ratzon of Hashem, man finds Divine favor, which is truly a fulfillment of his own ratzon. The Sifri is thus not self-contradictory.

3

Ha'tov V'ha'meitiv

This idea is reminiscent of the famous assertion of the *Kadmonim* that Hashem's sole intent in creating the world was to do good to His creations (*olam chessed yibaneh*).[6] To fulfill that objective He granted

---

them Torah and mitzvos[7] so that they could earn His goodness[8] and not be the recipients of "*nahamah d'kissufa*" (bread of shame), which would not have been a true reflection of the quintessential *ha'tov v'ha'meitiv*."[9]

There is, however, an important distinction between mitzvah performance in general and the offering of a *korban*. The performance of mitzvos allows Hashem, in His scheme of *mishpat*, to grant reward to the protagonist who has earned it. But the offering of a *korban*, particularly a *korban nedavah* (a voluntary offering), creates a sentiment of *ratzon* (favor and delight) in the Heavenly realms, which is reflected back to the world in turn.

Ordinarily, Hashem's trait of *chessed* is restricted by *mishpat*, for bestowing goodness on a person who has not earned it would not constitute good. However, in employing the trait of *nedivus* (munificence) and offering a *korban* amidst feelings of gratitude to Hashem, man allows Hashem to extend *chessed* beyond *mishpat* and release the enormous bounty of goodness that is His essence.

4

Nedivus

These two forms of Divine service, namely that of performing mitzvos in the scheme of *mishpat* or employing *nedivus* under the rubric of *hishpashtus ha'ratzon*, are both evident within our daily *tefillos*.

---

7   Chazal (*Avos* 4:2) say that "The reward of one mitzvah is another mitzvah, and the reward of one sin is another sin." The *Beis Halevi* (*Bereishis* 32:12, s.v. "*Ki yarei*") explains that this is because Hashem's desire is to bestow goodness upon us, and by allowing Hashem to reward us due to the performance of a mitzvah, we fulfill His will. It follows that the *s'char ha'mitzvah* (the reward we receive for a mitzvah), **is itself a mitzvah**, because it is Hashem's desire to grant us that reward, and we have facilitated Him doing so! And the reverse is true of sin. By giving Hashem the need to punish us due to sin, **we sin again**, for Hashem's will is to bestow goodness and not punishment.

8   *Sefer Hachinuch*, mitzvah 95.

9   *Derech Hashem*, 1, 2:1–2.

Chazal consider[10] *tefillah* to be an *avodah she'balev* (a service of the heart). This, at first glance, seems incongruous considering that the daily *Amidah* is replete with our *bakashos* (requests). How can making a request of our Master constitute "service" to Him?

In light of the above, this question may be resolved. Our Master wants nothing more than to bestow goodness upon His beloved creations. In order to do so, He needs nothing more than for us to recognize that He is the source of blessing, **and this is in fact the "service" that He desires.** By asking Him to grant our requests, we are serving Him in the most meaningful way, allowing Him to fulfill His true desire, which is to bestow goodness upon the world.[11]

There is, however, a higher form of service wrought by a servant for his master, which is to attempt to find favor in his eyes. In this dynamic, a servant does not merely seek that his requests be fulfilled but that his master should love and favor him. Rabbeinu Yonah explains:[12]

> And a person who is repenting shall also pray…that He [Hashem] shall desire him, and find favor in him, and accept his entreaty, as though he had never sinned. For it is possible that a sin may be forgiven and [its perpetrator] be freed of punishment or decree, but that Hashem will have no desire for him…But the desire of the righteous for success is to draw forth favor from Hashem, and that He shall desire them. And His favor—is eternal and genuine life, and the great light that comprises all delights…

Clearly, Hashem's love and *ratzon* are the goal of the righteous, and avail them of genuine, eternal life and "great light comprising all delights." They therefore seek to fulfill His *ratzon* and do not suffice by merely requesting that He fulfill their requests.

---

10   *Taanis* 2a. See also *Rashi* to *Devarim* 11:13, s.v. *U'l'avdo.*
11   And although we do not necessarily have this intention in mind, it is achieved regardless by the very fact that we pray to Him.
12   *Shaarei Teshuvah* 1:42.

5

Birkas Retzei

The weekday *Amidah* consists of three *berachos*: *shevach* (praise), thirteen *berachos* of *bakashos* (requests), and three *berachos* of *hodaah* (thanks). The middle set of *berachos* that culminate and are summed up by the *berachah* of *Shema Koleinu* are a means of performing the first sort of *Avodah* detailed above, namely, of recognizing that Hashem is the source of blessing and asking that He bestow it upon us. They may be compared to obligatory *korbanos* that a person must offer to atone for sin, but which do not stimulate a *rei'ach nicho'ach* to Hashem.[13]

Following that, we commence the final set of *berachos*, beginning with *Retzei*. These reflect the *Avodah* of drawing forth favor from Hashem and seeking *Hispashtus ha'ratzon ha'Elyon*, "*Retzei Hashem Elokeinu b'amcha Yisrael u'v'sefilasam*—Be favorable Hashem our G-d toward your people Israel and their prayers." They can be said to correspond to voluntary offerings, which do produce a *rei'ach nicho'ach* as described above.[14]

This second form of *Avodah* is only available to Am Yisrael, Hashem's beloved nation. The *berachah* therefore stresses, "*Retzei Hashem Elokeinu* **b'amcha Yisrael**." However, the first form of *Avodah* in which a person recognizes that Hashem is the source of blessing and asks Him to fulfill his requests, can also be performed by the nations of the world. This is stated explicitly in the *berachah* of *Shema Koleinu* of *nusach sefard*,

---

13   The Torah does not say that obligatory *korbanos* offered by an individual (rather than the *tzibbur* at large) produce a *rei'ach nicho'ach*, with the exception of the *Korban Chatas* (the sin offering) (see *Vayikra* 4:31). This may be because the admission of guilt by an average Jew to having committed a sin by accident (where guilt is minimal) creates a *rei'ach nicho'ach*. This is not the case with regard to the sin offering of the Nasi or Kohen Gadol (also detailed in that *parashah*) who should have known better. Their sin offering, therefore, does not produce a *rei'ach nicho'ach*.

14   The first three *berachos* of *shevach* may also play a role in drawing forth favor from Hashem. *Rashi* (*Berachos* 4b, s.v. "*Zeh ha'somech*") famously explains that the reason for the obligation to be *masmich geulah l'tefillah*, to mention redemption prior to the *Amidah*, is that a person should "approach Hashem and **seek to find His favor** with words of praise and honor." The same could be said of the first three *berachos* of *shevach*.

which declares, "*Ki Atah shome'a tefillos* **kol peh**—For you hearken to the prayers **of every mouth**."

The final three *berachos* of the *Amidah* are, as stated, considered to be *berachos* of *hodaah*. How does the *berachah* of *Retzei*, which is a heartfelt prayer for the return of the Beis Hamikdash and the sacrificial service, constitute *hodaah*?

The answer is that the request for Hashem's favor and grace (*bakashas ha'ritzuy*) is fundamentally different to making individual requests (*bakashas tzerachav*). When seeking his favor, we recognize that "our will is His desire," and that all that He wants is "*l'hispashet ha'ratzon haElyon*" among us. We are therefore inordinately thankful, for we are surely undeserving of such benevolence. When a person recognizes that he has received more than his share of blessing, he must thank Hashem as did Leah Imeinu who gave thanks when she was granted one son more than her share—"*Ha'paam odeh es Hashem*."[15] The *berachah* of *Retzei* therefore certainly belongs among the *berachos* of *hodaah*.[16]

6

L'maancha

We have described the *avodah* of *bakashas tzerachav* and that of *bakashas ha'ritzuy*, but there is a more elevated *avodah* yet. This *avodah* is known as *l'maancha*[17]—a *tefillah* on behalf of Hashem

---

15   *Bereishis* 29:35 and *Rashi ad loc.*, s.v."*Ha'paam*."

16   The Gemara (*Megillah* 18a) explains that the reason that the *berachah* of *Modim* follows that of *Retzei* is that "*Avodah v'hodaah chada milsa hi*—Service and thanks are one." *Rashi* (ad loc., s.v. "*Chada*") explains that "*Af hodaah avodah shel Makom*—Thanks is also service of the Almighty." Considering the above, we may also suggest that the reverse is true, "*Af avodah hodaah laMakom*—Service, namely *tefillah*, can also constitute a form of thanks to the Almighty."

The Gemara (ibid.) also explains that the reason that the *berachah* of *Retzei* follows that of *Shema Koleinu* is that "once *tefillah* was introduced, *avodah* follows." In light of the above, both *avodah*, which causes *rei'ach nicho'ach*, and *tefillah*, *Retzei*, seek to bring contentment to Hashem. It is therefore most apt that they seamlessly follow one another.

17   As invoked in the *tefillah* of *Elokai netzor* at the conclusion of the *Amidah*, "*Asei lemaan*

Himself and for His *Shechinah* which resides in exile.[18] This form of service is practiced by the righteous who are filled with the love of Hashem and are deeply sorrowful at any element of His dishonor.

The difference between the first two sorts of *avodah* and the *avodah* of *l'maancha* is marked. For while those pleading for their needs or seeking to draw favor ultimately have their own interests at heart, the proponents of *l'maancha* seek only to give pleasure to Hashem. They live constantly for a higher purpose and escape the boundaries of their desires and agendas, occupying a world of unlimited potential.[19]

And their reward is similarly immeasurable. The limitations of *mishpat* that curtail Divine favor are set aside, and the purest emanation of *ha'tov v'hameitiv* is their lot. Those who transcend their own agendas are afforded a taste of transcendent goodness.

The *avodah* of *l'maancha* may also be alluded to in the *tefillah*. The *berachah* begins by asking that Hashem accept our *tefillos*—"*Retzei Hashem Elokeinu b'amcha Yisrael u'v'sefilasam*," but it then appears to repeat the request with the words "*v'ishei Yisrael u'sefilasam b'ahavah sekabel b'ratzon*—the fire offerings of Yisrael and their prayer accept with love and favor." Why do we ask that Hashem accept our *tefillos* twice in the space of a few words?

The answer is that the two requests refer to two different forms of *avodah*. The first is that of *bakashas ritzuy*—*Retzei Hashem Elokeinu*; the second, *l'maancha*—an expression of immense *ahavah* (love). Thus the plea that Hashem respond in kind—"*u'sefilasam b'ahavah sekabel b'ratzon*."[20]

Shemecha—Act for the sake of Your name." In the *Selichos* prayers, we also implore Hashem to save us on account of His name—"*Hoshienu lemaan Shemecha*" (based on *Tehillim* 106:8).

18 See *Devarim* 30:3 and *Rashi* ad loc. citing the Gemara in *Megillah* 29a.

19 See *Maggid Mishnah* to *Hilchos Lulav*, 8:15.

20 The *avodah* of *l'maancha* is also invoked in the *Hoshanos* (prayers for redemption) recited on Sukkos. Those important *tefillos* are replete with requests that Hashem act for His own sake, "*L'maancha Elokeinu*, *l'maancha boreinu*" etc. The *avodah* of the Yamim Nora'im, which preceded Sukkos, was that of the first two forms of service—*bakashas tzerachav* (in the form of atonement for sin) and *bakashas ha'ritzuy*. The *Hoshanos* prayers bring us to a climax and allow us to assume the *avodah* of *l'maancha*.

The daily *Amidah* thus comprises three forms of service, *bakashas tzerachav*, *bakashas ritzuy*, and *l'maancha*.

7

L et us return to the sources with which we began. We noted that the *Sifri* describes a *korban* as simultaneously fulfilling the *ratzon* of Hashem and the *ratzon* of the man who offers it. According to Rav David Pardo, this reflects the notion that Hashem's will is to find favor in His people—"*l'hispashet ha'ratzon haElyon*." And this is a two-way dynamic—*middah keneged middah*. If a person offers a *korban* in order to give pleasure to Hashem, and not merely as a means for Hashem to help him fulfill his own aspirations, he will find favor with Him. As the *Sifri* declares, "Why did I command you to offer sacrifices to me? In order to fulfill My *ratzon*."[21]

We also noted that the Gemara in *Menachos* describes the objective of a *korban* only in terms of it fulfilling the *ratzon* of the person offering it, and that the *Ramban* felt that this is no contradiction to the *Sifri*. In light of all that we have said, this can easily be resolved. The Gemara meant to highlight the *avodah* of *bakashas ha'ritzuy*, the desire of man to find favor in the eyes of Hashem. Since this *avodah* is ultimately in his own interests, the Gemara stresses that "it is not due to My *ratzon* that you are sacrificing."

However, the *Sifri* refers to the *avodah* of *l'maancha*—service performed out of love. This service is indeed wrought with the intention of fulfilling Hashem's *ratzon* and bringing Him pleasure, with the benefits accrued to man as secondary.

---

21   The *Sifra* (6:9) similarly states, "*Nicho'ach l'shem nachas ruach*—the fragrance is pleasing when it is offered **for the sake of** bringing pleasure to Hashem."

8

The Beis Hamikdash was originally built by Shlomo HaMelech, but it was founded on the burning desire of his father David. Though David was ultimately not granted permission to do so, his desire to bring *nachas ruach* to Hashem, pervaded the *Mikdash* eventually erected by his son, making it a place of overwhelming *hispashtus ha'ratzon haElyon*.[22]

But Hashem's contentment in the Beis Hamikdash was not merely due to the yearnings of David HaMelech or the *rei'ach nicho'ach* engendered by the *korbanos*. The site of the Beis Hamikdash, specifically the *Even HaShesiyah* (the foundation stone situated in the *Kodesh Hakodashim* [the Holy of Holies]), was the place from which the entire world was established.[23] When Hashem rested His Shechinah there, He experienced, once more, the glorious contentment that existed upon the completion of creation; "And Hashem saw all that He had made and behold it was very good."[24] This was the greatest *nachas ruach* of all.

9

Yom Shabbason

Yom Shabbason ein lishkoach, zichro k'rei'ach ha'nicho'ach—
The day of rest, one should not forget, its mention is like a pleasant fragrance.

These are the opening words of the famous *zemer* of *Yom Shabbason* by Rabbi Yehuda HaLevi. Noticeably, they aver that the very *zecher* (mention) of Shabbos is a cause of *rei'ach nicho'ach*. That *zecher* likely refers to the *berachah* of Kiddush, which derives from the verse "*Zachor es yom haShabbos l'kadsho*—Invoke the day of Shabbos to sanctify it."[25]

22   See *Melachim I* 8:18 and *Divrei Hayamim II* 6:8.
23   *Yoma* 54b.
24   *Bereishis* 1:31.
25   *Yisro* 20:8.

The *Rambam* defines[26] the mitzvah of Kiddush as a *"zechiras shevach v'Kiddush*—an invocation of praise and holiness;" but how does invoking the praises of Shabbos produce a *rei'ach nicho'ach* comparable with that of *korbanos*?

In light of the above, the answer may be that the *zecher* and commitment to Shabbos invokes the very same glorious contentment as that experienced by Hashem when His Shechinah resided upon the *Even Hashesiyah* in the Beis Hamikdash. For just as the location of the Beis Hamikdash was infused with the spirit of Creation and of *"Vayar Elokim es kol asher asah v'hinei tov me'od,"* so does each and every Shabbos engender that very same *nachas ruach.*

How does every Shabbos recreate the *nachas ruach* of Creation? The answer lies within several seminal concepts articulated by Rav Hutner regarding Shabbos, which are discussed extensively in this *sefer.*

The Gemara asserts[27] that *"Kol hamispalel b'erev Shabbos v'omer Vayechulu, maaleh alav ha'kasuv k'ilu naaseh shutaf l'Hakadosh Baruch Hu b'Maaseh Bereishis*—Any person who prays on Friday night, and recites *Vayechulu,* the Torah considers it as though he becomes a partner with Hashem in the acts of Creation." The explanation of this extraordinary statement[28] is that the message of Shabbos, namely that all of Creation is a reflection of Hashem's unity, and that it contains nothing in the least bit contradictory, is promulgated by He who recites *Vayechulu* and observes Shabbos.

This is also why the very definition of Shabbos is *tov,* and why the *Shir shel Yom* (the Song of the Day) of Shabbos begins with the words *"Mizmor shir l'yom haShabbos, tov*—A song for the day of Shabbos, it is good."[29] Shabbos serves to reveal that everything is *tov,* for it not only helps us draw a clear distinction between the holy and the mundane, it reveals that the mundane itself exists to abet *kedushah.*[30]

---

26   *Hilchos Shabbos* 29:1.
27   *Shabbos* 119b.
28   See *Maamar* "The Song of Shabbos."
29   See *Maamar* "Good Shabbos."
30   See *Maamar* "Shabbos Chanukah," where this is discussed extensively.

The inherent *tov* of Shabbos—and its very *kedushah*—stem from the contentment (so to speak) felt by G-d when he observed that all that He had Created was "very good." *"Va'yar Elokim es kol asher asah v'hinei tov me'od...Vayechulu haShamayim...Va'yevarech Elokim es yom ha'shevi'i va'yekadesh oso*—And G-d saw all that He had created and it was very good...And the Heavens were complete...And G-d blessed the seventh day and He sanctified it."

Thus, the Jewish people who recite Kiddush accompanied by *Vayechulu* constantly invoke the *kedushah* and *tovah* of Shabbos and continue to spread its message to the world. This allows the sentiments of Creation to continue eternally, evoking the *nachas ruach* of Hashem each week.

And just as the *korbanos*, which are designed to instigate Hashem's *nachas ruach*, also draw down powerful *hispashtus ha'ratzon* and Divine favor, so do Am Yisrael in observing Shabbos and recreating the *nachas ruach* of Creation enjoy prodigious *ritzuy*. This is reflected by the mitzvah of *oneg Shabbos*,[31] which bids that they take pleasure on Shabbos and which is sourced in the *nachas ruach* of Hashem in Creation. The greatest *nachas ruach* to Hashem occurs when we recognize—as He Himself did—that everything is *"tov me'od,"* very good. Our assertion of that tenet opens up the unceasing flow of *ha'tov v'ha'meitiv*, as discussed herein.

Further, Am Yisrael is availed of a hallowed *neshamah yeseirah* on Shabbos, which is the vehicle by which they may somewhat partake of the marvelous reward of *Olam Haba* already in this world. That *neshamah* also seeks to create a mighty *hidduk* (bond) with their earthly bodies, availing them of a taste of immortality.[32] Lastly, on Shabbos their minds are put at rest from the searing questions and problems that accost them throughout the week—*"Baah Shabbos baah menuchah."*

Clearly, the invocation of Shabbos and the spreading of its message to the world is akin to the *rei'ach nicho'ach* of a *korban*, and provokes an

---

31 See *Maamarim "Kah Ribon"* and "Contentment or Satiation."
32 See *Maamar "Nishmas Kol Chai."*

enormous outpouring of *ritzuy* and *hispashtus ha'ratzon*. This affords Am Yisrael the inestimable joys of *oneg Shabbos*, *neshamah yeseirah*, and *menuchah*.

10

Nachas Ruach

The ongoing *nachas ruach* felt by Hashem following Creation was temporarily disrupted during the era that preceded the *Mabul* (the Great Flood). The evil of that generation was such that Hashem saw no choice but to wipe the slate clean. However, subsequently Noach found favor in the eyes of Hashem—"*V'Noach matza chen b'einei Hashem*,"[33] and this afforded Hashem the chance to persist with the world and to retain His sense of contentment in Creation.

This is alluded to in the very next words of the *zemer Yom Shabbason*, "*Yonah matzah bo mano'ach*—The dove found rest on it," referring to the dove dispatched by Noach from the ark, which found a place to rest from the floodwaters on Shabbos. The dove serves as a parable for the Jewish people,[34] and they, like it, find their *menuchah* on Shabbos. In spite of the ravages of the *Mabul*, Hashem regained His *nachas ruach* in Creation and this could once again serve as the source of the *kedushah* of Shabbos. Thereafter, the weary and those weighed down by the troubles of the world can find *menuchah* and calm on Shabbos, "*v'sham yanuchu yegi'ei ko'ach*—a means to restore their spirits."

The *tefillah* of Musaf of Shabbos states, "*Tikanta Shabbos ratzisa korbanoseha*—You established Shabbos and found favor in its offerings." The Shabbos *Musaf* offerings did not comprise a *Korban Chatas* (unlike the Yamim Tovim), for Shabbos is not a day of atonement but of *ritzuy* (*Ratzisa korbanoseha*) and of *rei'ach ha'nicho'ach*, a day of contentment both of Hashem and Am Yisrael.

---

33   *Bereishis* 6:8.
34   *Shir Hashirim* 2:14. See also *Rashi* to *Bereishis* 15:10, s.v. "*V'es ha'tzipor*."

Rav and Talmid

1

Torah, Sinai, Shabbos, and Creation— Unifying the Disparate

The Gemara relates[1] that Rabban Gamliel once extolled Rabbi Yehoshua as being his *"rebbi* who taught me Torah in public." This, at first glance, would seem a strange appellation, for the fact that Rabbi Yehoshua taught Rabban Gamliel in a public setting would not appear to enhance his status as his *rebbi*. While Torah that is disseminated in a group setting is more important than that learnt by individuals,[2] that in itself does not necessitate a teacher so long as people gather together to learn Torah.

The answer is that unlike any other wisdom, Torah can only be transmitted from one generation to another by a chain of *rebbi* and *talmid* (student). This is true even of intelligent students who could feasibly teach themselves, because creating a connection with a *rebbi* is not a matter of practicality or an expedient method of instruction, but an attachment to the chain of tradition (the *mesorah*) that dates back to Sinai.

---

1   *Rosh Hashanah* 25b.
2   *Megillah* 3b.

The Sinaitic Revelation is the model by which all future chains of the *mesorah* must progress. At Sinai, Moshe Rabbeinu stood and conveyed the words of G-d **to all of Israel as one**, and he did not do so merely out of convenience. The Gemara relates,[3] that in fact, Moshe would generally teach the Torah over and over again to the various groups who would come before him throughout the forty-year sojourn in the desert. Rather, this was the form that the *rebbi- talmid* dynamic was to take, namely, that **the *rebbi* stands in front of all of his *talmidim* together**—"*k'nesinasah mi'Sinai.*"

The notion of "*K'nesinasah mi'Sinai*" is already invoked by the Gemara, which rules[4] that Torah study must only take place in the milieu of the Siniatic Revelation: "*Limudah K'nesinasah, mah nesinasah b'eimah, b'yirah, b'reses u'b'zei'ah, af limudah b'eimah, b'yirah, b'reses u'b'zei'ah*—Just as the Torah was given amidst fear, awe, trembling, and sweat, so should its study be amidst fear, awe, trembling, and sweat."[5]

Why was it so at Sinai? This can best be explained by citing the famous Chazal which states "*Kudsha Brich Hu v'Oraisa v'Yisrael chad hu*—G-d, the Torah, and the Jewish people are one." At Sinai G-d taught His Torah to all of Yisrael together because He, His Torah, and His people are one—He was *Rebbi*[6] to His people and unified with them. And thereafter each and every *rebbi* was to similarly teach **his** Torah to all of his *talmidim* together, in order to emulate G-d at Sinai, "*k'nesinasah.*"

2

We have seen that the model of "*k'nesinasah,*" teaching one's *talmidim* all together, serves to **unite the *talmidim* with the**

---

3   *Eruvin* 54b.

4   *Berachos* 22a.

5   See *Pachad Yitzchok: Sefer HaZikaron,* p.15, which states that a *rebbi* is not merely the pipeline to learning and to the various methods of learning. Rather, appointing a *rav* for oneself is the fulfillment of the "*K'nesinasah*" of Torah that creates the *Maamad* of *Har Sinai* (reenactment of the revelation) in his soul from anew.

6   Clearly implied by *Rashi* to *Shemos* 19:16, s.v. "B"hyos boker."

rebbi **and with the Torah.** We should also note that gathering one's students in this manner **also serves to unify them and make each of them a crucial component of the** *rabbim*. At Sinai, G-d instructed Moshe to ensure that none of the people would touch the mountain "lest a multitude (*rav*) of them die."[7] *Rashi* adds that G-d was saying that He was concerned lest even one Jewish person die, "for any one of them who dies, even an individual, is considered to me like a multitude." We see, that the teaching of Torah serves to confer individuals with the power of the *rabbim*.

The Gemara relates[8] that when Yaakov wished to reveal the date of the final redemption to his sons the information was suddenly withheld from him. Suspecting that this was due to a flaw in his progeny, his sons needed to reassure him that this wasn't the case. They thus declared to him, "*Shema Yisrael Hashem Elokeinu Hashem echad*" conveying to him that, "Just as there is only One in your heart [the utter belief and conviction in the unity of G-d] so is there only One in our hearts."

The word "*echad*" invoked by the sons of Yaakov to demonstrate their unwavering belief in G-d, contains an allusion both to themselves and to their father Yaakov. The letter "*aleph*" (numerically equivalent to one) alludes to Yaakov himself. The letter "*ches*" (numerically equivalent to eight) alludes to the eight sons of Yaakov's two main wives, Rachel and Leah. The letter "*dalet*" (numerically equivalent to four) alludes to the four sons born to the maidservants, Bilhah and Zilpah.

These allusions may depict the concept outlined above, namely, that a *rebbi* (in this case Yaakov) must unite with his *talmidim* (his sons), and that his *talmidim* must also unify in the process. This is why Yaakov and his twelve sons are alluded to in the word "*echad*," as in that moment they were all utterly united.

The Torah relates that Yaakov then proceeded to bless each of his twelve sons individually. However, having done so, he then gave a general blessing to them all that they merit each of the *berachos* that

---

7 *Shemos* 19:21.

8 *Pesachim* 56a.

had been conferred upon each individual brother.[9] Rav Yonasan David explained[10] that the reason that Yaakov did so was that he first wanted to reveal the individual strengths of each of his sons, and he therefore gave each of them a unique blessing. However, he deliberately blessed them all together in order to unify them. In so doing, he demonstrated that although a *talmid* or child has individual strengths, he must be made a part of the *rabbim*.

From all of the foregoing, we may conclude that a *rebbi* must impact upon his *talmidim* in two ways. First, he must focus upon them as individuals, bring out their strengths, and help them fulfill their potential. This is a fulfillment of "*V'shinantam l'vanecha*,"[11] the mitzvah to teach Torah to one's students.[12] Second, he must seek to unite his *talmidim*, and emulate the model of "*k'nesinasah*"—the basis upon which the Torah was given and the *mesorah* established.

Rabban Gamliel was the Nasi, the ruler of the Jewish people. Unlike the *Av Beis Din* (the head of the *beis din*), whose job it is to issue Torah rulings and fulfill the mitzvah of *v'shinantam*, the mission of the Nasi was to direct the *rabbim* and guide them in *hanhagah* (appropriate conduct). This wisdom was received by Rabban Gamliel from Rabbi Yehoshua who "taught him Torah in public." In other words, he conveyed to him the Torah wisdom by **which one directs the** *rabbim*—the basis of the *mesorah* of *k'nesinasah miSinai*. Moshe Rabbeinu, with whom the *mesorah* commenced, was both the Nasi (see *Devarim* 33:5, "*Va'yehi biYeshurun melech*," with *Targum Onkelos* and *Yonasan ben Uziel*) and the *Av beis din* (teacher and leader).

---

9   *Midrash Tanchuma, Vayechi* 16, cited by *Rashi* to *Bereishis* 49:28.
10 As related by Rav C. Y. Kaplan.
11 *Devarim* 6:7.
12 *Berachos* 14b and *Kiddushin* 30a.

3
———

The notion that a *rebbi* must attempt to unite with his *talmidim* and unify them is reflective of a deeper truth. For in fact, the impression that a *rebbi* or his individual *talmidim* are somehow separate or disparate entities is nothing but an illusion. Given that *"Kudsha Brich Hu v'Oraisa v'Yisrael chad hu,"* the Jewish people, must, by their very definition, be one unified entity, just like G-d and his Torah.

The perception of unified concepts appearing to be disparate entities was caused by Creation itself. G-d, the epitome of *achdus* (unity), chose to create a physical universe, but in so doing, his *achdus* had to be, so to speak, separated into *pratim* (separate entities and details). This is why Creation took place over six days, for the very notion of physical Creation is one of separation and division.

Of course, the manifestation of division and *pratim* that were due to Creation, would only serve to conceal the *achdus* of G-d from the world. But this would all be rectified on the seventh day of Creation with the advent of Shabbos. After a week of *pratim*, too numerous to count, Shabbos would come and heal the divisions, connect the disparate, and resolve any contradictions by demonstrating that all,[13] in fact, stem from the singular *achdus* of G-d.[14]

In fact, though Creation was divided into six days, it was all contained in the letter *"beis"* of *Bereishis* at the beginning of the Torah as one sin-gle act of G-d.[15] This fact was brought to the fore by the Shabbos at the denouement of Creation, which revealed the *achdus* behind Creation.

The same message emerged on the Shabbos of Matan Torah. Then, too, disparate elements were shown to come from one unified source, as The Ten Commandments were first uttered **in one breath** before they

---

13   See the *Sefer HaZikaron* of Rav Hutner, which relates that in his youth Rav Hutner wrote to one of his friends, "I cannot be considered a person of *mussar* until I have a *hashkafah shleimah u'makefes* (a hashkafah that is complete and all encompassing)." In other words, Rav Hutner needed to gain a weltanschauung that explained everything in the world—a *hashkafah* that appreciated the *achdus* of Creation.

14   See *Maamar* "The Song of Shabbos," where we discuss this notion at length.

15   See *Rashi* to *Bereishis* 1:14: "All of Creation took place on the first day."

were uttered separately by Moshe Rabbeinu.[16] In the rendition of the mitzvah of Shabbos, the words "*shamor*" and "*zachor*" were also said simultaneously, which demonstrated how two apparently separate forms of service are no contradiction at all. This then served to reveal that all the myriad *pratim* of the mitzvos are just manifestations of G-d's *achdus* and can all be found in the single letter *aleph* (which represents *achdus*) of the word "*Anochi*"[17] at the beginning of the Ten Commandments.[18]

Thus, both the Shabbos of Creation and the Shabbos of Matan Torah introduced *achdus* to the world, joining together all of the *pratim* into one unified whole. In doing so, Shabbos plays the part of "*rebbi* to creation" joining together all of its students.

4

The unifying powers of Shabbos are present from the very beginning of the day—"*Baah Shabbos baah menuchah*." However, they are far more palpable and are truly felt (rather than just rationally understood) toward the end of the day, from *Minchah* time and onwards. This stage is the climax of Shabbos and the climax of the week, and, according to the Vilna Gaon, represents the era of the World to Come, which is a time filled exclusively by *menuchah*—a true feeling of tranquility and peace.[19] Though the entire Shabbos is described by Chazal[20] as *me'ein Olam Haba* (a miniature version of the World to Come), by the time of *Minchah*, this is felt more keenly.

For this reason, the *tefillah* of *Minchah* on *Shabbos* references *achdus*: "*Atah echad v'Shimcha echad*—You are one, and Your name is one," for

---

16   *Mechilta*, cited by *Rashi* to *Shemos* 20:1.

17   In fact, the word "*Anochi*" is said to be an acronym of "*Ana nafshi kesavis yehavis*—I am one with the Torah," (for I have written my essence into the Torah that I granted to Am Yisrael).

18   *Rav Saadya Gaon:* "All 613 mitzvos are included in the Ten Commandments. The Ten Commandments are all included in the verse of '*Anochi Hashem Elokecha,*' and the entire verse of '*Anochi Hashem Elokecha*' is included in the word '*anochi.*'"

19   See *Maamar* "The Song of Shabbos," where we discuss this comment of the Vilna Gaon at length.

20   *Berachos* 57b.

it is at this time of the week that *achdus* abounds. In fact, the *tefillah* questions how anybody could think otherwise, *"U'mi k'amcha Yisrael goy echad ba'aretz*—And who is like your people Israel, one nation in the world?" as by this stage of Shabbos, this notion is more generally felt.

And, as the *tefillah* continues, *"Yaakov u'vanav yanuchu vo,"* Yaakov and his sons—they who together uttered *echad*—will experience *menuchah*, the quiet bliss of tranquility of the World to Come—the utopia of *achdus*.

Shabbos Shuvah

1

The Gemara records[1] the following statement of Rabbi Levi regarding *teshuvah* (repentance):

Great is teshuvah for it reaches the Throne of Glory, as the verse states, "Shuvah Yisrael ad Hashem Elokecha—Return, Israel, to Hashem your G-d."

The verse cited by the Gemara is from the book of *Hoshea*.[2] Interestingly, there is an almost identical verse in *Sefer Devarim* which states, "And you shall return to Hashem your G-d."[3] Why does the Gemara cite a verse from *Neviim* (*divrei Kabbalah*) rather than one from *Chumash*?[4]

The *Rambam* rules:[5]

Today when the Temple is no longer in existence, and we no longer have the Altar of atonement, all we have is teshuvah.

---

1   *Yoma* 86a.
2   14:2.
3   *Devarim* 30:2.
4   The *Rambam* (*Hilchos Teshuvah* 1:1) implies that *"V'shavta"* is a prediction, not a command. It is difficult to discern the *Ramban's* position on this issue. See his comments to *Devarim* 30:2. The *pasuk* in *Hoshea*, however, implies a command.
5   *Hilchos Teshuvah* 1:3.

158

> *Teshuvah atones for all sins. And the very day of Yom Kippur itself atones for those who repent, as the verse states, "For on this day He will atone for you."*[6]

This halachah appears to be a contradiction in terms. The Gemara records[7] a dispute between Rebbi and the Chachamim regarding the atonement of Yom Kippur. According to Rebbi, the essential purity of the day of Yom Kippur itself absolves a person of his sins. According to the Chachamim, a person only attains atonement on Yom Kippur if he has repented. How can the *Rambam* state that "the day of Yom Kippur itself atones for those who repent"? This wording appears to be borrowed from both Rebbi and the Chachamim!

Teshuvah

The word "*teshuvah*," which literally means "to return," seems a curious expression. Its basic implication is that a person who repents **returns** to his original state pre-sin, and indeed, in many a case this is true. However, there are other cases where the term "*teshuvah*" would appear to be incongruous. Chazal maintain[8] that when a person repents out of love of Hashem (rather than fear of Him), he then occupies a **more elevated** state than he did previously for his sins are transformed into merits! How then can this be described as *teshuvah* (a return)?

The *Rambam*, in the following chapter,[9] issues another fascinating ruling, based on the Gemara:[10]

> *What constitutes complete teshuvah? If a person is given the test to commit the same sin that he committed in the past, in the same place, under the same circumstances, and he refrains and does not commit it because he has repented, and not due to fear or lack of strength—that is teshuvah.*

---

6   *Vayikra* 16:30.
7   *Yoma* 85b.
8   Ibid., 86b.
9   *Hilchos Teshuvah* 2:1.
10   *Yoma* 86a.

According to the *Rambam*, *teshuvah* is only complete if one is presented with the opportunity to commit a sin again, and refrains from doing so. But what if that opportunity never comes? Would that render his *teshuvah* incomplete?

Yode'a Taalumos

The answer lies in the very next halachah, where the *Rambam* clarifies:[11]

> *And what constitutes teshuvah? It is when a sinner forsakes a sin and removes it from his mind, and decides in his heart that he will not do it again, as the verse states, "A wicked person shall forsake his path."[12] Moreover, he is regretful of the past, as the verse states, "For after I have repented, I regretted."[13] And He who is aware of all hidden matters can affirm that the sinner will not return to this sin ever again.*

Many have toiled to understand this statement of the *Rambam*: Of what consequence is Hashem's affirmation, if it is unbeknown to us?

The answer to this question answers our previous question as well. To allay the fear of a *baal teshuvah* who wonders whether he will receive complete atonement when he has not experienced the same test as before, Hashem attests that he would indeed pass the test if faced with it again. This is something that only Hashem could know and is the *baal teshuvah's* consolation.

Thus, if a person truly repents, is regretful, has committed to refrain from sin, and has confessed, Hashem—who is aware of the strength of his commitment, will affirm that he will no longer err and considers it as if he had had the opportunity to sin and overcome it.

However, this notion appears to be an impossibility. How is it possible to reach a stage where one is certain not to commit a sin for which he has repented? Chazal assert that "a man's [evil] inclination attempts

---

11   *Hilchos Teshuvah* 2:2.
12   *Yeshayahu* 55:7.
13   *Yirmiyahu* 31:18.

to overcome him on every day,"[14] and that a person should "not trust himself until his dying day."[15] Clearly, even if a person has truly repented, he may regress in the future.

2

Circumcision of the Heart

Rabbeinu Yonah[16] makes the following, seminal statement about *teshuvah*:

> *For Hashem assists the repentant to reach a state that they could not naturally reach. He will rejuvenate them with a spirit of purity…and it further states, "And Hashem shall circumcise your hearts and the hearts of your children,"[17] namely, to attain the love of Him.*

In short, complete *teshuvah* is unattainable without Heavenly assistance. Rav Hutner explained that in Rabbeinu Yonah's view,[18] Hashem grants particular assistance to those attempting *teshuvah*, beyond what's granted to those who are involved in other Heavenly matters.[19] Thus, if an earnest *baal teshuvah* does all that he can to fulfill the command of "And you shall circumcise your heart,"[20] Hashem similarly commits to "circumcise your hearts and the hearts of your children,"[21] helping the contrite and repentant to go beyond their natural capabilities.

---

14 *Sukkah* 52a.
15 *Avos* 2:4.
16 *Shaarei Teshuvah* 1:1.
17 *Devarim* 30:15.
18 In contrast to the view of the *Ramban* (in his comments to *Devarim* 30:6) who clearly equates the two.
19 As Chazal say, "*Haba li'taher mesayin oso*—If a person comes to purify himself, they [Heaven] assist him" (*Shabbos* 104a).
20 *Devarim* 10:16.
21 The *Ramban* ibid. explains that this verse refers to the end of days when a spirit of purity will envelop the world. In invoking this verse in the context of a *baal teshuvah*, Rabbeinu

Perhaps this resolves the question we posed above, namely, how can a person reach a state in which it can be ascertained that he will no longer sin? The answer is that, indeed, if it were down to his natural faculties, man could never be sure of himself, never completely confident in his self-control. However, if he invests his heart and soul in repentance, Hashem will grant him unparalleled assistance and allow him to transcend his natural capabilities. He may thus reach a stage where "He who is aware of all hidden matters can affirm that the sinner will not return to this sin ever again."

3

L et us examine this idea more closely.

The Gemara rules[22] that if a person observes *Uchlusei Yisrael* (a group of six hundred thousand Jews),[23] he should recite the blessing *"Baruch chacham ha'razim*—Blessed is the wise one of secrets." *Rashi* explains[24] that the "secrets" are those contained in the hearts of the six hundred thousand present, and which are known to Hashem.

Why is this *berachah* only pertinent when one witnesses a group of six hundred thousand? Surely Hashem is aware of the secrets contained in the hearts of any group of people, no matter its size.

The Gemara also records[25] a famous statement of Rabbi Alexandri:

> *Master of the worlds. It is revealed and known to You, that our will is to fulfill Your will. But what prevents us [from doing so]? The leaven in the dough (the evil inclination[26]) and enslavement to the kingdoms [in which we reside].*

Yonah appears to convey the idea that a spirit of the end of days envelops every *baal teshuvah* even today.

22 *Berachos* 58a.
23 *Rashi* ad loc., s.v. "*Uchlusei.*"
24 Ibid., s.v. "*Chacham ha'razim.*"
25 *Berachos* 17a.
26 *Rashi* ad loc., s.v. "*S'or she'b'issah.*"

How can we excuse ourselves by invoking the evil inclination and the enslavement to the kingdoms? Ultimately, we are capable of choosing good over evil, regardless of the difficulties in doing so.

K'nesses Yisrael

The answer is that this Gemara does not mean to provide us with a litany of excuses. Rather, it reveals a profound idea about the true nature of a Jewish person. The *Maharal* explains[27] that unlike the nations of the world, Am Yisrael is a single unified entity and each individual Jew is hewn from one composite soul called *K'nesses Yisrael*.[28] This composite soul is essentially good, thus the natural tendency of every member of Am Yisrael is to do good, and evil is a deviation from that.

The cry of the Jewish soul, revealed by Rabbi Alexandri, "It is our will to fulfill your will," is the instinctive desire of a Jew is to aspire to fulfill the will of Hashem. In fact, Rav Hutner explained[29] that this intense, instinctive desire is even present **as a person commits a sin** and that is what forms the basis of repentance.

And this deep-seated desire is thoroughly unnatural—"*l'maala min ha'teva*." It was first introduced to the soul of Adam HaRishon, who essentially transcended sin, and was ultimately reintroduced to the composite soul of Am Yisrael upon their rebirth at *yetzias Mitzrayim*.[30]

When we state, "Our will is to fulfill your will. But what prevents us [from doing so]? The leaven in the dough," rather than excuse ourselves, we recall that our innermost desire is to do good. That which prevents us from doing so is the dastardly evil inclination, who prevents us from accessing our true selves and causes us to deviate from our natural path.

This idea may help explain a curious expression found in the *Amidah*. At the conclusion of the fifth *berachah* we say, "*Baruch Atah Hashem, ha'rotzeh b'seshuvah*—Blessed are You Hashem, Who desires repentance." This is the only *berachah* in the *Amidah* that references Hashem's desires; why so?

---

27   *Gur Aryeh, Ki Sisa* 30:12.
28   See *Maamar* "The Soul of a Torah Scholar."
29   *Pachad Yitzchok: Yom Kippur* 25.
30   See *Derech Hashem* 4:2 and *Maamar* "Nishmas Kol Chai."

Perhaps the answer is that this expression is a nod to the statement of Rabbi Alexandri—"It is our will to fulfill your will." We, in reflecting upon our sins, maintain that our true will is to fulfill Hashem's. We therefore specifically reference His will in the blessing of repentance—"He desires repentance."[31]

This also explains why we recite a *berachah* specifically when we encounter a gathering of 600,000 Jews. *K'nesses Yisrael*, the composite *neshamah* referenced above, comprises no more than 600,000 components.[32] Therefore, when 600,000 Jews gather—the combined might of *nishmas Yisrael*, the combined soul of the Jewish people is revealed. At that moment, we draw attention to Hashem's knowledge of the "secret" housed in every Jewish soul, which is that they are each the bearer of a fragment of *K'nesses Yisrael*—a piece of essential and intrinsic goodness carved out from beneath the Throne of Glory. To thank G-d for this secret we proclaim: "*Baruch chacham ha'razim*—Blessed is the wise one of secrets."

4

Now we may shed some light on the words of the *Rambam*.

When a person sincerely repents, though he cannot be certain that he will not sin again for he is only human, he activates the good will of Hashem who "desires repentance." Since Hashem is aware of all

---

31   My dear friend, Rav Moshe Nadler, added that this sheds new light on the *tefillah* we recite at *Musaf* on Yom Tov, "*Shuvah eileinu b'hamon rachamecha biglal avos she'asu retzonecha*—Return to us in your abundant mercy, on account of the forefathers who fulfilled your will." How do we invoke the merit of the forefathers when Chazal (*Shabbos* 55a) say that "*zechus avos tamah*—the merit of the forefathers has already been expended"? We must say that in fact we mean to invoke the *bris Avos* (the covenant with the forefathers), which is eternal (*Tosafos* ibid., s.v. "*U'Shmuel amar*"). Why then does the *tefillah* say that it is "on account of the forefathers who fulfilled your will"—does that not imply that we are invoking their good deeds? The answer is that in fact we are invoking the notion stated above, namely that the essence of the forefathers was to fulfill the will of Hashem, and that essence was inherited by us.

32   See *Rabbeinu Gershom* to *Arachin* 32b, and the Gemara in *Kesubos* 17a, "*Netilasah k'nesinasah*."

hidden matters, he is surely cognizant of the fact that the innermost desire of every Jew is to do good and to refrain from sin, and He can therefore affirm that this person will not sin again. For although he naturally does not have the ability to be sure of himself, if he delves into his essence—the segment of *nishmas Yisrael* that is his own—he can rise above his natural abilities and practically transcend *bechirah* (free will).

Yom Kippur

This also resolves the contradiction in the words of the *Rambam* regarding the atonement of Yom Kippur. As stated, man does not have the natural ability to utterly safeguard himself from sin. However, deep within his soul, he is connected to a world that is above *bechirah*, a world of essential goodness and perfection. If he accesses that point in his soul, he may indeed be sure not to sin.

And it is the day of Yom Kippur that enables man to do so. Though the atonement of Yom Kippur is only achieved via repentance, complete repentance in which Hashem may attest that we will not sin again is only affected due to the purifying effects of the day of Yom Kippur itself. Thus, "the very day of Yom Kippur itself atones for those who repent"—an atonement that could not be achieved by *teshuvah* alone. *Itzumo shel yom* (the power of the day) brings out the *itzumo* of the *neshamah*. Accordingly, there is no difference of opinion between Rebbi and the Chachamim, as we need *teshuvah* to access the power of *bechirah* and we need Yom Kippur to access the secret of the *neshamah*.

The *Rambam* also states[33] that "it is the way of *teshuvah* for a person to change his name, in other words, [he declares] 'I am another person, and I am not that person who committed those acts.'" The reason that he must consider himself to be another person is that the person he was previously stumbled and sinned. How can he be sure not to stumble again if he merely returns to being the same man he was before? That would not constitute complete repentance.

---

33   Ibid., 2:4.

Rather, complete repentance is **a return to oneself**—a return to the innermost essence of the soul where only good exists. There, the notion of a free-will choice of sinfulness over virtue simply does not exist. There, a person is "not that person who committed those acts." This also resolves our original question, namely, how can repentance be deemed a "return" when *teshuvah me'ahavah* catapults a person higher than he was before? The answer is that he is only capable of doing so **by means of returning to his essence.**

Those who embark on the path of complete repentance are transformed and remade. In the words of Chazal,[34] "In the place that *baalei teshuvah* stand, even complete *tzaddikim* cannot stand."

5

Kisei Hakavod

Now, we may also explain why Rabbi Levi chose a verse in *Hoshea* rather than one in *Chumash*. The verse in *Chumash* does indeed state that repentance reaches all the way to Heaven—"*V'shavta ad Hashem Elokecha*," but the verse in *Hoshea* places the emphasis on Yisrael—"*Shuvah Yisrael ad Hashem Elokecha*." This is extremely significant. For *v'shavta* (you shall return) operates in the theater of *teshuvah*, but Yisrael operates in the world of *l'maalah min ha'bechirah.*"

As we have noted, the special quality of the soul of a Jew is that it is a fragment of the collective soul of *K'nesses Yisrael*.[35] It is this quality that allows him to transcend his natural abilities and attain a scarcely believable repentance that lifts him higher than he was previously. In short, it is only due to the quality of "Yisrael" that *teshuvah* extends all

---

34   *Berachos* 34b.

35   The *Rambam* (ibid., 3:11) rules that "a person who separates himself from the ways of the community...and he doesn't join in their grief does not have a portion in the World to Come." The reason for this may be that by separating himself from the community, he divorces his soul from that of *K'nesses Yisrael*. This therefore leaves him no room for true repentance.

the way "*ad Hashem Elokecha*," "*ad Kissei haKavod*."[36] To reach Hashem's abode, a person must invoke the *chelek Eloka mi'maal* (the part of Hashem that exists within him), the part that is *chatzuvah mi'tachas Kissei haKavod* (sculpted from the Heavenly throne itself).

This also sheds light on a comment of the *Rambam*[37] regarding the *se'ir la'azazel* (the goat sent out to the wilderness on Yom Kippur):

> *The goat that is dispatched, since it is to effect atonement for all of Israel—upon which the Kohen Gadol confessed in the name of all of Israel—as the verse states, "And he shall confess upon it all of the sins of the Jewish people."*

Why do the Jewish people require collective confession and atonement? Each person must surely confess and repent for his sins individually.

The answer is that the *teshuvah* of each individual is dependent upon the entirety of Yisrael. Only as a facet and fragment of *K'nesses Yisrael* can a person truly atone for his sins.

This also sheds light on a fascinating comment of the *Ran*[38] regarding Rosh Hashanah. The *Ran* asks why man is judged on Rosh Hashanah rather than on any other day of the year; is the fact that he was created on Rosh Hashanah a reason to judge him on that day?

The *Ran* answers that since Adam HaRishon sinned on the very day he was created and was subsequently forgiven, all his descendants are similarly judged for their actions on this day.

In light of the above, this can be explained further. Absolute *teshuvah* can only be attained by accessing the pure recesses of the soul that was first breathed into Adam HaRishon. Therefore, the day on which every man is judged is the anniversary of the day on which he was given the keys to repentance.

---

36 Though the verse in *Chumash*, which does not mention "Yisrael" does not make this point, it is often the case that with regard to *teshuvah* greater detail is provided in the words of the prophets than in the *Chumash* itself (Rabbeinu Yonah, *Shaarei Teshuvah* 1:1).

37 Ibid., 1:2.

38 *Rosh Hashanah* 3a, *b'dapei haRif*.

It is this that distinguishes the repentance that takes place during the days of Elul and that takes place following Rosh Hashanah. It is not just that our efforts to repent are stepped up following Rosh Hashanah, but that we are granted the gift of Adam HaRishon—the pure soul that transcends sin and enables true and complete *teshuvah*.[39]

6

Teshuvah of a Ben Noach

Rabbi Elchanan Wasserman discusses[40] at length how *teshuvah* of a Jewish person retroactively uproots his sins, whereas the *teshuvah* of a *Ben Noach* is only effective going forward.

The reason for this is that a *Ben Noach* is occupied with the earthly concerns of the physical world. It is therefore impossible for him to rewrite the past. Once an act is performed, no thoughts in the world can erase it, "*Machshavah eino motzi mi'yedei maaseh*—Thoughts cannot uproot deeds."[41]

But the occupation of Am Yisrael is in matters of the World to Come, the world of *machshavah*. There, it is possible to uproot the past, for "*akiras ha'ratzon k'akiras ha'maaseh*—uprooting the desire is like uprooting the deed."[42] Since the true *ratzon* of a Jew is to fulfill that of Hashem, he may uproot his deeds retroactively, for deep inside him he never wanted to sin in the first place.

"*Shuvah Yisrael*—Return Israel." In the perspective of *kiyum ha'mitzvos* (fulfilling the mitzvos of Hashem) we are more than returning—for post *teshuvah* we occupy a more elevated state. But in the perspective

---

39   It could be said that the *teshuvah* of the month of Elul is that of the first chapter of the *Rambam's Hilchos Teshuvah*, whereas the *teshuvah* of the *Aseres Yemei Teshuvah* is that of the second chapter in which Hashem affirms that "he will not return to that sin again."
40   *Kovetz He'aros* 21:24.
41   *Kiddushin* 59b, *Shabbos* 52b and 58b, *Sukkah* 13b.
42   *Mesilas Yesharim* 4.

of where *teshuvah* leads us ultimately, namely, to the *Kissei haKavod*, we are indeed returning, precisely to where it all started.

Great is *teshuvah* for it reaches the Throne of Glory.

Shabbos HaGadol

1

Ahavah

The *Ramban* concludes his introduction to *Sefer Shemos* with the following words:

> But when they came to Har Sinai and built the Mishkan, and Hashem once again rested his Shechinah among them, they returned to the level of their forefathers described by the phrase "the secret of Hashem was upon their tents," for they were considered the chariots of Hashem. Then Am Yisrael was considered to have been redeemed.

What is the meaning of "the secret of Hashem was upon their tents" that describes the spiritual standing of the Avos?

Second, according to the *Ramban*, Am Yisrael only achieved the standing of the Avos when they built the *Mishkan*, following Matan Torah. But what did the *Mishkan* provide that Matan Torah did not? Chazal say[1] that everything can be found in the Torah—"*Hafoch bah, v'hafoch bah, d'kola bah*"—why the need for a *Mishkan*?

---

1   *Avos* 5:27.

A similar question arises in *Parashas Beshalach*. Toward the end of the *Shiras Ha'yam*, Am Yisrael declare: "You will bring them and implant them on the mountain of your heritage, the base of your dwelling place—Hashem, Your hands established the *Mikdash*."[2] The establishing of the *Mishkan* or Beis Hamikdash appears to be invoked as a goal of redemption rather than that of Matan Torah.

Yet, elsewhere, Matan Torah is explicitly referenced as the goal of *yetzias Mitzrayim*. For example, the Torah records in *Parashah Shemos* that Hashem said to Moshe, "When you take the people out of Egypt, you will worship Hashem on this mountain."[3] This clearly implies that the goal was Matan Torah. The *Sefer Hachinuch* also famously states[4] that the purpose of the mitzvah of counting the *omer* is to show our excitement for the forthcoming day of Matan Torah, which was the purpose of the Exodus. We do not continue counting the *omer* until the day of the inauguration of the *Mishkan*, on Rosh Chodesh Nissan of the following year!

Following the sin of the golden calf, Moshe Rabbeinu succeeded in achieving a reprieve for Am Yisrael, also ensuring that Hashem Himself would continue to lead them and not send an angel in His stead.[5] He also made a specific request of Hashem, *"V'niflinu ani v'amcha mi'kol ha'am asher al p'nei ha'adamah*—And I and your people will be made distinct from all of the other people upon the face of the earth."[6] *Rashi* explains[7] that Moshe was requesting that Hashem should never rest His Shechinah upon the other nations of the world, only upon Am Yisrael.

If Hashem had promised to rest His Shechinah upon Am Yisrael, why was it necessary to ask that He did not also rest His Shechinah upon others?

Moreover, there are sources that imply that the nations of the world do have a connection with Hashem. The verse states in *Shir Hashirim*,

---

2 *Shemos* 15:17.
3 Ibid., 3:12. See also 10:26.
4 *Mitzvah* 306.
5 Ibid., 33:14.
6 Ibid., 33:16.
7 Ad loc., s.v. *"Halo b'lechtecha imanu*," based on the Gemara in *Berachos* 7a.

"*L'rei'ach shemanecha tovim, shemen turak shemecha, al ken alamos ahevucha*—The scent of fine oils, Your name is flowing oil, therefore the maidens loved you."[8] The *Gra* explains that *alamos* (maidens) is a reference to the nations of the world whose connection with Hashem is akin to a scent that can be detected from afar. (This contrasts with the connection held by Am Yisrael that is akin to the sense of taste and can only be felt at close quarters). Clearly, the nations are also party to Hashem's love—what then, was Moshe's request?

2

Cholas Ahavah

Am Yisrael is described twice in *Megillas Shir Hashirim* as "love-sick" (*cholas ahavah*) for Hashem.

In the second chapter it states: "He brought me to the house of wine, and [placed] his banner of love upon me."[9] *Rashi* explains that the "house of wine" is a reference to the *Ohel Mo'ed* (the tent of meeting) in which the Torah in all of its details was conveyed to Moshe. Then, the following verse states: "Sustain me with exquisite cakes, spread apples out around me, for I am sick with love." According to the *Gra*, this refers to the seven days of the inauguration of the *Mishkan* when Am Yisrael longed for the final, eighth day in which the service in the *Mishkan* could commence.

In the fifth chapter it states: "I oblige you, daughters of Jerusalem, if you find my beloved, what shall you tell Him? That I am sick with love."[10] The *Gra* explains that this verse refers to the era when Am Yisrael are in exile and long for the return of the Shechinah that has seemingly deserted them.

One may surmise that the *Gra* understood these two verses from their context. In chapter 2, the verse previous to that cited above states, "In

---

8   1:3.
9   Verse 4.
10   Verse 8.

His shade I delighted and sat, and His fruit was sweet to my palate."
This denotes a feeling of contentment and enchantment, suited to the
period that led up to the *Mishkan's* inauguration. In chapter 5, however,
the previous verse states, "The watchmen who circle the city found me,
they struck me, they wounded me." This clearly refers to a period of
torment and exile.

There are thus two stages for *cholas ahavah*. The first is that of the
exile in which a powerful yearning for the Shechinah is engendered
and Am Yisrael become sick with longing. They channel these feelings
into Torah study, and this brings an even greater love of Hashem. The
Sifri states that the way to fulfill the mitzvah of "*V'ahavta es Hashem
Elokecha*—And you shall love Hashem your G-d,"[11] is to turns one's attention to the dictum of the very next verse—"*V'hayu ha'devarim ha'eleh
asher anochi metzavecha*," namely, Torah study. And although while in
exile the Torah is degraded—"Her king and her officers are among the
nations, there is no Torah,"[12] Am Yisrael's determined attachment to
Torah revives and comforts them.

However, there is a second, more powerful expression of *cholas ahavah*, where a person transcends his regular service of Hashem and is
practically divested of his earthly constraints (*hispashtus ha'chumri*[13]),
just like a sick person is divested of good health. This expression of love
only took place in the *Mishkan*.

These two forms of *cholas ahavah* were the twin goals of the exodus.
The first goal was Matan Torah and the love of Hashem that it would
engender. This love was immortalized in the fifth chapter of *Shir
Hashirim* that speaks of the *cholas ahavah* of the exile in which there is
only Torah and no *Mishkan*. And this *ahavah* also brings the Shechinah,
in the form of *Moshe Rabbeinu's* blessing to Am Yisrael, "May it be His
will that the Shechinah rests upon the work of your hands."[14]

---

11   *Devarim* 6:5.
12   *Eichah* 2:9.
13   See the *Shulchan Aruch, Orach Chaim* 98:1.
14   *Bamidbar Rabbah* 2:19, cited by *Rashi* to *Shemos* 39:43 and *Toras Kohanim, Miluim* 1:19, cited
      by *Rashi* to *Vayikra* 9:23.

But the Shechinah resting on the "work of their hands" wasn't enough. Am Yisrael longed for the closeness of the Shechinah within their hearts that could only be brought about by the *Mishkan*. They thus waited breathlessly during the seven days of inauguration of the *Mishkan* for the day on which they could attain it. Chazal say[15] that the command to build the *Mishkan*, "*V'asu li Mikdash v'shachanti b'socham*," implies that the Shechinah would not only reside within the four walls of the *Mishkan*, but within the confines of each and every Jew. The verse thus states "*v'shachanti b'socham*—and I shall dwell within them," rather than "*v'shachanti b'sochah*—and I shall dwell within it." The dwelling of the Shechinah within each individual brings forth his *cholas ahavah*, a deep and powerful love.

3

D'veikus

The attainment of the second, more powerful *cholas ahavah* is also known as *d'veikus* (attachment to Hashem) and is a fulfillment of an explicit command in the Torah, "*Es Hashem Elokecha tira, oso saavod, u'vo sidbak*—And Hashem your G-d you shall fear, Him you shall serve, and to Him you shall cleave."[16] The verse clearly states that fearing and serving Hashem does not suffice; *d'veikus* is required.

However, as the *Sifri* notes,[17] the injunction to attach oneself to Hashem appears unfeasible. Is a person expected to ascend to Heaven and form an attachment with the G-d who is described as an "all-consuming fire"!?[18] The *Sifri* therefore explains that the Torah's intent is that a person should form an attachment with "*talmidei chachamim* and their students," and this constitutes *d'veikus* to Hashem.[19]

---

15   *Bamidbar Rabbah* 2:3.
16   *Devarim* 10:20.
17   Ad loc.
18   *Devarim* 4:24.
19   See introduction to *Divrei Aggadah* where this idea is discussed.

One may have said that the *Sifri* concedes that actual *d'veikus* to Hashem is impossible and that the Torah only expects a person to form the closest possible attachment to Hashem, which is by means of *talmidei chachamim*. This would be akin to the notion of "*Mora rabach k'mora Shamayim*—The fear of your *rebbi* shall be like the fear of Heaven,"[20] where the fear of a *rebbi* ultimately remains secondary to the fear of Hashem.

However, in light of the glorious verses of *Shir Hashirim* above, it could well be said that a form of actual *d'veikus* to Hashem is achievable. For within the *Mishkan*, the notion of true *d'veikus*, a deep and undying love, was a reality, and was expressed by Am Yisrael in *Megillas Shir Hashirim*, "*Ki cholas ahavah ani.*" Though indeed we cannot ascend to Heaven to attach ourselves to Him, Hashem brings His Shechinah down to us, and rests it upon the *Mishkan*, and upon each and every individual.

Shlomo HaMelech in *Shir Hashirim* portrayed the love between Am Yisrael and Hashem allegorically, invoking the love of husband and wife. This same allegory was portrayed in the *Mishkan* by means of the *Keruvim*, which could be seen, thrice yearly, wrapped in embrace in the *Kodesh Hakodashim*, the quintessence of the *Mishkan*. There, the bonds of love between Am Yisrael and Hashem were revealed to one and all[21]; for while Hashem is indeed an "all-consuming fire," Am Yisrael who are ablaze with *cholas ahavah*, and feverish with love, can attach their fire to His. Though fire does consume all, it does not consume fire itself.

This may also have been the intent of the *Sifri*. The pathway to *d'veikus* can only be traveled by means of "*talmidei chachamim* and their students," for by observing the bond that *talmidei chachamim* form with Hashem and their students, one can also endeavor to form a bond with

---

20 *Avos* 4:12.
21 *Yoma* 54b.

Hashem.[22] Their relationship is thus a model for a person to fulfill the mitzvah of *u'vo sidbak*.[23]

4

Thus far we have ascertained that although love of Hashem can be cultivated by Torah study, *d'veikus* and an all-consuming love of Hashem can only be attained by attaching oneself to *talmidei chachamim* and their students. Doing so helps cultivate the *cholas ahavah* that allows us to draw close to Hashem, and which was manifested particularly within the confines of the *Mishkan*. Therefore, Matan Torah had to be followed by the creation of the *Mishkan*.

We reference this idea twice in the daily *tefillos*. In the *berachah* of *Ahavah Rabbah* we implore Hashem, "Open our eyes to Your Torah, and attach our hearts to Your mitzvos," but we then immediately continue with, "And you shall unify our hearts to love and fear Your name." Clearly, opening our hearts to Hashem's Torah is insufficient; we need to aim to love him dearly as well.

Similarly, in the *tefillah* of *U'va L'Tzion*, we first express the hope that Hashem will "open our hearts to His Torah," but, we then immediately continue with, "And he shall place in our hearts, the love of Him and the fear of Him."

This is why the *Shiras Ha'yam* concludes with a reference to the building of the Beis Hamikdash—"the base of your dwelling place, the

---

22 This is why the *Sifri* makes mention of the **students** of *talmidei chachaim*, even though they are eminent scholars in their own right. The lesson we may learn particularly from the students is that it is possible to form a bond with a *talmid chacham*, and this can then be extrapolated to forming a bond with Hashem.

23 These words of the *Sifri* may have served as the source for the assertion of the *Ran* (*Derashos* 8) who explains that today blessing flows to Am Yisrael by means of *talmidei chachamim*. Previously, it was the Beis Hamikdash that served as the conduit for blessing but following its destruction this role is played by the righteous. This is evident in the *Yehi Ratzon tefillah* of Monday and Thursday following *K'rias HaTorah* in which we first ask for the rebuilding of the Beis Hamikdash and then pray for the welfare of the *talmidei chachamim*. (This *derashah* of the *Ran* was cited by Rav Moshe Hillel Hirsch in his *hesped* for Rav Aharon Leib Steinman).

Temple." For although Matan Torah was indeed the first goal of the exodus, the building of the Beis Hamikdash was to be the ultimate goal.

Shiras Ha'yam

Am Yisrael, who were traversing the Yam Suf, were in fact best placed to perceive the ultimate goal. Chazal say[24] that the Divine revelations experienced at that time, even by the lowliest maidservant, were greater than those experienced by the great prophet Yechezkel ben Buzi. They thus declared, "*Zeh Keli v'anvehu*—This is my G-d, and I will glorify Him," referring to Hashem with the demonstrative pronoun "*Zeh*," as though they could point to Him with their fingers.

In so doing, they were casting forward to a time in the future, when "Hashem will make a circle of the righteous and sit among them, and they will all point with their fingers, and say 'Behold this is our G-d that we hoped for and for His salvation.'"[25] Their prophecy was akin to that of Bilaam who stated that "There is destined to be another time like this in which Hashem's love of Yisrael will be revealed to all, for they will sit before Him, and learn Torah from Him, and their realm will be closer to Him than the ministering angels..."[26]

Am Yisrael's vision of a future Beis Hamikdash was a vision of the *d'veikus* that would exist there and, by extension, of the *d'veikus* that would be utterly complete in the utopian times of the future. In those times, they would be utterly loyal to Hashem, whose "left-hand" denoting strict justice would be transformed into a "second right-hand," which would perform nothing but *chessed*.[27] Those "two right-hands" of *chessed* would join forces to create a Mikdash, "*Mikdash, Hashem konenu Yadecha*," a place of pure *chessed*, love, and *d'veikus*.[28]

---

24 *Mechilta* to *Shemos* 15:3 and *Shir Hashirim Rabbah* 3:9.
25 *Taanis* 31a, citing the verse in *Yeshayahu* 25:9.
26 *Rashi* to *Bamidbar* 23:24.
27 *Mechilta*, cited by *Rashi* to *Shemos* 15:6.
28 And within the *Mikdash* they would feel Hashem's loving embrace, as the verse states, "His left arm is beneath my head, and His right arm embraces me" (*Shir Hashirim* 2:6). In fact, His left arm would be transformed to being a right arm and tighten the embrace.

The *d'veikus* and love of those times is the very purpose of Creation. Chazal say[29] that this world will last for seven thousand years, and then there will be "*Shamayim chadashim v'eretz chadashah*—New Heavens and new earth,"[30] where Creation will come full-circle and achieve its purpose. The objective of the first moment of Creation, the *aleph*, will combine with the seven thousand years of its existence, the *zayin*, and will together form a *ches*, denoting a supernatural world of perfection and *d'veikus*.

And this was alluded to by Am Yisrael in the *Shiras Ha'yam*, which begins "*Az yashir Moshe*." The word "*az*" comprises the letters *aleph* and *zayin*, the letters that combine to create the utopia of the World to Come,[31] and which also allude to the eighth day of the *Mishkan's* inauguration upon which the *d'veikus* of the World to Come could already be established in this world. Am Yisrael were thus simultaneously expressing their yearning for the eighth day of the *Mishkan* and the eight thousandth year of the world, and the *d'veikus* that they represent.[32]

In the physical world, the designs of the first day of Creation were completed on the seventh day, Shabbos, "*Sof maaseh b'machashavah techilah*—Last in deed but first in thought." In this *sefer*, we have discussed on numerous occasions[33] how the lessons of Shabbos impact upon the entire week, completing and perfecting it. But the World to Come—the abstract, non-physical world of reward—adds another layer of perfection yet. There, and in the *Mishkan* upon its inauguration, the first and the seventh days, the *aleph* and the *zayin*, combine to form,

---

29   See *Sanhedrin* 97a–b.

30   *Yeshayahu* 65:17.

31   This may also be alluded to in the word "*yashir*," which, as *Rashi* (ad loc) notes, is curiously written in the future tense. *Rashi* cites a *Midrash* which states that this teaches us that Moshe and Am Yisrael will again sing in the future following the Resurrection.

32   This is also alluded to in the words of the *piyut* of the *Baal HaCharedim*: **"Nafshi cholas ahavasecha...az *tischazek v'sisrapei, v'haysah lah simchas olam*—My soul is sick due to Your love...then** it will be strengthened and healed and it will partake of everlasting happiness."

33   See *Maamarim* "The Song of Shabbos," "To Declare that Hashem is Just," "Good Shabbos," "Source of Blessing," "*Kah Ribon*," "Shabbos Chanukah," "Sanctity and Blessing" and "The *Gra* and the *Baal Shem Tov*."

and are subservient to, the letter *ches*, the letter of the supernatural and of unparalleled *d'veikus*.[34]

5

Sun and Moon

Rabbi David Tevil, at the end of his *sefer Nachlas David*, makes a number of delightful observations contrasting Am Yisrael with the nations of the world. Chazal note[35] that the nations of the world abide by the solar calendar, whereas Am Yisrael use the lunar calendar. This, attests Rabbi David Tevil, strongly alludes to their respective roles and relative status in this world.

The moon does not produce its own light; it merely reflects the light of the sun. During a lunar month, the moon goes through various phases; when it is closer to the sun it reflects less light, when it is more distant from the sun it reflects more. On the fifteenth of the month, when it is at its most distant stage from the sun, it glows most brightly of all.

Am Yisrael, who are compared to the moon,[36] do not, in this world, "produce their own light." Yaakov and Eisav, the progenitors of Am Yisrael and the nations of the world, had made an agreement between them; Eisav was to take this world, and Yaakov the World to Come.[37] Yaakov can therefore only partake of the scraps of this world that Eisav deigns to give him.

Though it may seem counterintuitive, Yaakov receives the most from Eisav when he distances himself from him. Just as the moon shines most brightly when it is at its furthest from the sun, so may Yaakov

---

34 Witness the **eight** days of Chanukah, which commemorate supernatural events, as well as the **eighth** day of *bris milah*, which commemorates the imprint of the spiritual upon the physical.

35 *Pesikta Rabbasi* 15:1.

36 *Shemos Rabbah* 15.

37 *Seder Eliyahu Zuta* 19.

partake of this world to the greatest extent when he keeps his distance from his nefarious brother.

But in the future things will be different. The moon will return to its former size and glory and begin to produce light of its own.[38] Am Yisrael will similarly be renewed and shine as powerfully and brightly as the moon, *"she'heim asidim l'hischadesh kemosah*—for they are destined to renew themselves like it,"[39] and will no longer be beholden to the nations of the world for anything.

6

The Yamim Tovim of the year begin on the fifteenth of the lunar month. Pesach and Sukkos begin on the fifteenth of Nissan and Tishrei respectively, and Shavuos is slated to begin on the fiftieth day after Pesach, in other words, fifty days after the fifteenth of Nissan. This teaches us that the brightest days of our year are dependent upon keeping our distance from the nations of the world, just like the moon, which is most distant from the sun on these days.

Much of the *avodah* of the Yamim Tovim centers on this concept. The very first stage of the Seder on Pesach is that of *Kadesh*, which alludes to the nascent *kedushah* of Am Yisrael upon the exodus. They were chosen from all the nations to become G-d's people, for He had seen in them the lofty traits of their forefathers. Mired in forty-nine levels of impurity and almost irredeemable, He nevertheless saw that their essence was pure and was being purified further by the *kur ha'barzel* (the steel furnace)[40] of the Egyptian exile. And although on the surface they acted like their Egyptian neighbors,[41] they retained a sense of

---

38   *Yeshayahu* 30:26.

39   Text of *Birkas HaLevanah*.

40   *Devarim* 4:20.

41   The angels protested to Hashem that Am Yisrael were no more worthy than the Egyptians—"These are worshipers of idols and these are worshipers of idols (*Yalkut, Va'eschanan* 828).

Jewish identity by not altering their Jewish names, or modes of dress and speech.[42]

By retaining their Jewish identity and staying apart from the Egyptians, they allowed themselves the chance of *d'veikus* with Hashem. Later, upon their redemption, they instigated one of the broadest expressions of love of Hashem in marching faithfully out to the desert to follow him, "*Chessed ne'urayich, ahavas kelulosayich, lechtech acharai ba'midbar*—The kindness of your youth, the love of your nuptials, you followed Me out to the desert."[43]

Haggadah Shel Pesach

The *Haggadah Shel Pesach* emphasizes that "even if we were all wise and erudite men, or had extensive knowledge of the Torah, it would still be incumbent upon us to discuss the Exodus from Egypt." This is because Torah knowledge is not sufficient. Just as Matan Torah was followed by the creation of a *Mishkan* and a place for *d'veikus*, so does the mitzvah of recalling the exodus require not just the retelling of the Torah sources, but of recreating the intense love and *d'veikus* between Hashem and His people as of those times. Then, we may truly feel as though we ourselves were redeemed from Egypt, as the Haggadah requires.[44]

Shemini Atzeres

The climax of the *Shalosh Regalim* drives this point home and brings this *avodah* full circle. On Shemini Atzeres we celebrate our special relationship with Hashem as He invites us to a private meal, just Him and us.[45] The nations of the world are discarded, the bulls offered on their behalf gradually reduced on each of the days of Sukkos hinting at their eventual decline.[46] But we remain eternally as Hashem's faithful partner and loved one.

---

42 *Shir Hashirim Rabbah* 4:25.
43 *Yirmiyahu* 2:2.
44 *Pesachim* 116b.
45 *Sukkah* 55b.
46 Ibid.

Korbanos

The *Rambam*, in describing[47] the mitzvah to build the Beis Hamikdash, explains that "it is a positive mitzvah to create a house for Hashem, such that *korbanos* can be offered there, and celebrations can be held there three times a year." Ostensibly, in the view of the *Rambam*, the Beis Hamikdash serves two main purposes: the sacrificial service, and the celebrations of the pilgrims on the *Shalosh Regalim*. In light of the above, we may say that these two are designed to achieve the same objective, namely *d'veikus*.

Korbanos are designed to remove the distance that has been created between man and Hashem due to sin. Though he may have only sinned unintentionally (or else a korban would not be sufficient to atone for him), the act of sin itself distances a person, regardless of his intentions. His solution is to draw close, *l'hiskarev*, to Hashem once again by means of a *korban*.

And if the offering of a *korban* is an **act** of drawing close to Hashem, the Yamim Tovim are the **times** to draw close. "Three times a year, all of your males shall see the face of the Master Hashem"[48]—Am Yisrael are bid to ascend to the *Mikdash* for there the "face of the Master" is in evidence, and it is possible to approach Him. On the holiest of days, in the holiest of places, they can rekindle their holy relationship with the Holy One, Blessed is He.

7

Now we may begin to understand Moshe's urgent prayer that Hashem not rest His Shechinah upon the nations of the world. The *d'veikus* between Am Yisrael and Hashem, manifested most prominently on the festivals, can only be created when they are exceptionally distant from the nations of the world. If the nations were also to enjoy

---

47   *Hilchos Beis HaBechirah* 1:1.
48   *Shemos* 23:17.

a form of loving relationship with Hashem, no matter how tenuous, it would dissolve the *d'veikus* of Am Yisrael.

Moshe succeeded in his prayers and indeed the nations will never enjoy even the slightest hint of *cholas ahavah* of *Shir Hashirim*. Though indeed the *Gra* asserted that the nations do have a **scent** of a connection with Hashem, "the scent of fine oils," that is only due to their obedience in fulfilling the seven Noahide mitzvos, and does not engender *d'veikus*, love, or warrant a *Mishkan* or *Mikdash*. That connection is akin to that of a Jew who fulfills the dictates of Matan Torah and the second chapter of *Shir Hashirim*, but does not scale the heights of *cholas ahavah* and the fifth chapter of *Shir Hashirim*.

8

Tents of the Avos

Said Rabbi Akiva: "If all of the songs [in the Torah] are holy, *Shir Hashirim* is holy of holies."[49]

Shir Hashirim tells a story of love—but it is "holy of holies"—for it is an allegory for the powerful love between Am Yisrael and Hashem. Their love is like that of a husband and wife, which precludes all others, thus the nations of the world are sidelined and kept at a distance.

This is alluded to in the words of the *Ramban* with which we began. He asserts that upon the creation of the *Mishkan*, Am Yisrael "returned to the level of their forefathers" using the singular expression "*maalas*" (level), rather than the plural "*maalos*" (which would have called to mind their numerous, noteworthy character traits[50]). This alludes to a singular, unique achievement of the Avos, which was that they recognized Hashem when nobody else did. This created an extraordinary closeness between them and Hashem, for there is no greater kinship than when one's affiliation with another is utterly exclusive.

---

49   *Mishnah Yadayim* 3:5.
50   Such as "Merciful, bashful, and purveyors of loving-kindness" (*Yevamos* 79a).

And this may also be the intent behind the *Ramban's* cryptic words, "the secret of Hashem upon their tents." The "secret of Hashem" is the notion of the Shechinah coming to rest upon the Avos, and of their utter *d'veikus* that were a result of the "secret" housed within their hearts which were veritable *Batei Mikdash*—"*V'assu li Mikdash v'shachanti b'socham.*" "Upon their tents" is a reference to the holy abodes that the Avos shared with the Imahos; Avraham with Sarah, Yitzchak with Rivkah, and Yaakov with Rachel and Leah. Their holy marriages were a reflection in miniature of the holy sparks of *cholas ahavah* that connected them with Hashem.

The *Avos*, due to their unparalleled greatness, could create a *Mishkan* within their hearts and within their tents. Their descendants could only attain their level of *d'veikus* by means of an actual *Mishkan*, or by attaching themselves to "*talmidei chachamim* and their students." However, ultimately, in achieving that level of *d'veikus*, they return full circle to "the level of their forefathers"[51] and could then be considered to be "redeemed."[52]

---

51   See the *Ramban* in *sefer Emunah U'Bitachon* 15.

52   With all that has been said, we should not lose sight of the unparalleled greatness of Moshe Rabbeinu who certainly achieved both the *ahavah* of Torah and the *d'veikus* of *Mishkan*. Rav Hutner (*Pachad Yitzchok: Pesach, Reshimos* 6:2 and 4) observed that the letters of the name "Shlomo" are the same as those of the word "l'Moshe," which connects the longing of the *avodah* of Shlomo to the Torah of Moshe. Our stress of the chronology in which Matan Torah takes place first, followed by the erection of a *Mishkan*, is only to facilitate the understanding of the role of each in the psyche of the people, not to imply that the *avodah* of Moshe Rabbeinu was inferior.

Shabbos Chanukah

An Epilogue to Erev Shabbos

The Jewish people hail the Shabbos that coincides with Chanukah as "Shabbos Chanukah," which surely hints at a powerful connection between the two.[1] That connection may be that they each promote both the unconcealed message that Torah is *ikar* and science is *tafel*, and the concealed message that holiness and godliness can be found in the physical world, as we will explain.

The Yom Tov of Chanukah celebrates the victory of *chochmas Yisrael* (the wisdom of the Jewish people) over *chochmas Yavan* (the wisdom of Ancient Greece and, subsequently, Western civilization). *Chochmas Yisrael*, which is the Torah (the *chochmah* of Hashem), insists that *teva* is *tafel*, and on Chanukah it overcame the *chochmah* of Yavan, which claimed that *teva* is *ikar*. According to Rav Tzadok HaKohen,[2] the credo of Yavan is that "seeing is believing;" but according to the Torah, "believing is seeing." In short, Chanukah yields the unconcealed message of Shabbos that Torah is *ikar*.[3]

---

1 The *ruach hakodesh* (the Divine spirit) that rests upon the Jewish people would not have coined the expression "Shabbos Chanukah" to merely reflect the coincidence of Shabbos occurring during the eight days of Chanukah.

2 *Pri Tzaddik, Bereishis, Chanukah* 2. See also *Derashos HaRan* 1 and 11, which define the *Ran's* battle against Aristotelian philosophy.

3 In fact, Chazal note (*Pesikta Rabbasi* 23a, to *Shemos* 20:8) that the Jews are the only people

But Chanukah teaches the **concealed** message of Shabbos as well. The *Beis Yosef*[4] famously asks why Chanukah is celebrated for eight days considering that the flask that was found in the Beis Hamikdash did contain enough oil to burn for the first day. The *Taz*[5] answers that in fact, the miracle did begin on the first day, for a small amount of oil that should have burned remained at the end of the day. The reason for this is **that G-d does not perform miracles out of thin air; He ensures that they are rooted in the natural world**. A small amount of oil must therefore have remained after the first day so that a miracle would be able to occur on the following seven days.[6]

Miracles and Nature

Why must a miracle always be rooted in the natural world? Perhaps it is to teach us that in fact, **the natural world is also nothing less than a miracle**. This is referenced by the *berachah* of *Modim* in the *Amidah*; we thank G-d for "*nisecha she'b'chol yom imanu, v'al nif'l'osecha…she'b'chol eis*—Your miracles that are with us every day, and for Your wonders…in every season." In the famous adage of Rabbi Chanina ben Dosa (whose daughter accidentally kindled her Shabbos candles with vinegar), "The One who dictated that oil shall burn, He is the One who may dictate that vinegar will burn."[7] In other words, it is essentially no more miraculous for vinegar to burn than oil—both are dependent upon the dictates of the Creator of the world. The miraculous oil of Chanukah illustrates that what we perceive to be only natural, is really not so at all, for why should oil produce fire? Fire produced by friction could be understood logically but which scientific principle dictates that oil produce fire?

who count the days of the week in their relation to Shabbos: Sunday is *chad b'Shabsa* (or *yom rishon l'Shabbos*) and Monday *sheni b'Shabbos*, etc. This may allude to the idea that according to *chochmas Yisrael*, Shabbos impacts and enlightens the rest of the week and reveals that it is *tafel*. Since this is anathema to the other nations who are under the influence of *chochmas Yavan*, they see no need to name the days of the week in this manner.

4   *Shulchan Aruch, Orach Chaim*, 670.
5   Ibid., 1.
6   See *Sefer Melachim II*, 4.
7   *Taanis* 25a.

The *Ramban* similarly asserts[8] that "Man has no share in the Torah of Moshe Rabbeinu unless he believes that all of our affairs and experiences are miracles." And perhaps the reason that he references Moshe Rabbeinu is because Moshe was a man of miracles with whom G-d spoke face to face, *"Panim el panim Adaber bo,"* yet who nevertheless occupied an earthly existence. This alludes to the notion that earthly existence is no contradiction to miracles.

The opening words of *Kah Ribon* depict how very concealed these miracles are. The word for "world" in Hebrew is *"olam"* which is related to the word *"he'elem"* meaning "hidden" or "concealed." The words *"Kah Ribon alam v'almaya"* therefore paint a picture of utter *he'elem,* a world of mystery and veiled secrets.

But behind the veil is G-d Himself, the orchestrator of it all. The word *"alam,"* which depicts the *"he'elem,"* is spelled without a letter *vav,* which is the *"Os ha'chibbur* (the letter that acts as a conjunction). This alludes to the fact that G-d has no *chibbur* (conjunction) with the physical or spiritual worlds, for His holiness supersedes all.[9] But on Shabbos, the *machshavah techilah* (the original masterplan of the world) becomes revealed in the *sof maaseh.* On Shabbos one may find Hashem and get to know Him and his master-plot, for Shabbos is *me'ein Olam Haba,* in miniature.

It follows that the *zemer* of *Kah Ribon* is truly pertinent to every day of the week, for it tells of the Godliness hidden in our world. But it is nevertheless set aside for Shabbos because it is then that we may sense G-d's presence in our world and almost point to Him with our fingers, *"Ant Hu Malka Melech malchaya*—You are the King who reigns over kings."

The Midrash relates:[10] *"Kevod Elokim haster davar, u'chevod melachim chakor davar*—It is the honor of G-d to conceal, but it is the honor of kings to reveal."[11] Rabbi Levi commented: "Until this point [the onset

---

8   At the end of his lengthy comments to *Shemos* 13:16.
9   *Responsa Rashba* 5:52: "G-d is **revealed** in terms of His existence but **hidden** in terms of His essence."
10   *Bereishis Rabbah* 9:1.
11   *Mishlei* 25:2.

of Shabbos], the honor of G-d was *"haster davar—a* concealed matter."
Thereafter, the honor of the King can be revealed. During the week,
the world is beset by *he'elem.* On Shabbos, it may perceive the "*Malka
Melech malchaya*" amidst the "*alam v'almaya.*"

Kabbalas P'nei Ha'rav on Shabbos

1

"Why are you going to him today? It is not Rosh Chodesh or Shabbos!"[1]

These words were uttered by the husband of the distraught Ishah HaShunamis (the Shunamite woman) who rushed to the prophet Elisha in a desperate bid to revive her stricken son. Interestingly, this verse also serves as the source for the Gemara's ruling[2] that a person is obligated to visit his *rebbi* on each *Mo'ed* (Yom Tov), known as the mitzvah of *kabbalas p'nei rabo*." The Gemara explains that the implication of the verse is that if it had been a *"Chodesh* or Shabbos" it would have been eminently understandable why she was intending to visit Elisha.

However, the Gemara gives rise to an obvious question. If the source of the mitzvah of *kabbalas p'nei ha'rav* is the aforementioned comment of the husband of the Shunamis, why does it only apply to Yom Tov and not Shabbos and Rosh Chodesh?

---

1   *Melachim II,* 4:23.
2   *Rosh Hashanah* 16b and *Sukkah* 27b.

This question is posed by the *Ritva*, who offers[3] a fascinating answer. The regularity with which a person must visit his *rebbi* depends upon their relative proximity. If the student resides nearby, he must visit his *rebbi* daily; if further away, weekly; if further still, monthly. If he lives at a great distance from him, he must make the effort to visit him at least on Yom Tov. The Gemara only mentioned Yom Tov because it intended to exhort even those who live at a distance from their *rebbeim* to still exert an effort to visit them several times a year.

The universal *minhag* does not accord with the *Ritva*; people are unaccustomed to paying a special visit to their *rebbeim* on Shabbos or Rosh Chodesh. The *Rambam*, moreover,[4] does not imply that there is an obligation aside from Yom Tov.[5]

There therefore must be another approach to understanding why the Gemara does not derive from the conduct of the Shunamis that there is an obligation to visit one's *rebbi* on Shabbos or Rosh Chodesh.

2

The *Noda BiYehudah* issues[6] a remarkable ruling with regard to *kabbalas p'nei ha'rav*. The Gemara forbids[7] a person from rising in respect of his *rebbi* more than twice in one day, for he may not treat his *rebbi* with more respect than he does Hashem, "*She'lo yihyeh kevodo merubeh mi'kevod Shamayim.*" Since he only recites *k'rias Shema* twice in a day,[8] he may also not rise for his *rebbi* more than twice.

The *Noda BiYehudah* contends that the same logic should be applied to the mitzvah of *kabbalas p'nei ha'rav*. Since the destruction of the Beis Hamikdash, we have been unable to visit Hashem's presence on the Yamim Tovim. Therefore, it should be forbidden to pay a special visit

---

3   *Rosh Hashanah* ibid.

4   *Hilchos Talmud Torah* 5:7.

5   See *Biur Halachah* in the name of the *Magen Avraham*.

6   *Tinyana* 94.

7   *Kiddushin* 33b.

8   See *Hagahos HaRadal* ad loc.

to a *rebbi* on the Yamim Tovim, *"She'lo yihyeh kevodo merubeh mi'kevod Shamayim!"*

The *Noda Bi'Yehudah* clearly equated the mitzvah of *aliyah la'regel* (the pilgrimage to the Beis Hamikdash on the *Shalosh Regalim*) with that of *kabbalas p'nei h'arav*. His reasoning is likely that a *rebbi* is compared to a Malach of Hashem as the verse states, "For the lips of the Kohen should safeguard wisdom, and people should seek Torah from his mouth, for he is a Malach of Hashem."[9] Therefore, receiving his presence is comparable to receiving the presence of Hashem in the Beis Hamikdash.

Chazal moreover state[10] that "the fear of your *rebbi* shall be like the fear of Heaven," which, according to the *Maharsha*,[11] should be taken literally—the fear should be like that of Heaven itself. Since a *rebbi* teaches a person to fear Heaven, which is the purpose of *aliyah la'regel*, there is similarly an obligation to conduct a pilgrimage to the *rebbi*.

There does, however, appear to be an obvious question on the reasoning of the *Noda BiYehudah*. If it was forbidden to visit one's *rebbi* following the destruction *"She'lo yihyeh kevodo merubeh mi'kevod Shamayim,"* it should similarly have been forbidden to visit him during the era of the Beis Hamikdash on any day other than the *Shalosh Regalim* when one would visit the Beis Hamikdash. How then was the Shunamis permitted to visit him on Shabbos or Rosh Chodesh as she pleased?

3

And it shall be that at every new moon, and on every Shabbos, all of mankind will come to prostrate themselves before me, says Hashem.[12]

---

9   *Malachi* 2:7.
10   *Avos* 4:12. See also *Pesachim* 22b, *Bava Kama* 41b, *Bechoros* 6b, and *Kiddushin* 57a. "Hashem your G-d you shall fear," "this comes to include *talmidei chachamim*."
11   *Bava Kama* ibid., s.v. *"Keivan"* and *Kiddushin* ibid., s.v. *"Darish."*
12   *Yeshayahu* 66:23.

According to the *Radak*,[13] these words of Yeshayahu HaNavi refer to the time in the future following the Resurrection. He thus explains that the words of the following verse that describe the condition of "the men who had previously rebelled against Hashem" who will "lie in disgrace before mankind," refers to the disgrace they will suffer **after the Resurrection**, also described in *Sefer Daniel*.[14]

The *Radak's* conclusion appears to be supported by the previous verse to this one, which states, "For just as the new heavens and the new earth that I will make will endure before me, the word of Hashem, so will your children and your name endure." When will Hashem create "new heavens and new earth"? It is surely not in the era of Mashiach, for "there will be no distinction between this world and the days of Mashiach other than that of subjugation to the kingdoms."[15] We must say that this passage relates to the period following the days of Mashiach, namely the period following *techiyas ha'meisim*.

Regardless, the verse states explicitly that in those times the people will come to pay homage to Hashem on Shabbos and Rosh Chodesh and not just on the *Shalosh Regalim*. If so, according to the *Noda BiYehudah* there will also be an obligation in those times to visit one's *rebbi* on Shabbos and Rosh Chodesh, for the mitzvah of *kabbalas p'nei rabo* is, as stated, dependent upon the mitzvah of *kabbalas p'nei haShechinah*.

This may help us resolve the question we posed above.

The eminent Ishah HaShunamis may have seen with *ruach hakodesh* that in the distant future Am Yisrael would flock to the Beis Hamikdash on every Shabbos and Rosh Chodesh. She therefore understood that this was an essential, meaningful practice, even though it was not practiced yet in her times. Realizing this, she made it her practice even then, for although a person should not take on pious measures randomly,[16] if they are rooted in basic halachah, it is permissible.[17] Since the essential halachah of *kabbalas p'nei ha'rav* was already in practice, and the notion

---

13   Ibid., 66:24, s.v. *"V'hayu dera'on"* from *"V'yesh mefarshim"* onwards.

14   *Daniel* 12:2–3.

15   *Shabbos* 63a.

16   A person who does so is dubbed by Chazal (see *Sotah* 21b) as a *"chassid shoteh."*

17   This is how the *poskim* (see *Mishnah Berurah* 17:4) explain the custom of women to fulfill

of extending it to Shabbos and Rosh Chodesh was to become a reality in the future, she was free to take on this custom as she pleased.

Perhaps, this is why she would also not have violated the injunction of *she'lo yihyeh kevodo merubeh mi'kevod Shamayim* by visiting her *rebbi* more than she did the Beis Hamikdash. She did not assume the practice of visiting Elisha out of **obligation**; she took it on voluntarily, *b'toras nedavah*, due to her perception of the times of the future. Just as it was always permissible to voluntarily visit the Beis Hamikdash, it was similarly permissible for her to voluntarily visit Elisha at times other than the *Shalosh Regalim*.

If this is correct, then we may also resolve the difficulty posed by Rabbeinu Chananel and the *Ritva*. Certainly, the Shunamis visited Elisha on Shabbos and Rosh Chodesh but she did so *b'toras nedavah*, not as an obligation. In fact, had she done so out of obligation, she would have been in contravention of *she'lo yihyeh kevodo merubah mi'kevod Shamayim*. For this reason, the Gemara could only derive from her conduct that there is an obligation of *kabbalas p'nei ha'rav* on Yom Tov, and visiting one's *rebbi* on Shabbos and Rosh Chodesh did not become a uniform practice. The *Rambam* would similarly not cite a practice that is not an obligation.

For this reason, the conduct of the Shunamis also does not serve as proof that the mitzvah of *kabbalas p'nei ha'rav* applies to women.[18] Since she acted only voluntarily, we cannot adduce a proof that women are subject to an obligation in this regard.

---

the mitzvos of various time-bound positive mitzvos though they are exempt from performing them.

18   See *Magen Avraham, Orach Chaim* 301:4.

4

Techiyas Ha'meisim

W hy was the Ishah HaShunamis chosen as the vehicle to impart the mitzvah of *kabbalas p'nei rabo*?[19] Perhaps, in view of all of the above, we may suggest an answer.

The basis in the Torah for the mitzvah of *kabalas p'nei rabo* is likely to be that of *u'vo sidbak* (the mitzvah of cleaving to Hashem).[20] Since "the fear of one's *rebbi* shall be like the fear of G-d," one may gain an attachment to Hashem by means of attaching oneself to Torah scholars.[21] This notion lends new meaning to the correlation made by the *Noda BiYehudah* between the mitzvah of *kabalas p'nei rabo* and that of *aliyah la'regel.*

The mitzvah of *u'vo sidbak* was fulfilled in an exemplary fashion by the Shunamis,[22] who would provide Elisha with comfortable lodgings each time he visited her town.[23] Not only that, but she trusted his promise that she would yet bear a child, no matter how unlikely it seemed. Since she fulfilled the dictum of attaching herself to a Torah scholar to such a great degree, she certainly attained a commensurate attachment to Hashem, which is the very purpose of the mitzvah of *kabbalas p'nei ha'rav.* She was thus the perfect vehicle through which to convey this mitzvah to others.

In addition, she was also the perfect means to convey the lesson that the mitzvah of *kabbalas p'nei ha'rav* essentially applies to Shabbos and Rosh Chodesh as it will in the time following *techiyas ha'meisim.* For not only did she envisage the nature of *kabbalas p'nei haShechinah* in

---

19   This seems particularly curious considering that we have concluded that she acted voluntarily.

20   *Devarim* 10:20.

21   *Sifri* ibid. See *introduction to Divrei Aggadah* and *Maamar "Shabbos HaGadol"* for further treatment of this topic.

22   We should point out that the *Sefer HaChinuch* (*Mitzvas U'vo Sidbak*) rules that women are obligated to fulfill the mitzvah of *u'vo sidbak.*

23   *Melachim II*, 4:9-11.

the times to come, she also lived with the notion of Resurrection in her everyday consciousness. Thus, when her son suddenly died, she did not despair, but hastened instead to the Navi Elisha to perform *techiyas ha'meisim*, certain that he could do so.

The Ishah HaShunamis understood the implication of the second *berachah* of the *Amidah*, in which Hashem is described as a "**Mechayeh Ha'meisim** (a **reviver** of the dead) in the present ongoing tense rather than a "**Yechayeh Ha'meisim**" (a **future reviver** of the dead) in the times to come. With this certainty she strode to Elisha, her *rebbi*, strongly attaching herself to him and thereby to the Shechinah, thus serving as the model for the fulfillment of *kabbalas p'nei rabo* and of *u'vo sidbak*.

Kedushas Ha'guf
and Guf Ha'kedushah

Written in honor of the first yahrtzeit of Rav Yitzchok Hutner, 20 Kislev 5741

1
—

The account of the passing of Rabbi Yehudah HaNasi ("Rabbeinu HaKadosh" or "Rebbi"), is recorded in both the *Talmud Bavli* and *Yerushalmi*. However, there are several differences between their respective accounts:

The *Talmud Bavli* states:[1]

> The Ereilim and Metzukim (the angels and the righteous[2]) **seized the Aron Hakodesh**. The Ereilim **defeated** the Metzukim and the Aron Hakodesh was **taken captive**.

The *Yerushalmi* states:[3]

> The Yetzukim and Ereilim **grasped** the **Luchos**. The Erelim **prevailed over** the Yetzukim and they **snatched** the Luchos.

What is the meaning behind these discrepancies?

---

1   *Kesubos 104a.*

2   *Rashi ad loc., s.v. "Ereilim u'Metzukim."*

3   *Kesubos 12:3.*

2

R av Hutner would explain that *kedushah* can assume two forms. The first is *guf ha'kedushah* (the essence of holiness itself), such as that of Torah and mitzvos. The second is *kedushas ha'guf* (the impression of holiness upon the earthly).

Kedushas ha'guf can affect mediums that are essentially physical or mundane and would not generate *kedushah* of their own accord. The task of man is to elevate them in the service of Hashem and transform them from physical to spiritual, mundane to sacred. This fulfills the directive of *"B'chol derachecha da'eihu—*Know Him in all of your ways"[4] and can be achieved in any realm of life, in the *beis ha'midrash* and workplace alike.

Targum

The two forms of *kedushah* each have a language specific to them. *Guf ha'kedushah* is manifested in *lashon hakodesh*, the essential language of *kedushah*. *Kedushas ha'guf* is represented by *Targum Aramis* (Aramaic), a language that comprises elements of both *lashon hakodesh* and secular dialects.

The *Targum* contains the key to impressing *kedushah* upon the secular, material world, and to uncovering the mask of *teva*. Hashem's presence is hidden in this world as alluded to by the verse, *"Zeh shemi l'olam, v'zeh zichri l'dor dor—*This is My eternal name, and this is My remembrance from generation to generation."[5] The word *"l'olam"* is spelled in this verse without a letter *vav* and could thus be pronounced *"l'alam,"* which means "for obscurity." This hints to the fact that Hashem's name, or in other words, His presence in our world, is obscured, and it is our duty to search for and find Him.[6] This duty is represented by the language of the *Targum*.

---

4   *Mishlei* 3:6.
5   *Shemos* 3:15.
6   See *Rashi* ad loc., s.v. *"Zeh Shemi"* who explains that Hashem's name is hidden in the sense that (in the case of the Tetragrammaton), it may not be pronounced as it is written. This likely also alludes to the same concept.

3

Man is expected to occupy himself both in the realm of *guf ha'kedushah*, by means of Torah and mitzvos, and in the realm of *kedushas ha'guf*, by serving Hashem in all walks of life. Regarding *guf ha'kedushah*, man's *avodah* is not unique; he is matched by the Malachim who are similarly occupied.[7] However, in regards to *kedushas ha'guf*, man is unmatched, and his *avodah* is unique. For unlike Malachim who are spiritual beings and who can only impact upon matters of inherent *kedushah*, man comprises both a *guf* and *neshamah* (body and soul) and has the capacity to infuse the physical with holiness.

This is why man has the capacity, and indeed a mitzvah, to translate the Torah into *Targum*. The Torah is *guf ha'kedushah*, and its translation into *Targum* represents the channeling of that *kedushah* to all aspects of existence, *kedushas ha'guf*. For this reason, the Chachamim instituted that each person is obliged to read the weekly *parashah* twice, accompanied by *Targum Onkelos*, "*shenayim mikra v'echad Targum.*"[8]

The Malachim, however, do not understand the language of *Targum*,[9] or believe it to be a *lashon meguneh* (an abhorrent language).[10] Since they have no grasp of the notion of *kedushas ha'guf*, they look askance at a language in which *lashon hakodesh* appears to coalesce with the secular world.

4

Rav Hutner made use of these concepts to offer a marvelous explanation of the three versions of *kedushah* we recite each day during *Shacharis*.[11]

---

7   Though, unlike man, they have no *bechirah* (free-will).
8   *Berachos* 8a–b and codified by the *Shulchan Aruch, Orach Chaim* 285.
9   *Shabbos* 12a.
10   *Rosh* to *Berachos* 2:2.
11   See *Maamar "Kesser Yitnu Lecha,"* where we offer an alternative explanation.

Malachim

The first *Kedushah* appears in the *berachos* of *k'rias Shema* and represents the *avodah* of *guf ha'kedushah*. We thus recite it while enveloped in the *kedushah* of the tallis and tefillin and preparing to accept the yoke of Heaven upon ourselves. Here we long to reach the spiritual level of the Malachim who excel in all matters of *guf ha'kedushah*. We therefore invoke their praises at great length, "*Kulam ahuvim, kulam berurim, kulam gibborim, v'chulam osim b'eimah u'v'yirah retzon konam...kulam k'echad onim v'omrim b'yirah Kadosh, Kadosh, Kadosh...*"

The second *Kedushah* appears in the repetition of the *Amidah*. At this stage we stand in front of Hashem, with our feet together, aspiring, as the *Shulchan Aruch* dictates,[12] to "divest ourselves of physicality, and allow the power of the mind to prevail, until we virtually reach the level of prophecy." Now we may join the Malachim in their praises, "*Nekadesh es Shimcha ba'olam keshem she'makdishim oso bi'shmei marom*—We will sanctify Your name in the world, just as they sanctify it in the Heavenly realms."

The third *Kedushah*, known as *Kedushah D'Sidra,* is recited in the *tefillah* of U'va L'Tzion following the *Amidah*. It is here where Am Yisrael come into their own, and where Hashem chooses their praises over that of the Malachim, "*V'Atah Kadosh yoshev tehilos Yisrael*—You are the holy One, thriving on the praises of Yisrael."[13]

Why are our praises chosen over those of the Malachim? The answer is that in the course of our *tefillos*, we have labored not only in the realm of *guf ha'kedushah* but also in that of *kedushas ha'guf*. We have made sure to mention *geulah* before the *Amidah* in order to praise Hashem immediately prior to making our requests,[14] and we have married our material and spiritual needs within the *Amidah* itself.[15] In so doing, we have brought the physical into the realm of the spiritual, something

---

12   *Orach Chaim* 98:1.

13   *Tehillim* 22:4.

14   *Berachos* 4b and *Rashi* ad loc., s.v. "*Zeh ha'somech.*"

15   See *Maamar* "A Pleasant Fragrance," where this is discussed at length.

beyond the capabilities of Malachim. Hashem therefore dearly loves those praises and is "enthroned" upon them.[16]

It is at this point that we introduce the language of the *Targum*, interspersing each line of the *Kedushah* with its explanation in Aramaic. Since we have managed to incorporate *kedushas ha'guf* into the *tefillah*, and transformed *chol* into *kodesh*, *guf* into *neshamah*, we invoke the *Targum* that represents that very same notion, and which the Malachim simply cannot fathom.

According to Chazal,[17] it is in the merit of *kedushah d'sidra* that the world endures. In light of the above, this can be easily understood. The physical world would have no reason to endure from the perspective of the Malachim and *guf ha'kedushah*. It is only due to Am Yisrael who imbue it with sanctity, *kedushas ha'guf*, that it may serve any purpose at all.[18]

The three *Kedushos* thus reveal the process of Am Yisrael's ascent to glory. First, they aspire to the *guf ha'kedushah* of the Malachim. Then, they impart *kedushah* to the world in a manner unique to them, *kedushas ha'guf*. Finally, they achieve the extraordinary—the transformation of this world to *kedushah* itself.

This process may be reflected in one of the methods of fulfilling the mitzvah of *shenayim mikra v'echad Targum*. There are those who are accustomed to reciting the *Mikra* followed by the *Targum*, then the *Mikra* once more,[19] and this might allude to the process above. *Mikra*, as stated, represents *guf ha'kedushah*—the aspiration of Am Yisrael. *Targum* represents their *avodah* of *kedushas ha'guf*. The return to *Mikra* symbolizes their successful transformation of *kedushas ha'guf* into *guf ha'kedushah*.

---

16 Chazal (*Bereishis Rabbah* 47:6) say that the Avos were the *Merkavah* (the chariot) of Hashem. Here we learn that the very *tefillos* of Am Yisrael act as a form of *Merkavah* for Hashem, for they are the vehicle that brings their rider, namely Hashem, to His destination, which is to shower favor upon His nation. See *Maamar "Kesser Yitnu Lecha."*

17 *Sotah* 49a.

18 See *Rashi* ad loc., s.v. *"A'kedushah d'sidra"* who offers a different interpretation.

19 See, however, the *Rosh, Berachos* 1:8 with *Divrei Chamudos* 41, s.v. *"V'echad Targum,"* cited by the *Shaar HaTzion*, 285:10.

In tribute to the extraordinary prowess of Am Yisrael in transforming the world, Hashem declares, *"Am zu yatzarti li, tehillasi yesaperu*—This nation that I formed for myself, they declare my praise."[20] Ultimately, the *Metzukim (tzaddikim)* of Yisrael do prevail over the *Ereilim* (detractors) in Heaven, and in this merit they implore Hashem to continue to shield and protect them, *"Shomer goy kadosh, shemor she'eiris am kadosh, v'al yovad goy kadosh ha'meshalshim b'shalosh kedushos l'kadosh*—Guardian of the holy people, protect the remnant of the holy nation, who declare the three-fold sanctification to the Holy one."

5

Talmud Bavli and Talmud Yerushalmi

Guf ha'kedushah and *kedushas ha'guf* not only have different languages, they also have different lands and different versions of the Talmud. The land of Israel—the holiest of lands—represents *guf ha'kedushah*, and its version of *Talmud* is the *Yerushalmi. Bavel* (Baylonia) represents *kedushas ha'guf,* and its version of *Talmud* is the *Bavli.*

The Gemara relates[21] that *Talmud Bavli* is alluded to by the verse, *"Ba'machashakim hoshivani*—He has placed me in darkness,"[22] for it comprises the great battle for clarity amidst the profane, the secular, and the impurity of exile.[23] This battle is that of *kedushas ha'guf,* the attempt to impart *kedushah* to the physical. The *Talmud Yerushalmi,* by contrast, wages no such battle, for Eretz Yisrael, the land of *guf ha'kedushah,* does not pose that sort of challenge.

This distinction sheds light on a number of differences in expression between the *Bavli* and the *Yerushalmi.* The word for "according to" found in the *Yerushalmi* is *"adaatei,"* which stresses the *"daas,"* the understanding of the person in question. The word utilized by the *Bavli* is

---

20   *Yeshayahu* 43:21.
21   *Sanhedrin* 24a.
22   *Eichah* 3:6.
23   *Rashi* ad loc., s.v. *"Ba'machashakim"* offers a different interpretation.

"*aliba*," which is related to the word "*libah*" (heart). This alludes to the idea that the *Yerushalmi* represents *guf ha'kedushah*, the intrinsic and essential truth found in the *daas* (the mind). But the *Bavli* represents *kedushas ha'guf*, whereby the *lev*, which is the repository of emotions and character traits, must be imbued with the wisdom of the *daas*.

On a similar note, the expression utilized by the *Yerushalmi* to denote a statement that is unanimous is "*kol ama lo peligi*—the entire nation would not disagree," referring to the Jewish nation. The *Bavli*, however, uses the expression "*kulei alma lo peligi*—the whole world would not disagree," referencing the nations of the world as well. The reason for this distinction is that the *Yerushalmi* only considers Am Yisrael, the nation that is inherently holy, whereas the *Bavli* also considers the impact of *kedushah* upon the nations among whom the Jews in *Bavel* lived.

Lastly, and perhaps most famously, there is a clear distinction between the expression utilized by the *Yerushalmi* to adduce a proof and that which used by the *Bavli*. The *Yerushalmi* uses the expression "*puk chazi*—go out and see," for in the land of *guf ha'kedushah* the truth was clearly in evidence—one only had to **go out** and **see it**. The halachos of the *Yerushalmi* are moreover, more clearly stated. The *Bavli*, however, uses the expression "*ta shema*—come and hear," for in *Bavel* the truth could only be discerned by straining to **hear it** and by drawing close to it, and, as Chazal say,[24] "there is no comparison between hearing and seeing."

6

In light of the above, we may begin to understand the varying accounts of the death of Rabbi Yehudah HaNasi by the *Yerushalmi* and the *Bavli*.

Rabbi Yehudah HaNasi, Rabbeinu HaKadosh, excelled in all aspects of *kedushah*, both *guf ha'kedushah* and *kedushas ha'guf*. However, the

---

24   *Rosh Hashanah* 25b.

Yerushalmi subtly focuses upon his prowess in *guf ha'kedushah* whereas the *Bavli* stresses his conquering of *kedushas ha'guf*. This is clearly depicted by the differences in their accounts, as referenced above.

The *Yerushalmi* used the metaphor of the *Luchos* to describe Rebbi for they represent *guf ha'kedushah*, the intrinsic holiness of the Torah. The *Bavli*, by contrast, described Rebbi as the *Aron Hakodesh* (the Holy Ark) for the *Aron* would house the *kedushah* of the *Luchos* and symbolized *kedushas ha'guf*, the spreading of *kedushah* to the *guf* by dint of its housing the *neshamah*. The metaphor of the *Aron Hakodesh* thus served as a tribute to Rebbi's unparalleled success in spreading *kedushah* to the physical world.

In fact, the Gemara relates[25] that Rebbi would accord great honor to the wealthy. This perhaps reflects the fact that he considered material wealth to be a means to serve Hashem.[26] Not only that, but Rebbi was himself enormously wealthy,[27] yet he claimed on his deathbed to have not taken pleasure in his wealth throughout his life.[28] This demonstrates how he used his assets only as a means to serve Hashem, thus imbuing them with *kedushah*.

The *Yerushalmi*, moreover, describes the *Ereilim* as having "grasped" and "snatched" the *Luchos,* which seem to indicate a **temporary** coup rather than a permanent state of affairs. The same is implied by the description of the *Ereilim* "prevailing" over the *Metzukim*, rather than defeating them. The *Yerushalmi* thus implies that the *Ereilim* could have no permanent impact on Rabbeinu HaKadosh.

Perhaps the reason for this is that in the realm of *guf ha'kedushah* death is irrelevant. A person's *neshamah* is unaffected by death; it was essentially holy before and remains essentially holy afterwards. The temporary feat of the *Ereilim* in the demise of Rebbi was only in causing a parting between his *neshamah* and his body that housed it.

---

25   *Eruvin* 86a.
26   See, however, *Gilyon HaShas* ad loc., who cites the *Maharil* as offering a different explanation.
27   *Avodah Zarah* 11a, cited by *Rashi* to *Bereishis* 25:23, s.v. *"Shnei goyim."*
28   *Kesubos* 104a.

The *Bavli*, however, describes the *Ereilim* as having "seized" the *Aron Hakodesh*, "taken it captive," and "defeated" the *Metzukim*. These are expressions that denote a permanent victory, for in the world of the *Bavli*, death does indeed have almost a permanent effect, for it puts a halt to the potential for *kedushas ha'guf*. Upon the *neshamah's* departure, man can certainly no longer sanctify his *guf* or the physical world around him.

7

Luchos Rishonos and Luchos Sheniyos

These ideas also help to explain an important difference between the *Luchos rishonos* (the first set of *Luchos*) and the *Luchos sheniyos* (the second set of *Luchos*). According to the *Ramban*,[29] Moshe was only instructed to build an *Aron* to accommodate the *Luchos sheniyos* and not the *Luchos rishonos*, because Hashem was aware that the *Luchos rishonos* would ultimately be broken.[30] Perhaps, in light of the above, this may also allude to a fundamental change of state that Am Yisrael underwent at that time.

Chazal state[31] that had Am Yisrael not served the *eigel ha'zahav* (golden calf) and received the *Luchos rishonos* they would have become immortal and existed in as pure a state as Adam HaRishon before he had sinned ("*paskah zuhamasan*").[32] This is portrayed by the verse that states, "I said, you are like angels, and you are all children of the lofty ones."[33]

Had that occurred, the nation's state of being would have been that of *guf ha'kedushah* (just like the *Luchos* themselves) whereby the *neshamah* and *guf* utterly unite and where the *Ereilim* have had no power over the

---

29   *Devarim* 10:1, s.v. "*V'taam v'asisa lecha.*"
30   See the *Ohr Hachaim* ad loc., s.v. "*Ba'eis ha'hi*" for an additional explanation.
31   *Avodah Zarah* 5a.
32   See *Maamar* "*Nishmas Kol Chai*," where we discuss this concept at length.
33   *Tehillim* 82:6.

Metzukim at all. This state of being needs no *Aron Hakodesh*, for there is no element of physicality that needs to be sanctified, no need to imbue the physical with holiness by compelling it to serve *kedushah*.

However, following the sin of the *eigel*, the state of the people dropped precipitously, and they became mortal once again. This is captured by the very next verse, "But like men you shall die, and like one of the princes you shall fall." At this point the *avodah* of the nation reverted to that of *kedushas ha'guf*, where the immortal soul must impact upon the mortal body. This is depicted by an *Aron Hakodesh*, a physical structure which served the holy *Luchos*.

Chazal say[34] that the *Aron Hakodesh* would miraculously not take up any space in the *Kodesh Hakodashim*, "*Makom haAron eino min ha'midah*." Perhaps, this alludes to the idea that the marriage between the physical *Aron* and the spiritual *Luchos* it contained—a veritable marriage of *guf* with *neshamah*—was nothing short of miraculous. The *Rama* explains that this is in fact the intent behind the words of *Asher Yatzar*, "*Rofei kol basar u'mafli laasos*—Who heals all flesh, and who does wondrous things." The wonder of man is that he comprises both *guf* and *neshamah*, and they remain together for the duration of his life.

8

The Mishnah relates[35] that when those bearing their *bikkurim* (first fruits) would arrive in Yerushalayim, all of the workmen would stand and greet them. The Gemara attempts[36] to adduce a proof from this Mishnah to the principle of "*chavivah mitzvah b'shaatah*—beloved is a mitzvah at its time," which has several halachic ramifications. Since the workmen would stand for those bearing their *bikkurim*, **but would**

---

34   *Bava Basra* 99a, *Megillah* 10b, and *Yoma* 21a.
35   *Bikkurim* 3:3.
36   *Bavli, Kiddushin* 33a and *Yerushalmi* ad loc.

not do so for passing Torah scholars,[37] we see that a mitzvah that is in the process of being fulfilled is immensely beloved.

The *Talmud Yerushalmi* indeed accepts this as proof, but the *Talmud Bavli* dismisses it, arguing that the workmen would only rise to greet those bringing their *bikkurim* as a special dispensation to ensure that they would come again the following year.

What underlines the difference in reaction of the *Bavli* and *Yerushalmi*? Perhaps it depends upon the principles delineated above. According to the *Yerushalmi*, *guf ha'kedushah* is paramount; according to the *Bavli*, *kedushas ha'guf* is also profoundly important and worthy of focus.

Torah scholars, in front of whom the workmen would not rise, represent *kedushas ha'guf* like the *Aron Hakodesh*, for their *neshamos* imbue their earthly bodies with *kedushah*. Mitzvos, however, represent *guf ha'kedushah*, as do those who are in the midst of performing them. Therefore, according to the *Yerushalmi*, it is eminently understandable that greater honor would be accorded to those bearing their *bikkurim* than to Torah scholars. However, according to the *Bavli*, *kedushas ha'guf* must also be afforded great honor, and there should have been no greater reason to rise and greet those bringing their *bikkurim* than a Torah scholar. It therefore attempts to dismiss the proof.

The Mishnah also relates that delegations would be dispatched from Yerushalayim to meet those arriving with their *bikkurim* and that the size of the delegation would depend upon the eminence of those who were arriving. The *Yerushalmi* asks, "Are there people of greater or lesser stature among Israel?" In other words, can any distinction be made between those arriving with their *bikkurim,* allowing us to attribute different levels of importance to them?[38]

The *Yerushalmi's* question is hard to understand—are there not people of different stature among Am Yisrael? The answer is that according to the *Yerushalmi*, those occupied with a mitzvah attain the status of

---

37   As dictated by halachah, for any endeavor other than their work would constitute a breach of contract.

38   This follows the text of the *Maharshal* in the *Yerushalmi* and not the text or explanation of the *P'nei Moshe*.

guf ha'kedushah, and in that realm no distinction can be drawn between people of different stature. Only in the realm of *kedushas ha'guf* are differences apparent between those who have sanctified themselves to lesser or greater degrees.

9

Rabbi Yehudah HaNasi

The *Talmud Bavli* states that prior to Rabbi Yehudah HaNasi's demise, the Chachamim decreed a fast and issued a sharp statement forbidding the announcement of his death: "Anybody who says that Rebbi has died shall be stabbed by a sword."[39] Nevertheless they dispatched Bar Kapara to check on Rebbi's condition and he endeavored, upon his return, to hint to them that Rebbi had in fact died, and not state it directly. He therefore uttered the famous words cited above, "The *Ereilim* and *Metzukim* seized the *Aron Hakodesh,* etc."

Why was Bar Kapara trusted with the mission to check on Rebbi, and why was he unafraid of the threat of being "stabbed by a sword"? Perhaps the answer is that Bar Kapara had a special insight into the character of Rebbi, for he was a *badchan* who would entertain him. In fact, his effect was such that Rebbi would even dance in joy in Bar Kapara's presence![40] According to Rav Hutner, dancing is an act that impresses the spiritual upon the physical for it combines the most physical of activities with the power of song, which is of the most spiritual. By jumping and leaping from the ground, man expresses the innate desire to take leave of his physicality and become a more spiritual being. Bar Kapara, who witnessed the dancing of Rebbi, clearly perceived this in him.

Bar Kapara knew how to make use of the physical to promote the spiritual, and having witnessed Rebbi's exalted dance, he perceived this facet of Rebbi's character better than anybody. He saw that Rebbi had

---

39   *Kesubos* 104a.
40   *Nedarim* 51a.

succeeded in the *avodah* of *kedushas ha'guf* to an astonishing decree, expressing that in his immortal words, "The *Ereilim* and *Metzukim* seized the **Aron Hakodesh**."[41]

Ultimately, as Bar Kapara concluded, "The *Ereilim* defeated the *Metzukim* and the *Aron Hakodesh* was taken captive." However, even this defeat is temporary for in the times to come the dead will rise from their slumber and *guf* will become *neshamah* once more. As the *Midrash Tanchuma* proclaims,[42] "There is destined to be another time like this, in which the dearness of Yisrael will be revealed to everyone, for they will sit before Him, and learn Torah from his mouth, and their sphere will be closer to Him than the ministering angels."

---

41   The Rosh Yeshiva Rav Aharon Shechter, in his eulogy of Rav Hunter, stated: "His *inyan* (main trait) was not *neshamah* alone and not *guf* alone, but the *kesher* (the tie) between *neshamah* and *guf*. This also clarifies his avid interest in *neginah*."

42   *Balak* 14, cited by *Rashi* to *Bamidbar* 23:23, s.v. *"Ka'eis yei'omer."*

About the Author

R abbi Yitzchok Alster was born in Cologne, Germany. Together with his family, he emigrated to the US shortly before WWII. He was attracted to Yeshiva Rabbi Chaim Berlin and became a close *talmid* of the great Rosh Yeshiva, Hagaon Rav Yitzchok Hutner, *zt"l*. After marriage, he continued in Kollel Gur Aryeh, founded by the Rosh Yeshiva in 1955.

Rabbi Alster taught in Kamenitz high school in Brooklyn and founded the Yeshiva Gedola of Pittsburgh, a high school and *beis midrash*, as well as the Yeshiva of Seagate. Rabbi Alster also established Kollel HaTorah in the *beis midrash* of K'hal Veretzky for businessmen and professionals who dedicate their mornings to a true yeshiva learning atmosphere. Kollel HaTorah became the flagship for many such *kollelim*, catering to *bnei Torah* who left the *arba amos shel halachah* for *parnassah* pursuits and then returned to serious learning.

He fulfilled his lifetime aspiration of *"shivat Tzion"* and moved to Eretz Yisrael in 2004. There he established Kollel Nachlas Zvi, in memory of his father, *z"l*, for outstanding *talmidei chachamim* from English-speaking countries, such as the US, Canada, and South Africa.

Rabbi Alster is the author of the *Sifrei Olas Yitzchok*, containing his treatises on various topics in halachah (Jewish jurisprudence) as well as his *maamorim* on topics of Aggadah, relating to the fundamental principles of Torah philosophy and ideology. The sections on Aggadah are currently being translated for the English-speaking public.

MOSAICA PRESS

BOOK PUBLISHERS

Elegant, Meaningful & Bold

info@MosaicaPress.com
www.MosaicaPress.com

The Mosaica Press team of
acclaimed editors and designers
is attracting some of the most
compelling thinkers and teachers
in the Jewish community today.
Our books are available around
the world.

HARAV YAACOV HABER
RABBI DORON KORNBLUTH